WITHDRAWN

# THE PERSONAL VISION OF
## INGMAR BERGMAN

*Translated by Holger Lundbergh*

# THE
# PERSONAL

## VISION OF
# INGMAR
# BERGMAN

By JÖRN DONNER

*Biography Index Reprint Series*

 BOOKS FOR LIBRARIES PRESS
FREEPORT, NEW YORK

PN
1998
.A3
B46153
1972

Copyright © 1964 by
Indiana University Press

Reprinted 1972 by arrangement

PUBLISHER'S NOTE

The publishers and the author wish to express their gratitude to Professor C. Leonard Lundin of the Department of History at Indiana University for his invaluable assistance on editorial problems.

Translated from Jörn Donner, *Djävulens ansikte: Ingmar Bergmans filmer* (Stockholm: Bokförlaget Aldus-Bonniers, 1962)

Library of Congress Cataloging in Publication Data

Donner, Jörn.
    The personal vision of Ingmar Bergman. Translated by Holger Lundbergh. Freeport, N.Y., Books for Libraries Pr. [1972, c1964]
    276 p. illus. 23 cm.
    (Biography index reprint series)
    Translation of Djävulens ansikte: Ingmar Bergmans filmer.
    Bibliography: p. 255-265. "Film index": p. 266-276.
    I. Bergman, Ingmar, 1918-  I. Title.
PN1998.A3B46153  1972  791.43'0233'0924 [B]  73-38310
ISBN 0-8369-8119-7

PRINTED IN THE UNITED STATES OF AMERICA
BY
NEW WORLD BOOK MANUFACTURING CO., INC.
HALLANDALE, FLORIDA 33009

*This book is dedicated*

*to the co-workers of*

*Ingmar Bergman*

# Contents

# Illustrations

For permission to use the photographs in this
book, the author wishes to thank the following
producers of Ingmar Bergman's films: Svensk Filmindustri, Terrafilm, Nordisk Tonefilm, Sandrew-
Aateljéerna, Sveriges Folkbiografer, and Filmhistor-
iska Samlingarna.

# THE PERSONAL VISION OF
# INGMAR BERGMAN

# 1

## FAME AND SIGNIFICANCE

In varying shapes, the Devil's deputy is lying in wait for the characters in Ingmar Bergman's films. The actors are searching for their face, their chance to live. They are hunting their true identity. They wish for a moment of happiness. To be conscious of evil and the danger of the world is a step toward happiness.

For this reason this book might be called The Devil's Face.* It deals with Bergman's films. It does not touch upon his life otherwise, on his work in the theater, nor any other of his varying artistic activities. I have seen very little of his theater. What I have seen has confirmed my preconceived opinion that B is not one of its regenerators. He himself frequently asserts that he can very well live without the film, but not without the theater. The theater is his faithful wife, the film his mistress. That is B's own affair.

As a theater man, he subordinates himself to a text. He tries to be its faithful and obedient interpreter. At times, what he interprets is his own text. He never takes such liberties as, say, Brecht, Strehler, or Vilar. He does not seem to have any theories about what the theater should be. He works within the frame of a given tradition, and tries to create a quality important to all theater,

---

* _Djävulens ansikte_ is the Swedish title of the book.

3

old or new. He emphasizes the feeling for the ensemble as a unity. His staging is plastic, graphic, mobile. The theater man B seems possessed by the same demanding pride as the old conductor Sönderby in *To Joy*. Sönderby is satisfied with "interpreting the works of the old boys in spirit and in truth." He advises his young friend, the violinist Stig, to give up his heaven-storming plans. Stig replies disdainfully: "It is terrible to hear you talk. Like hearing someone already dead." Stig's utterance reminds one of B's ambitions during his artistic *Sturm und Drang* period—to conquer the world. At least, however, Stig, too, seems ready to accept the life wisdom which is Sönderby's: to know one's limitations.

B's path leads to brilliant results in the theater, and can do the same in film. Several critics, Swedish and foreign, have suggested that even in the film he ought to strive to subordinate himself more to others. He could, for instance, film Strindberg or Shakespeare, or in general refrain from using his own manuscripts. This view is based on what I consider the false premise that B is weaker as film author than as film director. But the weaknesses in, for instance, *The Virgin Spring*, from a manuscript by Ulla Isaksson, do not spring from the medieval legend which is the ultimate material of the film, nor from B's direction. The weaknesses are found in the dialogue, and in certain superfluously added scenes which not even B's direction could manage to make convincing.

This advice, however, is founded on a strange conception of B's position as a movie director. After Strindberg, Lagerlöf, and Garbo, he is today the only world celebrity created in and through Swedish art. Many of Sweden's writers, who quite justly are regarded as significant creators of characters or as visionaries, unfortunately have never reached beyond the boundaries of the North. Even if B stood out as a renewer of the theater, as an original writer of the word, he would hardly enjoy in these fields the same chance for worldwide renown as in the medium of film.

The motion picture is today the universal art form, which crosses national and political frontiers. The film is the democratic art form above all others, easily accessible to people in all corners of the world. It has means of expression which others lack. The word artists may answer that the film lacks means of expression which the word possesses. This may be countered with the statement that the film combines the word and the picture, the fascination of movement and the suspense of immobility, the influence of music and the power of silence. Within this art form, B has achieved his fame, not by being like others, but by being himself.

The theater he has created has had a great influence in Sweden; his films have influenced the whole world. Perhaps the skeptics are right when they say that much of his fame is only a fashion, hence transitory in nature. He often speaks along these lines himself, conscious of the fact that the economic foundations of his work are insecure. Still, B's fame in today's world is significant enough to be discussed. As an artist in film he interprets and transfers his private dreams and imaginings to the celluloid. As an artist he is firmly anchored in a Swedish and European tradition in which Strindberg, Kafka, and Proust were pioneers. And still he has succeeded in convincing, not only a cultured, intellectual world, but also masses of people who perhaps know nothing of the spiritual background of his work.

An analysis of B's pictures evolves into a series of questions of how he has succeeded in realizing his vision. To try to find the reason for his fame is to trace his importance. Even up to the festival in Cannes in 1956, when *Smiles of a Summer Night* was shown and won a prize, B was on the whole a director for the few. In Sweden, to be sure, he became well known in a short time. As early as 1944, when he produced *Torment*, he was a name. He was the country's youngest theater director, and many labels were pinned on him. He was called a demon director. Still, when one reads the Swedish articles about him and his work down to more recent times, they are remarkably lacking in perspective. Praise is as devoid of nuances as is criticism. Not a single Swedish reviewer has tried to establish his position in Swedish culture.

On the other hand, many have tried to find out what B "really means" in his films. The question returns hauntingly every time a new B film has a premiere. The reviewers neither describe nor analyze the picture. They try to explore B's real face, his real intentions. For Swedish critics and audiences B is one of those Chinese-box artists: "each film yields a riddle, each one seems to move a little closer to the centre. Then comes the moment when one begins to wonder: are we always being offered the same riddle; and is the centre going, after all, to be just another empty box?"[1] What they are searching for here, in other words, is B's face, his soul, but they forget to look for the face his film shows. When he is dead, his films will remain. Only a few will then care to seek out the private personality. It is my conviction that B has succeeded in transforming his private perception into a general one, understandable to other people. This is his strength as an artist. It does not then become a question of seeking the truth about his private personality, but rather, as much as possible, of hiding it and not talking about it. Perhaps there is no consistency in B's private life. The consistency I have sought is enclosed in his work, in his development from 1944 until today. This is why Ingmar Bergman in this book is designated by the letter B. The person behind the work is a fictitious figure who undoubtedly resembles the private person B. Such resemblances do not interest me.

B's name is today mentioned with those of the greatest artists in film history. Of these great names, few have survived. Most of them are like mayflies. The men who have written film history have most often, unfortunately, been historians rather than critics and analysts. The values they have sought are in the realm of cultural history. They refrain from saying which works, in today's perspective, may retain their reality and strength. Most films from the old days strike us as laughable. They are worthless as works of art. They are reminders of the cinema's childhood, when the most daring tried to learn the alphabet of the new medium. In one respect, a confrontation with the past is a fascinating experience: the beholder may follow the birth of an art form, its first hesitant steps and its first great conquests.

The film is typical of our time in the explosive speed of its growth. In my opinion it has only now begun to achieve maturity, its status of manhood. As early as 1947 B wrote: "I do not believe the film is in a crisis. I believe it finds itself in puberty, the stage when its voice is changing; that it is facing an almost existentialist decision. I believe the greatest care, boldness, and love are needed. What happens in the immediate future can be of great and decisive importance."[2]

The tricks of the trade used today have been employed a long time. However, the transition from the silent film to the talking picture meant a temporary retrogression, the effects of which stretched all the way to the end of the second World War. I have a different opinion from that of those historians who proclaim the eternal value of a mass of pictures from the 'teens and twenties. I reject the theoreticians, such as Rudolf Arnheim, who characterize the talking pictures as a corruption. I find that we are today on our way toward something new, which breaks radically with most in the film's past. We are on the way toward a film art where the personality of the individual artist puts its stamp on the work. The film has learned to write. It is now learning to create form and to compose poetically. In this renewal, B is in the foremost ranks.

The above restrictions make a list of the giants of filmdom a very short one. Yet there are many lessons from the past that are very valuable today. I am thinking of the rich imaginativeness of the early films, their feeling for the landscape. I am thinking of the unrestrained whipping rhythm in the films by Eisenstein. Certainly Chaplin, Sjöström, Pudovkin, Dreyer, Ford, and many others will keep their place. Some of them are pioneers. Some of Eisenstein's theories are valid today, as a foundation for the still unwritten esthetics of the talking picture.

In his own films B has expressed his admiration for George Méliès and the old farces. In *The Devil's Wanton* he has a comical vignette which alludes to this. He has maintained that the film has "not found its limits, nor even its expressions," that it is fettered by dangerous conventions. "I believe that the film cannot recapture its artistic power until it is freed from an imagination-killing and earthbound rendering of a reality which becomes indifferent and unreal just because of the exactness of the reproduction. It is not a fault, nor is it degrading, for the film to have been originally an amusement of the marketplace, a juggling or conjuring trick; but it is a fault and degrading to deny this origin, to be on the verge of losing its magic and the imagination-stimulating qualities of the juggler."[3]

B and the other directors who may be regarded as the vanguard of film art give expression to qualities which the pioneering men could not, perhaps did not even wish to, evoke. The intensely personal film art created by a group of artists in different countries undoubtedly has more qualities which separate than which unite. What unites is, to be sure, important enough. It is the chance to realize a deeply personal vision. It can be done in B's way, as a series of questions put to eternity and to mankind. It can be done in the manner of Buñuel, Antonioni, Kurosawa, Renoir, Ford, Rossellini, or Mizoguchi. I have chosen to write about B, not because I consider him a more important artist than those mentioned above, but because certain conditions have made it possible for me to follow his development year by year. Between 1944 and 1962 B wrote and directed thirty pictures. He has therefore almost always been able to realize his personal intentions. One can follow his development from an eclectic yet individual beginning to the maturity he now possesses. He has not let himself be obstructed by commercial considerations—a fate which, for instance, John Ford has often been forced to accept in silence.

The essential thing that has happened in motion pictures since the second World War has been summed up under the term *Cinéma d'auteurs*. All movements of revolt have aimed at a liberation from "an imagination-killing and earthbound rendering of a reality which becomes indifferent and unreal just because of the exactness of the reproduction." The Italian neorealism became perhaps a new dogma, tied as it often was to a social determinism. Its aim, however, was to give freedom to the storytelling quality of the picture. The height of this development is found in such films as *Last Year in Marienbad*. Here the art form is on its way toward liberation from the conventions of storytelling technique, conventions of contemporaneousness, and general literary conventions which have been a stumbling block in its development. The big freebooters naturally have the right and the opportunity to oppose the tendencies of the times, which can be said of Ford. By emphasizing his dependence on the Swedish cinematographic tradition, B has underscored that he is not only a child of his time. The general direction, however, is toward a liberation from a classic film dramaturgy, from patterns which habit and convenience have long made repetitious.

He who reads the analyses of B's work soon becomes aware that the same arguments are used by those who accept and by those who reject him. The assertion that he projects his private world on the screen can be used both to blame and to praise. His grappling with Christian problems is regarded as praiseworthy or cramping. I think this is all based on a strange confusion of thought. In dealing with films, many critics employ dogma-fettered criteria which they would apply to other arts with the greatest hesitation. B's films have become conversation pieces, something that "everybody" feels he can discuss with authority. The question of whether to accept or reject B becomes for these people first and foremost a question of whether to accept or reject the personal opinions that they believe they find behind his work. Applied to literature, such a point of view would be devastating. Only those who fully shared Strindberg's *opinions* would be able to read him.

Ever since I saw the first of B's films, I have put up a determined but somewhat fluctuating struggle against the thought of accepting them. B's world actually seemed to me to be limited, in a dangerous sense. At times one got the impression that he was a director, at other times that he was an author. It seemed as if some of his characters expressed a dangerous criticism of rationalism. They tended to deny the whole world of social resolution and social action on which the Swedish society of welfare and affluence was, after all, built. His opposition to forces that he regarded as obstructive appeared to be misdirected. The antibourgeois line seemed like a Bohemian flirtation with an impossible freedom. To praise such an artist was perhaps the same as to abandon without resistance the thought that art can exert an influence on society through the individuals who are the recipients of art. In a word, B's world seemed to me one of conformity.

The fact that B nevertheless managed to engage me personally arose from the rich possibilities of choice, the deep analysis of action and thought, that were to be found in his pictures. The perspective in his works varied continually. This richness of fancy could only in part be directly attributed to biographical circumstances. He himself and his critics often stress the fact that he is the son of a man of the church and that his upbringing bore the stamp of the Protestant religion. Those who are not Christians find it difficult to estimate this information correctly— as well as all the other facts that have been told of B's life. It is much more interesting that the Last Judgment which the artist B holds over his head and those of his characters has a general application. Of general application are Knight Antonius Block's questions in *The Seventh Seal* and Professor Isak Borg's dread in *Wild Strawberries*. All this is understandable even for the irreligious. The questions in B's films often deal with man's relationship to eternity, but broaden their scope to include all the painful experience that plagues the man of our time. The dread in B's films relates not only to the petty concerns of a materially thriving society, but dread about the future of man and of life on our threatened planet.

It has been said that the characters in his films seem to live in faulty contact with "the times" as a social and political field of action. A biographical light may of course be thrown on this in the form of a statement that B was represented in earlier portraits as totally uninterested in social and political problems. In a radio play, *A City*, he has mocked artists who engage themselves politically. I think this point of departure is wrong. It is more important to raise a question about B's cultural roots, about why his international fame found its beginning in France, and about the reason why an artist of this type is, even with respect to the intellectual fashion, *primus inter pares*.

An Italian critic has voiced exactly the same question. The sense of crisis, approaching and full of threat, present and overwhelming, is never distant from B's pictures, even the most idyllic ones. This feeling corresponds to the spiritual unrest that has troubled Swedish society during the last thirty years. Guido Oldrini[4] speaks of the Swedish neutrality complex. The country did not join in the common European struggle against Nazism. The traditional Christian religion has gradually weakened. Its solidarity and moral edicts have not been replaced by anything. At the same time, certain Protestant norms have been retained. A "decline and dissolution of what holds the social unit together" has influenced B's work. He has not been able to solve or to ignore the historic social crisis in which he finds himself. In common with Swedish culture in general, he has taken over only the Christian middle-class aspect of the decline of Hegelianism. The bridges have been destroyed by objective and materialistic dialectics. This concerns primarily art and the intellectuals.

Oldrini maintains, however, that attempts are not lacking in B's work to "see clearly," nor endeavors toward objective dialectics. It is also conceivable that B is a great artist regardless of whether he can overcome the limitations of his intellectual milieu. His background is that of the Swedish literature of the forties, which proclaimed (according to a very often quoted statement) that the new poetry had a nihilistic touch, that it was "a necessary cleansing process," "a catharsis of impotence."[5] The great European and American writers, such as Eliot, Kafka, Hemingway, Joyce, etc., had very slowly reached the consciousness of the intellectuals in Sweden. At the same time, both during and after the war, the country found itself in a strange transition. On the social level, an uninterrupted series of reforms took place; they had been inaugurated when the Social Democrats came into power in the early thirties. Simultaneously, movements appeared in the art world that seemed to oppose in every way the social reforms and the collective ideals of society.

There is a marked difference here between the leading tendencies in Swedish literature of the thirties and the forties. An artist of B's kind would have been inconceivable in the thirties. The new poets proclaimed a credo of pessimism, an action of inaction: "there is intrinsic action in the very analysis of cowardice, terror, and impotence. Yes, it may be asked whether this analysis, in the situation in which we now find ourselves, is not simply the correct action. For it reveals *the blindness of us all* [the italics are mine—J.D.] and beyond all systems of thought restores the central complex of problems to man and to man's nature."[6] The foremost critics of the forties put their stamp on the debate in a manner that manifestly could not help but influence B's work. Camus, Kafka, and Sartre were the names of the day. Man was analyzed, not as a product of his class and surroundings, of the concrete circumstances under which he lived. Mankind was transformed into the abstract collective concept. Man, a

Sisyphus, a K, a suffering Mankind. This is reflected in B, so that persons of completely different background and upbringing still seem to possess the same conceptions. They are abstract shapes, parts of the infinite idea, Mankind.

French motion picture criticism of the fifties has partly the same spiritual roots. Therefore it was able so quickly to approve the purpose of B's work. According to Oldrini, this is reflected in the common middle-class foundation, and partly in "the development toward attitudes which, when viewed superficially, are nonconformist and rebellious in the directions most popular in French culture, all of varying forms, but with common aims, arising from Kierkegaard's 'conservative irrationalism.' " While Sweden has proceeded toward more and more collective solutions, where society's care for all is regarded as self-evident, its literature has developed away from this doctrine. Art has become ever more individualistic. This spirit finds its extreme expression in the sentence: "The evil form which we suffer is metaphysical." And the term *we* means all mankind.

Earlier it had been possible to put the blame for man's lack of happiness on circumstances outside himself. Now this seemed impossible. For this reason, therefore, Sartre's philosophy, offering abstract opportunities of choice, seemed modern and right. For this reason the lonely Sisyphus became a hero of the intellectuals. B's films are not uninfluenced by this. They are influenced by a certain individualistic, intellectual tradition, related to Kierkegaard's. This, however, has not checked his development as an artist. Perhaps it is difficult for him, as Guido Aristarco points out, to join in rebuilding the "ruined cathedral," a new unity of thought. That is because this question has never been one of great importance to him: "the direction-determining resolve which in our day could lead to a real and fruitful conclusion is: Toward anguish or away from it? Shall anguish be eternal or vanquished? Must it again be reduced to one of the innumerable effects which together form the structure of man's inner life, or must it still be displayed as the deciding factor in man's existence?"[7]

Aristarco maintains that B is one of the many artists who take part in the revolt against reason. The antirationalistic trend has a dominating place in the European literature of the twentieth century. In contrast to Tolstoy's great realism, in contrast to the conception of the position of art and its influence that Goethe proclaimed, the artists and writers of the new era stand ready to criticize rationalistic values. Man's road to happiness and harmony becomes a miracle, accomplished without rational activity. Only "the educated, problematic, intellectual persons, in a word 'the middle class,' "[8] seem able to achieve that higher form of consciousness, needed to conquer life's innermost contradictions. Only the intellectuals suffer. The rest of mankind just lives on, without asking for the meaning and aim of life.

Yet it must be borne in mind that the values B's films aim at are always of a moral nature. The importance of economic and social barriers is underestimated. Still, the social conventions are questioned and examined by the very concentration on moral values. In this respect B becomes a writer of his time just as much as any other. Nevertheless, we can call it a paradox that this poet of the film—exclusive in his selection of dramatic material, marked in an overwhelmingly one-sided way by the intellectual milieu in Sweden, by the spiritual situations of Protestantism—is able to convince great numbers of people. There are greater creators of characters in Swedish literature. Since Strindberg, there has not come forth a poet who intuitively is so attuned to his own time as B. Note, for instance, how in *Winter Light* he lets the dread of the threatening unknown, nuclear warfare, become the film's main dramatic material.

His writing, that of the film, describes and interprets a situation of chaos and insecurity in the Western cultural world, but it also manages to push outside it. The great penetrating thinkers, who stick at nothing in their criticism of the human condition, have found it much more difficult than he to win an audience. They are too nonconformist. We find in B a strange blend of conformity and nonconformity. The battle between these two poles is documented in *Smiles of a Summer Night* and *The Naked Night*, which Jacques Siclier considers rose and black versions of exactly the same theme. B's analysis of the human condition, of man's attitude toward the great abstract questions, is almost as merciless. But beyond this he is seeking a solution, which may appear romantic and false because it often originates in a defective, purely individual analysis of man's being. But the important thing is that he, thanks to his tremendous ability to narrate on the screen, can make his world clearly visible. He is thereby able to satisfy demands of many different kinds—and arouse dissatisfaction of many different kinds. One might wish for another world for B to depict than the one he shows us. But his skill in showing us his world is not lessened thereby.

He often objects to a "literary" judgment of films. In Sweden this means an ordinary review which, basing its opinion exclusively on the word content, tries to estimate the value of the picture. It is important to reject a judgment of this kind. The film is not only a unique art form: in its best moments it is able, more adequately than other art forms, to express our time. But not even B's arguments seem quite tenable. He says that "the picture story hits our emotions directly, without any intermediate landing in the intellect."[9] He thinks—or thought—that a movie adaptation of a literary work more often than not kills the irrational dimension of the work of art. B finds it true that the film produces "real dreams, lightly stringing games, poisonous wriggling snakes of association, bright, reflecting soap bubbles." With these words he proclaims an irrationalism of art, to which fortunately he himself has not often succumbed.

The motion picture meets the spectator through both emotion and intellect, a fact which is true of all art forms. A literary estimate need not only aim at interpreting the words in the film. It may just as well try to analyze the ideas in the work of art. If we think that modern art at some stage should free itself from "the chaos of time," and thus, in other words, should not itself become chaos, then we must also seek the roots of the irrationalism which sometimes characterizes B's art.

There is another, more important, reason for a literary estimate of B's work. One tries to find the moral and social center, the nucleus of thoughts, around which B's films revolve. One wants to explore to what extent the film, despite its unique gifts of narration, is bound to traditional art forms. B once wrote: "I have long felt a certain aversion to telling stories on the screen. This is not because I find narrating in itself objectionable, but I feel that one of the curses of the film is its bondage to the epic and dramatic."[10] Only his later pictures have tended toward a loosening of the epic grip which earlier was the dominating factor. Furthermore, one can say with Lionel Trilling: "As long as the cinema makes use of story, it is captive to the concepts that control story in literature, it is bound by Beginning, Middle and End."[11] The film as an art form is new. In its construction, however, the film drama has been bound by rules laid down during the long development of literature. Today's feature pictures have an average length of about 100 minutes. They follow certain conventions of action. The film has borrowed from literature, painting, and sculpture. To compare the film with these art forms is not wrong. At the same time we must remember that the artistic development of the twentieth century has been strongly affected by the movies.[12] The film has influenced the other art forms, and has become influenced by them.

Why so? Why not in another way? Why not something else?

These questions have been asked B in connection with almost all his pictures, whether they were regarded as pessimistic, 1940-ish, Christian, or too amusing. Even if I do not like certain sides of B's artistic talent, such as some of the ways in which he analyzes man, that does not mean that I would believe it possible to change the character of B's films by well-meant advice. Through the years he has ruthlessly hewn to his own line. *The Magician* gives the answer to those who ask: "Have you a face? What happened to your heart?"[13] B's answer has been his films. Outside his own art he is, as a creating person, defenseless before his critics and adversaries. Within his art he finds his security and great danger, his nightmare and his victory. There he must each time show the courage to demonstrate some side of himself, to stand naked before the world. The work of art, as such, becomes "in the end the positive evidence of his security, and for the Swedish director, as with Renoir, the work of art is the best argument for, the only right solution to, the problem of being."[14] Art becomes the goal of art, but still not art for art's sake.

I do not share the opinion of those who maintain that B is best when he stages the manuscripts of others. Neither do I find a profound difference between his direction of his own scripts and those of others. The creation is stamped by his own personality. The pervading tone of the films, dialogue, and instruction, the way the camera is placed in a room, the visual rhythm, are all B's own. B almost always reshapes the manuscripts written by others. Today he chooses freely what he wants to film. He is like his opposite pole in the theater, Brecht, in that he steals ideas from others and blends them with his own. Thus the screen preamble to *The Devil's Eye* says nothing about the fact that B adapted a Danish radio play, though certainly very thoroughly.

## Crisis

B's first work as director is *Crisis*, in 1945. The picture is built on Leck Fischer's drama, *Moderdyret* (The Mother Animal). There are many Swedish films from about the same period which are considerably better. A poll taken by the trade paper *Biograf-*

*bladet,* covering the season 1945-1946, gave *Crisis* fourth place after *Blod och eld* (Blood and Fire), *Vandring med månen* (Journey with the Moon), and *Åsa-Hanna.* In explaining his choice, one critic wrote about *Crisis* that it was "a daring shot by an eager hunter—in the right direction but shy of the mark."[15] Still only *Crisis* has survived these other films. This is not just because it is B's film. His production is a totality, in which his knowledge of the parts enriches our vision. But even though *Crisis* objectively is poorer and technically less polished than comparable products from the first postwar years, it is personal in another way, which today we find easier to discover than when it appeared at the beginning of B's career.

In many ways, *Crisis* is conventional—tied to the theater. Gradually, however, one becomes genuinely interested. The reason for this is Jack, the person B has introduced in the play's listless action.

The plot is laid mostly in a small town, introduced by a speaker, who shows a number of introductory, postcard-like stills. The town "bathes its feet in the river, and sinks quietly to sleep in the lush verdure. No railroad station disturbs with its bustle the idyll's meditating peace. No industries, no shipping jar the lazy rhythm of the day or the evening's soothing stillness . . ." Nelly has spent eighteen years of her life here. She lives with her foster mother, Ingeborg, is courted by Ulf, an agronomist, and that night will attend her first ball. During the day Nelly's real mother, Jenny, arrives in town and somewhat later also Jenny's lover, Jack. Jenny is now better off: she runs a beauty parlor and she wants her daughter back.

At the ball, Jack offers Nelly from his pocket flask a drink which he calls "Jack the Ripper's Evensong." They cause a scandal in the small-town society, and rush outdoors. There they are forcibly separated by Ulf. Nelly now decides to leave town, and takes a job with her mother. The pattern of her life changes. Ingeborg comes to visit her, and returns, full of disappointment.

One dreamlike evening Jack succeeds in seducing Nelly, who is alone in the beauty parlor. They are surprised by Jenny, who reveals that Jack's stories about his misfortune are sheer lies. Jack leaves, and shoots himself outside the beauty salon. Nelly returns to the small town, presumably to stay.

B found Jack to be the picture's central figure: "Besides hoping that the film will have a successful run, I do hope that I may some day develop Jack, completely and without any respect. He deserves it. And he must be *seen*, not read. But not seen on the stage, for he belongs to the film."[16]

The best scenes in the picture are played in the beauty parlor between Jack, Nelly, and Jenny. *Torment* was B's own film, and its characters bore his stamp. In *Crisis* Jack seems to be the only person entirely imagined by B. He deepens the action and gives sharpness to the drama. Bent Grasten has said that B reveals his characters layer by layer.[17] The action disentangles the complexity of the characters. This transition is brought out by Jack. He might have been picked from one of Hjalmar Bergman's plays.

His sudden appearance gives to the small-town ball a cuttingly ironic perspective. Jack stands on the platform with Nelly and looks down on the confusion they have created. "Have you ever seen such crazy marionettes—Do you know who set it all in motion? I did." Jack is a marionette, "a creature of moonlight," who can love nobody but himself. The scenes in the beauty parlor bring out a theme that becomes a permanent one with B. Here the characters are unveiled, and here he pictures the contrast between illusion and reality. The mood is eerie and haunting, with the "decapitated heads"—the row of wig models. From the other side of the wall comes the sound of music from the theater, next door to the salon. During his conversation with Nelly, Jack tells her that he has murdered a woman. Nelly can become his "anchor in reality." It is not the seduction scene as such, but the humiliation and disillusion that follow, that give the scene its strength. Jenny reveals that Jack has told all this to her, too. He has talked about his revolver and threatened suicide: "I suppose you're going to shoot yourself now? You have your little revolver, and it's loaded with caps. You know where your head is, so that you won't hit anything else, little Jack."

Jack replies: "You are so right, little Jenny. I don't think I will shoot myself. People like me don't take their own lives. That would be out of character."

He leaves, and the shot is heard.

The street scenes after the suicide have a dreamlike poetic atmosphere. Even here, B is inclined to shroud his sequences in a chiaroscuro. It is obvious that he has been influenced by Carné and Duvivier, by the stylistic patterns of the French films of the thirties. The similarity in feeling for life is less obvious.

*Crisis*, however, is to a still greater extent a product of a certain comic tradition in the Swedish cinema and theater. The uncertainty of cinematographic grasp is compensated for by the freshness in conception of the people. The music—which he later strives to eliminate—underscores the emotional nuances of the various scenes, according to the custom of the time. The remarkable thing about this in many ways amateurish adaptation and unsure direction is that the film shows traits which later are to reappear in strengthened form. Nelly runs away and returns home, although in another direction than Monika and Harry, who flee from the city in *Monika*. Nelly wants to get out; she is possessed by the thought of freedom. She wants to keep her independence, her free choice. Jack is a living dead man. Such figures of pain and suffering we shall often meet again. Disillusion shatters the pretty dreams.

The striving for disharmony finds a gruesome expression in one scene during Ingeborg's visit to the city. Jenny begins to read aloud from Nelly's diary, which describes how young and beautiful Jenny looks when she is naked. Ingeborg, suddenly worn and old, interrupts the reading; she finds Jenny insolent. Ingeborg has aged, doomed by her physician to death. Jenny feels herself alive. The fear of growing old, the consciousness that the only purpose of life seems to be death (or life), these are motifs that soon will emerge even more strongly. At the same time we are reminded of the fact that the diary, that intimate form of confession, is employed by B in his entire production. His characters have the ability to speak directly to the spectator, past all the technical devices which all too often seem to make the film impersonal and frighteningly cold. B's pictures are confessions of a child of this century, who lives in the time of the Apocalypse.

Ingeborg has become accustomed to give without taking. The film proves that such self-sacrifice is seldom rewarded. *Crisis* shows that it is practical advantage and a narrow selfishness that ultimately direct man's action. *Crisis* is an appealing debut work, behind which the forces of misfortune and disharmony brood.

## Brink of Life

B's peculiar talent imparts his own reality to all material from other sources. *Brink of Life* is built on a manuscript by Ulla Isaksson. Here we find not a trace of the pictorial mystery which characterized parts of *Crisis*. Each movement of the camera is exactly calculated, the pictures are drenched in the disinfected whiteness of the hospital. *Brink of Life* is, so far as one can conceive of such, an objective study of three women yet in words and action it expresses an ideology that is B's own. Most of the action takes place in one room, and it never leaves the hospital. Three women are central in the narrative.

Cecilia Ellius is married and by profession secretary of the Board of Education. She is three months pregnant and has a miscarriage. Hjördis Pettersson is a "nineteen-year-old factory girl with a childlike appearance: dangling pony tail, uncertain carriage, and frightened eyes."[18] She, too, is pregnant, but unmarried, and she wants to have an abortion. The film story convinces her that she should give birth to her child, even against the wish of its father. The third woman is Stina Andersson, "twenty-five-year-old wife of a workman, in the tenth month of pregnancy, a big, handsome wench, one of our Lord's best creations."[19] She longs intensely to have her child. Her labors are painful and difficult, and the baby is stillborn.

The picture is marked by far-reaching visual asceticism. *Brink of Life* might be called an examination test in perfect technique. But this does not mean an objective distance from the women: "We are with them; never outside the door. Whether we are women or men, we share completely their thoughts and their physical sensations. . . . Identification with the screen characters is founded not on sympathy, but on respect."[20] The drama of the white hospital room is caught objectively, at a certain clinical distance from the characters. The power of the drama comes from the director's ability to lead us to sympathy and a feeling of participation. Of this film it can be said that it "tells us truths which no other means of expression could reveal in such a blinding light."[21] One need only think of Cecilia Ellius, the story's central figure. Her miscarriage is a confirmation of the fact that her husband never wanted a child. When he comes to call on her, their conversation is a jarring clash between two worlds that never can meet, never understand each other. Anders Ellius is one of those Bergman intellectuals who have built up an armor against the world and against emotion. The dialogue between him and his wife is remarkable because of what is not said, because of the small gestures and nuances that B's acute direction is able to convey. On this plane, B has taken a long stride from *Crisis*.

Typical of the conception of the film is also the conversation between Hjördis and the social welfare director at the hospital. It is later explained that the welfare director's interest in other women bearing children is based on the fact that she herself has become sterile. Her words describe the security an unmarried mother enjoys in contemporary Swedish society. What she says lacks understanding for Hjördis, and it is presented in such a way that progress, the very fact that this security exists, appears as something repulsive. Just as Ulla Isaksson does in *Brink of Life*, B in his films turns against institutional care. He seems to dream of a free humanity with a strong sense of responsibility. The welfare director says: "You don't need to worry. We will do nothing you won't agree to. But you must understand that society's point of view in these matters has changed drastically. Today it is neither a shame nor a misfortune for a girl to have a baby. You can call yourself Mrs., and set up a little home."[22]

Hjördis answers: "And where would I get the money? From the bank?"

The perspective in which *Brink of Life* is here seen is the question whether B also in this instance has been able to impress upon the film his own personality. Whether or not there exists a conscious or unconscious kinship between him and Ulla Isaksson, it is remarkable that she is able to incorporate into her manuscript the vital questions which are perhaps the central ones with B. Or, as the preface to the manuscript reads: "There is a secret with life, with life and death, a secret as to why some are called to live, while others are called to die. We may assail heaven and science with questions—all the answers are still only partial. But life goes on, crowning the living with torment and with happiness."

The abortion motif often recurs with B as a reflection of two processes in Swedish society: the new relations between men and women, and the freer sexual relations. Abortion or miscarriage means that a bond is broken between man and woman— perhaps the only bond. Cecilia is a stranger before her husband, the father of Hjördis' child does not wish it to be born. Only Stina's husband, who visits her in the sick room, wants to have a child. But she fails. The picture has a general character that seems to follow completely B's philosophical pattern: Chance becomes the deciding factor for the weal of man.

B has succeeded in raising the individual drama to the level of universally valid truth. His work as director is faithful to the material. Everything in the shaping of the film emphasizes the play between faces: the women who are the fruit of the film. *Brink of Life* follows the Ingeborg Holm tradition in Swedish film:[23] a tradition of social perception, of simplicity and faithfulness to the emotions depicted. Happy motherhood is viewed as the fulfillment of a union between man and woman, in fact, its real meaning. The conclusions are not negative, as many have believed. Cecilia is revived by sympathy toward the fate of the other two. To be sure, Stina loses her baby; but she does not lack possibilities. She is vital and happily married. The fact that Hjördis decides to accept her fate alone is a result not only of isolated ideas within herself, but also of talks she has had with other people.

No words in *Brink of Life* imply a nonmaterial explanation of man's predicament. The film tries to show that man's fate rests within himself. If B is an existentialist, he is a positive existentialist. Life does not exist only for the end, death. All forces, even those of death, can be transformed to serve life. Man is not condemned to the impossible. He continually finds escapes. He revises his earlier views, and faces new decisions in order to "try, as an outside risk, the right ways of living, which he earlier rejected."[24]

*Crisis* and *Brink of Life* are among B's least interesting films, because the narrative form, although in a certain harmony with the story, leaves no opportunity for the rich deepening of character which we meet in his major works. Still these pictures show how B manages to create a total vision of the world in which he lives. There are film artists who manage to achieve this in a manner that appeals to me more, because their opinions and style are closer to my own ideas. But there is hardly anyone who with greater stubbornness than B follows the path of his inspirations.

It is impossible to make an exact tabulation of B's productions according to the themes of the various films. In the following, his pictures are on the whole treated chronologically. This means that I find the theories advanced by Béranger and others erroneous, namely that B has passed through a series of metamorphoses. The spiral is a better symbol for his development. His work moves back to the same starting point, but also outward, to greater creative freedom.[25] *Wild Strawberries* is a film that touches upon all the themes previously found in B's work, while at the same time containing something new.

It would be possible to follow the development of a character, such as the moonlight-being, Jack, or the pubescent romantic Jan-Erik Widgren in *Torment*, up to its embodiment in the persons he has depicted in his latest works. One might perhaps also say that his central characters grow old with himself. While such a thematic analysis surely is not unfamiliar to those critics who continually search for B's real intentions, it has one fault—it leaves no room for an examination of the completeness which B has reached so far. *Crisis* of 1945 is an end result just as much as is *Illicit Interlude* of 1950 or *Through a Glass Darkly* of 1960-1961. The French-inspired form of *Crisis* is an end result, like the expressionistic baroque in *The Naked Night*. A chronological analysis must emphasize these traits, to show how his conception of man and society gradually changes and becomes more finely shaded.

B has fashioned comedy and tragedy. The distance between these poles is shorter than is usually believed. One of his many unscreened manuscripts is entitled *The Fish*, a film farce. We there meet a man, Joakim Naken, whom we encounter elsewhere in B's productions. He is a pioneer film artist, mostly concerned with farces. When he at last gets up enough courage and has the chance to do a love story, a calamity occurs: "To our great distress, something has gone wrong with the camera. Everything happened at a frightfully high speed, and looked extraordinarily funny. I was mortified, but the cameraman suggested that we do the whole picture in the same way, and change the tragedy into a farce. I refused for a long while, since I felt that into that strip of horribly funny pictures I had, after all, poured something of myself. At last I yielded to the argument of the photographer, and we laughed until we shrieked as we walked home through the deserted nocturnal streets."[26]

What turned out to be a comedy could just as well have become a tragedy, and vice versa. B, like Joakim Naken, works in this way. In the end, Joakim escapes being executed by crawling into the stomach of his beloved Susanna. When B has learned his profession, his cinematographic craft, and learned to avoid the mistakes of his first years, he is indifferent to what form he chooses. In his tragic films, the comic element is very strong.

It is conceivable that his fame will not last, that within twenty years he will have been succeeded by film artists who regard their medium with the same eyes with which a lyric poet or a prose writer contemplates the empty sheet of paper before him. Any way one interprets B's success and fame—whether as a testimony to the unsuspected possibilities of the art form or as an instance of the confusion of our time, or as a victory for the art of the film, or as a decadent element in the intellectual history of the West—it remains a remarkable career. Siclier finds it unnecessary to "establish prognoses regarding the work's place in the history of the film, since the only important factor just now is that it exists."[27] Thereby, the question is left open on what level B's contribution will remain a lasting one.

He has created a synthesis between the two refashioners in modern Swedish film, Victor Sjöström and Mauritz Stiller. The remarkable thing is that he has been able to combine them, overcome them, and still remain himself. The difference between these two predecessors has been characterized thus: "One can distinguish between Sjöström's inclination to express himself mainly through character studies, faces, and the natural movement of bodies, and Stiller's to express himself through rhythm, through a refined montage."[28] B combines the qualities of *Stroke of Midnight* and *The Story of Gösta Berling*. The banality he is often accused of is not real. The film was born as an equivalent and competitor to simpler popular amusements. It has retained this naïveté of pioneer days. Even today, it must have the right to use both the lurid effects (*The Naked Night*) and the subdued ones. B transmits this tradition, which has never quite been broken in the Swedish film. In earlier years he seemed ready to reject most of the values of his own cultural group. He has returned to them, reshaping the tradition.

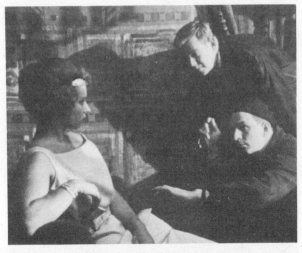

Ingmar Bergman
at work on
THE SILENCE.

CRISIS. Inga Landgré
(*Nelly*) and Marianne
Löfgren (*Jenny*).

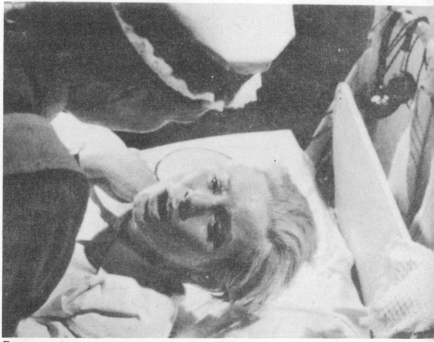

BRINK OF LIFE. Ingrid Thulin (*Cecilia*).

# 2

## THE ROAD FROM *TORMENT*

"What caused Sivert the greatest torments was scriptwriting itself. This was because most critics were interested in the esthetics of the content and usually concerned themselves with the story; moreover, they tied his private person to the content, pointed him out, and made him easily understood and labeled. And Sivert abhorred being seen, pinpointed, and defined. Nobody surmised how inexhaustible his talent was, not a soul understood that he had not yet really shown himself. He searched and experimented, he presented one facet at a time, a great deal was accident and chance. But one day he would reveal himself life-size—and then look out!"[1]

During his first years as a director, B advocated that Swedish fiction of the forties should be filmed. Nothing ever came of it. The above quotation is from Lars Ahlin's novel of cultural criticism, *Bark och Löv* (Bark and Leaves), and describes the movie director Sivert, who has certain similarities to B. Ahlin and B planned a collaboration. Regardless of this, B was termed a film exponent of the forties. In the popular jargon this meant an insight into the darkness and difficulty of living, the feeling of dread that dominated the feeling of life. This was present in B's production during that decade. At the same time it can be seen that even in the most somber of his tales from the forties, he

30

sought a compromise, a *modus vivendi*. Not even *The Devil's Wanton* leaves all roads closed.

It may be said that both the pessimism and the optimism of these films bear the stamp of romanticism. This is true even of the first manuscript by B ever filmed, *Torment*. Since the fall of 1942 he had been writing adaptations of literary material for Svensk Filmindustri. According to the company's archives, his first work was *Katinka*, after a novel by Astrid Väring. During the 1940's, up to his great breakthrough, he wrote many scripts, alone or in collaboration with others (Herbert Grevenius and Lars-Eric Kjellgren). Only a few of them have been made into pictures; some are preserved. They contain ideas that later were used in films actually shot. Among the suggestions he turned in were *Prison* and *The Fish*, both of which were rejected by Svensk Filmindustri. B often wrote prefaces to his manuscripts. His notes indicate that he had also become familiar with the economic difficulties of production.

## Torment

*Torment* became an important international success, by many regarded as proof of an era of greatness in Swedish film. The merits of the picture are often attributed mostly to Alf Sjöberg. Lasse Bergström[2] maintains that the frenzy is B's, while the muting of the film to a psychological credibility is Sjöberg's. He calls B uncontrolled, and Sjöberg controlled. In *Crisis*, B is supposed to have imitated Sjöberg as a "creator of images and a man of visual strength." The argument has not convinced me. The shaping of *Torment* is dominated by Sjöberg's narrative style. As early as the opening scenes on the stairway he is tempted to use compositions and visual effects, peculiar camera angles, which are an inheritance from expressionism and the early Soviet pictures. The intimate tone of B's manuscript is eliminated. The tale becomes dangerously esthetic, with its long, threatening shadows, its quivering of light on the walls, and its primitive epigonic technique.

What remains of lasting value are certain ensembles, in which the drama of the dialogue and of the built-up mood break the esthetic pattern. *Torment* is an important picture, as B's film, not Sjöberg's. It examines a youthful revolt against society that continues all through the production of the 1940's.[3] What fascinates B is the chance of a reconciliation with the world. It is easy for him to find this reconciliation, even if in *Torment* it is expressed by the leading character's being forced to keep aloof from society and the powers that threaten his independent life, family, and school.

The original manuscript was written in 1942. In its attitude toward Caligula, the teacher who is a sadist and reads the Swedish Nazi newspaper, *Dagsposten* (probably an idea of Sjöberg's), the picture is contemporary criticism. Jan-Erik's father reads *Svenska Dagbladet*. It is a middle-class home in the middle-class Östermalm section of Stockholm. The film comes very close to being a political parable on taking a stand toward the world war then raging. The young generation, filled with revolt against the ideals of the elders (school, family, middle-class ease), puts all these forces on about the same plane: the sadist Caligula, Nazism, the school. The makers of the film share Stig Dagerman's agonized awareness that the Swedes perhaps have been too well off, since they have not experienced the evil of the world. At the same time it is said that "there is no reason for a poet not to write about anguish and suffering only because there are those who have felt greater anguish and suffered more. If he believes that it is his task to examine human potentialities, he is dishonest if he allows himself to be checked in his probing of the effects of pain by the knowledge that there exist fakir beds with longer spikes than his, for they will always exist. But pain itself concerns him more than the length of the spikes, which admittedly also is his business, but on another plane than the literary one."[4]

*Torment* wants to wake up the spectator. The picture is an accusation, written with heart's blood. Every detail bears an imprint of ruthless subjectivity. Externally however, the contemporaneously critical in the film is a side issue. In the program, B recalls that the original idea was born in the thirties, the summer after he had passed his university entrance examination. The timely allusions are by both the scriptwriter and the director. The picture deals in the first place, as many have said, with the problem of authority. The community in which Jan-Erik and his friends live seems today romantic. Sandman is a materialist, a disciple of Nietzsche. He says of the teachers that they never get any farther than the matriculation examination; their growth has been stunted. B draws the same contrasts later in *The Last Couple Out*, written around 1950, but screened several years later—this, too, by Alf Sjöberg.

The part of *Torment* that criticizes social conditions is formulated, as always with B, in an apolitical and asocial manner. His observations of the middle-class family, its habits, and its inflexibility seem to be his own. It is an extreme subjectivity that gradually yields to a more understanding, yet still personal, point of view. What the narrator seeks is a norm for the action. The story opens at the beginning of a day in school. Already in these shots, the subjectivism of the picture is intimated. A little boy is hunted down and captured by a zealous teacher. School is a prison. Everything is seen through the eyes of Jan-Erik. The moment is truth.[5] During morning prayers some of the pupils are doing their lessons. Caligula, the Latin teacher, is presented as a "home sadist," which refers to an eliminated sequence concerning his home life. Caligula is infinitely lonely, and B hopes that the audience may feel some sympathy with his weakness. He also wishes that Caligula "may be unmasked, exterminated, rendered harmless. For there are many kinds of Caligulas, large and small, rather innocuous ones and repulsive monsters, obvious or insidious. But a Caligula can always be recognized by one thing: He creates hatred, staleness, destruction among people. He is alien to all fellowship, he lacks natural ability and the ability to make contact."[6] During a lesson that follows upon the morning prayers, Caligula's insinuating, treacherous, and dangerous nature is clearly shown. Jan-Erik Widgren obviously is his victim, and receives a bad-conduct mark. In the classroom scenes Sjöberg's direction is very effective. The atmosphere achieves a tightening and a hateful concentration that are rare in Swedish films of that time. The strongly subjective becomes a source of strength, which permits the spectator to identify himself with the pupils, who are the oppressed.

The dramatic action of the picture is skillfully constructed. Jan-Erik makes the acquaintance of the beautiful Bertha at the tobacconist's. He discovers her blind drunk in the street, and follows her home. She wants him to stay. She has a strange fear—a man, an evil ghost is following her. He visits her and they have a drink together. We do not know then, though we suspect it, that this man is Caligula. To Jan-Erik, Bertha becomes a passion, an escape from school and responsibility and home. The story reaches its climax when Jan-Erik finds Bertha dead in her bed. In the hall sits Caligula, crouching in a corner like a rat. He is taken to the police, where the inspector removes his glasses, revealing a strange expression suggesting a mask and trichina. Bertha, however, has died from a weak heart, and not as a consequence of his advances. He is set free, and reports Jan-Erik to the school principal. In a violent scene, Jan-Erik turns his wrath on Caligula, who has destroyed the only happiness he ever had.

In the final sequence, Jan-Erik stands in the rain outside the school, watching while his graduating classmates emerge in their white caps* and are greeted by family and friends. In a window

* In the Northern countries the donning of the white cap is a symbolic gesture showing that one has completed the work of the secondary school and is ready for the university.

stands Caligula, waving gaily to them. As the students take leave of the teachers, only Jan-Erik's friend Sandman gives voice to his feelings about Caligula by calling him a swine. Jan-Erik has moved into Bertha's empty apartment. There he is visited by the principal, who offers him support. During all this scene, and in spite of the young man's insecure attitude, one gets the feeling that he is the victor, because he is the living one. As Jan-Erik leaves, he meets on the stairs Caligula, who is trembling with fear that the principal may have maligned him. Jan-Erik denies this. Caligula remains in the darkness of the stairs, ridden by a disease that is malevolence. Jan-Erik steps out in the sunshine; he is the one who has matured most, not the others.

The construction of the picture suffers from the fact that Sjöberg is a very uneven, often theatrical, director. A predeliction for the theatrical returns in B's own, later films. The world beyond Jan-Erik is drawn in caricature fashion, from the outside. Yet *Torment* does not fail in its effect, because its feelings are subjectively true. Swedish audiences probably recognized in Caligula certain of Hitler's traits. Many years later it is difficult to see this resemblance. Caligula is a sadist, the first of B's many evil characters who oscillate between the normal and the insane. In a poem Brecht describes a Chinese mask of the evil one, and discovers that it is burdensome to be wicked. This discovery is made by the narrator of *Torment*. But the shapes of evil do not leave B. They represent the world of benumbed life against which he protests.

Caligula's opposite among the professors is the class superintendent Pippi, who once, in the school map room, upbraids Caligula for his misanthropy. The clearest picture of Caligula, however, is given in the scenes with Bertha and at the police station. Caligula reiterates steadily that he is sick. He tries to conciliate Jan-Erik, but cannot endure the boy's quiet and defiant look. When he is with Bertha, he tells her, in his whining, childish, undeveloped voice, a story about a cat. Outside a house he has seen a big cat and stroked its back. Thereupon the cat bit him tenaciously: "He dug all his twenty claws in my hand, hung on to it, buried his teeth in it. He suddenly grew and became enormous. I shall never forget my panic. I think I screamed. Do you know what I did? I plunged the cat and the hand and the arm in a water barrel near by. The cat was locked in a cramp. It drowned, but did not let go its grip. A doctor had to cut it loose. See—I still carry the scar. See—see how I look. . . That's the way to be. . . Bite and hold on. Don't let go. If I don't bite, you will, and therefore I bite first."

*Torment* outlines the contrast between the generations. Moreover, the film gives an unprecedentedly accurate portrait of a school life, whose portal is the prison door. The romanticists demand the impossible; the classmates take the road of compromise. Jan-Erik is chosen to suffer, as is Caligula. But the boy conquers his suffering, and does not turn it into evil. The strength of his revolt may have appealed to the generation of Swedes who experienced the clashing transition in their country between different principles of upbringing, between an authoritative and a free system. Out of the paradoxical combination of Sjöberg's and B's temperaments, severity of form and *Sturm und Drang*, there issued a film which seemed real, despite its many literary ideas (Bertha as a figure, the middle-class milieu) and the sometimes hackneyed description of the milieu. And it was genuineness, psychological truth, that the Swedish film needed.

The early pictures present B's world naked and raw. In them, one can decipher the basis for ideas that later were given a more convincing artistic form. The road onward from *Torment* is a road between two opposite poles. B wants to solve on the one hand the moral questions that are presented, and on the other— and perhaps especially—the director's problems. Nothing is self-evident. The artist B need not seek a material to shape and fashion. He is seeking a way in which to do it.

## *It Rains on our Love*

*It Rains on our Love* is more strongly influenced by the French than *Crisis*.[7] This is evident in the night pictures, in the poetic mood the narrator has tried to evoke. Aside from this, however, the film is weighted by a deterministic view of life. Neither the clergy nor the profane world can offer any help. But the two main characters do still go toward a happier future. They are not doomed, like Carné's actors. This is perhaps due to an optimism, an in-spite-of-all attitude which is present even in the most somber of B's works.

As in *Crisis*, he makes use of a narrator. It is an old man, who, in the courtroom sequence toward the end, defends the young couple. The point of departure for these two is their homelessness, freedom from the fetters of society. David has recently been released from prison. Maggi, who once wanted to become an actress, carries a child whose father she does not know. The two meet at the Central Station in Stockholm. Time, and their struggle against the outside world, bring them gradually together, until their union reaches its fulfillment with their acquittal in court. The film lets society shoulder the blame for David and Maggi's difficulties. Society—that is once more the good people, regimented by bourgeois habits. Society is hypocrisy itself.

When they have bought a small cabin, they visit a clergyman to have the marriage banns published. The general satirical tone is struck by the minister, who says, "Well, young lady, first you will have to send your birth certificate to the registrar's office, and give them the new address. They will notify Furusele and us, and you'll get it back direct from them and then you can come here with it, and we'll publish the banns. It takes a little time, but then your fiancé must also ask for removal." *Night is my Future*, on the other hand, treats the clergy with more sympathy. On the whole, though, all through B's films there is a picture of ministers as being completely blind to the realities of fellowship. They are narrow bureaucrats, absorbed by paper work. Their malevolence is unconscious. They are not rascals, but clowns, like the minister in *A Lesson in Love*, who tries in vain to mediate between the adversaries by shouting "Peace!" The ministers stand on the same side of the boundary line as the social welfare workers.

David finds employment with a gardener, Håkansson, but there, too, he gets into trouble. Many of the characters in the film seem to have been lifted from some simpler folk tale. Hjalmar Bergman, too, may have inspired the character delineation. When David at last manages to buy his small cottage, a civil service official, Herr Purman, appears and tells David that he and Maggi must move. Misfortunes are heaped on the heads of the young couple. Maggi loses the child she wants to give birth to. The film seems to deny "the intervention of all transcendental powers in meaningless life."[8] One critic, finding the picture more than social satire, calls it "a salute to young, homeless love, in a world where it rains, but not porridge."[9]

*It Rains on our Love* is not improvement, visually, upon *Crisis*. The story appears improvised. In spite of the strong influences, it has a very special tone of its own, tender, bantering, something of a canticle or a ballad. One may agree with Siclier's appraisal of B's earlier films: "For Bergman, life is a sort of monotonous journey, and the pictures of human existence are of interest only to the extent that they mirror this monotony. The great problem for his characters is not so much to act as to be happy."[10] It is strange that an ideal of passivity may be glimpsed behind B's early films. The people want to *be*, rather than to act. The man of action, whether intellectual or not, is an object of suspicion. Perhaps it can be explained by the notion, frequently harbored by intellectuals, that "happiness, that's for the others,"—in other words, the people who are not tormented by inner conflicts as much as "we" are. The happiness ideal then becomes a conflict-free condition. This thought, too, is typically romantic.

The most interesting of B's original manuscripts from the 1940's (with the exception of *The Devil's Wanton*) were not filmed at all, or were done by others. The pictures he directed himself were based on outside literary material, and written in collaboration with Herbert Grevenius, to whose contribution B himself attributes great importance.[11] Grevenius wrote a quick and easy everyday dialogue. But it cannot be said that the dialogue in the films that were written entirely by B and staged by others was inferior. The two pictures treated below, *Woman without a Face* and *Eva*, were directed by Gustaf Molander. It was generally agreed that Molander with these works regenerated himself, and that the frenzy in B's narrative contributed to this.

### *Woman without a Face* and *Eva*

For both these films Molander wrote the final acting version of the script. The original of *Woman without a Face* was a short story, "The Puzzle Represents Eros," written in 1946. While some changes in the time element have been made in the script, nothing essential has been added, and the dialogue is exactly the same as in the printed story. An American critic, Hollis Alpert, is amazed at B's loose manuscripts. But that seems to be the general rule in Swedish films. In other words, the Swedish manuscripts cannot be compared with the Anglo-Saxon shooting scripts. The final planning is done by the director on the lot.

The interesting thing about *Woman without a Face* and *Eva* is that Molander's treatment of the material does not differ much from what one might have expected from B. The work of both artists at this time built on a common tradition in Swedish film and theater. The style, in fact, is strongly influenced by the theater, and individual scenes leave little space for creative work in the cutting room. The film cutter has only a narrow margin to work with. He is bound by the story's dramatic demands (if he decides to follow the conventional drama structure). These pictures, directed by Molander, are made without surprises, within the framework of a certain tradition. The method has held back creative cinematographic activity. This, unfortunately, is also evident in those of B's own pictures where he is most free. This has meant that a director like Molander, the connecting link between the two great periods in Swedish film—Sjöström-Stiller and B—was able to fashion *Woman without a Face* in B's spirit.

The short story from which *Eva* is taken was also made into a movie script by Molander with small changes. The story is not told in flashbacks, as is the film. Of these two works, *Woman without a Face* is considerably more interesting. This is because of the strong and caustic portrait of the leading character, Rut Köhler. The plot is told in a long flashback, beginning with the attempted suicide of the leading male character in a hotel. He takes this desperate step when Rut leaves him. The narrator is Ragnar Ekberg, an old friend of Martin Grandé. He happens to watch Rut's departure from the hotel, and manages to save the life of his friend. Martin Grandé's name appears also in *The Devil's Wanton* and in the comedy *Kamma Noll*. B often plays with names in his pictures. But identical names do not necessarily mean identical characters.

B describes Rut thus: "Her face is not beautiful. Her irresistible attractiveness is found in something else, something indefinable—in the soft smile and the hard laugh, in the voice, ingratiating and devoted, caustic, scornful, and brutal, in her quickly changing moods, the facial play of emotions in her springy and delectable movements, in the catlike grace and elasticity of her body. A little *femme fatale*, a cuddly little puma with deadly claws."

The film is set during the years 1944 and 1945, which is not clearly indicated in the story. Martin Grandé is a middle-class married man with one child. He attends Stockholm University. He becomes acquainted with Rut, by chance, just as Jan-Erik Widgrens meets Bertha in *Torment*. Rut lives alone, but often visits her mother and her mother's lover, who is one of B's evil spirits. He is Victor, who, when Rut was twelve years old, seduced her. Victor is played by the same actor who in *Illicit Interlude* appears as the personification of evil.

The picture deals with people possessed. During his military service, Martin disappears, and looks up Rut. Their life together leads to a catastrophe. At first they find quarters at the home of a chimney sweep and his family. Later, via a fourth-class hotel, they move to a warehouse, where Martin leaves her. But their reconciliation in the end (at the beginning of the film) leads to Rut's taking her revenge by leaving him. To relive the past means for Martin that he can get well—a means many of B's characters resort to. To remember is to be able to forget, and this obtains also with Martin. He returns to his family. His attempts to break loose from his middle-class circle have failed. He has sought a freer life, but has not been able to realize his hopes. His retreat is described here without surprise, but rather as a self-evident matter.

The contrasts in the story are very plain. On the one hand, the middle-class milieu, safe and quiet; on the other, the restless, unsure, but fascinating life outside. The representatives of the latter are Rut, the author Ragnar Ekberg, and the jovial chimney sweep, Sam Svensson. But since *Woman without a Face* is not a satire, there is nothing of Strindberg's nausea in the description of the middle-class people. The conflicts later receive a more convincing, artistically integrated description. Moreover, it often reveals the oversimplified and adolescent nature of the solutions sought. B the artist seems here to evade the opposition between artist and bourgeois, only to come to grips with it later. But

*Woman without a Face* is, of course, not his film, his visual creation. It is done by Molander with a frenzy that corresponds to the tone of the narrative. The film is unified, but very melodramatic when it tells exclusively about Martin and Rut.

This lack, a certain inability to achieve an artistic (read dramatic) balance, is even more evident in *Eva*, which, however, contains richer material. This film, too, is influenced by war's proximity. When the two lovers are staying in the Stockholm archipelago, the corpse of a German soldier is washed ashore. Eva, who is pregnant, finds it meaningless to bring children into this world, where bloody strife seems inevitable. The storm, the sense of apprehension and uneasiness, the brooding mood of autumn, all seem very clearly influenced by the international situation. It is a belated, a weakened Swedish reflection of the big European problems, a searching examination that turns inward because there is no external enemy.

The delineation of Eva is typical of B's artistic courage, or naïveté. In the preamble to the film, Bo Fredriksson goes home to see his parents. During the course of the picture he remembers the incident which set its decisive mark upon his life. This is typical of B's way of letting a key situation interpret a character: A shocking experience becomes the background to a person's life. Thus chance often plays a deciding role, an individual trauma, which only clear awareness can turn into a source of strength. *A Ship to India, Night is my Future*, and *Port of Call* all contain such key episodes. These episodes have often occurred far in the past, and are given as an introduction to the story, or are told in flashbacks. In *Ship to India* the father tries to drown his son; the last trust between them breaks. In *Night is my Future* the main character becomes blind. In *Eva* Bo runs away from his family and joins a band of strolling musicians. He discovers another world, in which he finds Marthe, who is blind. She becomes his companion and confidante. One day he guides Marthe to a switch engine and sets it in motion. She experiences the fascination of speed. His fright increases with the acceleration. The locomotive overturns and is derailed, and Marthe is killed. Bo's father, who is a station inspector, arrives at the place of the wreck, and beats his son mercilessly. Together they lift up Marthe's limp lifeless body.

With this tragedy, Bo leaves childhood forever behind him, perhaps more because the bond with the father has broken than because Marthe has died. In the synopsis, this event is told in such a way that death, to Bo, becomes "a frightening executioner and a headsman. I vowed to hate God. An icy chill filled me, and I thought it was my guilt for having killed Marthe and my hatred of God and the nothingness of life that made me so cold. Gradually, all this melted away, and there was only left a gnawing silent ache, which I almost did not feel. But something like a veil clouded my eyes."

Childhood, beyond sin and guilt, appears to the poet behind this film as a promised land. He looks for the dividing line between childhood and maturity, for the painful realization of time's passing. The film narratives become a sort of penance, from which the compromise emerges, whether it is shameful or not. Death is viewed as "a part of life and its waves."[12] Bo's return means a reconciliation with the family. He sees Eva again, a childhood friend; in her home an old man is dying. These scenes have a full and definitive tone of resignation. Eva's and Bo's fellowship stands in contrast to the old man's death. Life becomes a balance sheet, perhaps without any result.

In the description of Bo's visit to the city, B's worst sides are shown—a mixture of melodrama and comedy—while in the scenes of their life beside the archipelago the film regains its power. The struggle for the child is tied to the discovery of the German soldier, the storm with Eva's labor. The dramatic contrasts are not invented or literary. They are real because they can be given direct form in the film. For that reason, the end of the picture with its tone of vanquished death becomes convincing, even psychologically. In an essay from the 1940's, B is described, on the basis of this film, as a proclaimer of "in-spite-of-all."[13] This characteristization can be applied to all of B's films.

## A Ship to India

As with many of B's less important works, *A Ship to India* could be summed up as a scene, a fraction from one of his richer films. His later and more mature works analyze and mirror a deeper world. The choices are more difficult, the positions taken more subtle. On the other hand, influences of other directors and schools of the film are less prominent in his more recent output. *A Ship to India* shows traces of its theatrical origin. Like *It Rains on our Love*, it is "almost a Swedish-French film."[14] Something in the tone of the film suggests also Ford's *Voyage Home* as well as the German expressionism of the twenties. This eclectic attitude need not be regarded as a weakness. It is the expression of a searching artist's exercises in the medium. As films, *Eva* and *Woman without a Face* are purer; they are firmly anchored in the Molander tradition of good craftsmanship. As a director, B is groping his way; he fails, only to achieve more important victories later on.

The main story is once more told in one single flashback. If it had not been so, B's artistic philosophy would not have been able to reach its equilibrium, its conciliatory conclusions: "We know, when the film's introductory passage is over, that Johannes is well, that the father's suicide attempt has failed, as well as his attempt at murdering his son. We also know that Sally herself has become entangled in what she helped Johannes out of. Sensation for its own sake has disappeared. . . ."[15] Johannes Blom returns to his native city after seven years at sea. He looks up Sally. She is alone and says she does not need his pity. He goes down to the shore, and begins to recall his past. His father, Alexander

Blom, was a sea captain and the master of a salvage vessel. As a young man, Johannes was hunchbacked (obviously a psychological disability). Alexander Blom dreams of voyages faraway with Sally. He leads her to the salvage boat, which is the family's home, and violently demonstrates his intentions. Deep inside he is a dreamer, constantly frustrated in his attempts to escape. He has a room in the city where he is able to dream of India in peace. He is about to become blind. His worn-out wife Alice hopes it will happen soon. Then he will be completely dependent on her.

The great shock for Captain Blom comes when he discovers the mutual sympathy between Sally and Johannes. Sally can cure Johannes of his repressions and his hatred of his father. The gospel of fellowship is eloquent. It is somewhat similar to that which is projected in *Port of Call* but in a sterner form:

Johannes: I have always been alone. There has never been anybody who bothered about me.

Sally: One cannot just be lonesome. One must have somebody to care for. One must have somebody to love. Else one might as well be dead.

This leads to the brilliant sequences that condense the action of the film. The father forces Johannes to work in spite of the fact that the son wants to go to the city. Johannes dives; the father does not feed him any air, but Johannes is saved. The father flees in desperation to his room and destroys the symbols of his yearning, the ships and the exotic objects. Then he tries to commit suicide.

*A Ship to India* does not treat any problems of faith, but discards them entirely for the subject of happiness and the possibilities of fellowship. Love is regarded and analyzed as a means of help. Ulrichsen[16] believes that the attitude is almost one of "mental hygiene." Sally is the helper, who cures Johannes. In his turn, he wants to help her. It is not a question of love. The film ends in conciliation, when Johannes, at the end of the flashback, still prevails upon Sally to go with him. He accomplishes what his

father, bound to his wife and his boat, has failed to achieve—the
journey away. This departure motif in B's production must be
seen against a historical and social background. Symbolically, it
may be regarded as an attempt to break the routine of Swedish
life. One wants to see the world. One wants to act. In a transferred meaning, Sweden becomes a symbol of something middle-
class and stagnant. But it is also the question of the romanticist's
eternal dream: the attempt to solve problems by running away
from them.

The problems in the picture are personal, private. There arises
a contrast between the philosophic meaning of the idea of flight
and the characters' own, rather simple motives. The characters
cannot carry the manifold meanings with which they have been
saturated.

## Port of Call

The motifs from *A Ship to India* return in a considerably more
credible and successful manner in *Port of Call*. The picture was
made exactly one year later. It is not so strongly melodramatic
as *A Ship to India*. B leaves the French influences and seeks a
realistic line, which later is followed up in *Monika*. Both films
move in a proletarian milieu. The acerbity in the social narrative is an acerbity of style. B is working under the influence of
the Italian neorealism, in which he has suddenly discovered "the
melody of postwar thought." He considered this neorealism (he
specifically mentioned Rossellini's *Open City*) to be one of the
most significant trends in films in some decades.[17] To move from
the fictitious, the enacted, in a search for the documentary seems
to come naturally to B. *Night is my Future*, done before *Port of
Call*, becomes gripping as a story when it deviates from the plot
and describes children in a school for the blind. They are reading
*The Wonderful Adventures of Nils*, by Selma Lagerlöf, in

unison. *Port of Call* is important for its close-to-reality touch.
Here B makes use of a more mobile, more expressive camera
than in the majority of his earlier pictures. The film is made in the
harbor of Gothenburg, on ships, piers, in factories, that is, in
authentic surroundings. The photography abandons almost all
effects of estheticism, except in one of the final scenes, where the
despair of the sailor Gösta is told by expressionistic, stylistic
means. *Port of Call* abandons the social idealization that weighs
down much of the Italian neorealism. It is Rossellini's ideal that
comes back. It is true that some of the early morning shots of
workmen remind one of the harbor sequences in *Potemkin* and
the lyric tone of the British documentary pictures of the thirties.
But the influence of the Italians is the most fruitful. B returns to
reality, as did the classic names in Swedish films in their most
important pictures. This is a path which B's later productions unfortunately has not followed. He has instead gone as far as can
be imagined from society and surroundings.

B is not slavishly faithful to his predecessors, whether Swedish
or foreign. He is an "autodidact of the form,"[18] ready to repeat
the mistakes of others. It is from this that his photographic vision
receives its unusual naïveté, its great insecurity, and its ability
later on to shape an observation which is masterly in its sharpness
of detail.

As a story, *Port of Call* is surprisingly firm, although scenes
and figures are recognizable from B's earlier pictures. The story
was originally written by Olle Länsberg, but large parts have
been rewritten by B. He also did the scenario and made many
changes while shooting. In everything essential, the film is exclusively his work.

Merchant sailor Gösta Andersson, twenty-nine years old, returns home after eight years at sea. Simultaneously, a tragedy
begins to unfold in the harbor. A girl wanders somnambulisti-
cally down to the pier and jumps into the water, but she is fished
out. As Gösta passes the group of people that has gathered, she

is carried away in an ambulance. There is in her fate, as the film projects it to the very end, an obvious social determinism. In contrast to the individualism in Swedish literature, there is a naturalistic line which presents people solely as products of their environment. These two lines were already broken with Strindberg. Sweden has lacked the explosive events that forced other European authors to express the possibility of a social change. While the climate for a revolt against the established order has not been missing, the harmony and the even rhythm of development have left their mark on the presentation of social problems in literature.

Gösta is a serious young man, who in one scene is shown reading Harry Martinson's *Journeys without Aim*. In a dance hall, he meets Berit, the girl who attempted suicide. He follows her home and stays over night. But from his farewell it is obvious that no emotional bond will hold him. His promise to see her again seems halfhearted. The picture's social criticism is concentrated in the description of Berit. Nothing is told of Gösta's past. Berit is under the surveillance of a guardian. Her mother is divorced from her father, and is described as a repulsive pedant. One remembers especially a scene in the girl's room. The mother moves about, straightening things, nervously, aimlessly. She is religious. She has spoken to a minister and managed to have the father promise to return home. All flashbacks in the film concern Berit. In one of these is shown the parents' wearying quarrel about the daughter; in another, how Berit, who attends a milliner's school, is locked out of her home late one night. On the stairs she meets a man who, like Jack in *Crisis* (played by the same actor), is half unreal, romantic. She moves in with him, but her mother sends her to a correctional institution. She escapes, but is caught and sent back. At the time she meets Gösta, she is working in a ball-bearing factory. But her mother tells her guardian that Berit has had a visit from a man. This gives rise to new conflicts.

The film's observation of details is sharp and visually clear. The difference between a picture such as *Port of Call* and those made ten years later is not that the more recent ones appear as philosophical debates on a higher plane. The difference is that B manages to utilize *all* cinematographic methods. Berit's guardian, Mr. Vilander, wants to see the girl returned to the institution. Her brother, an engineer in the plant where she works, wants the girl to be given another chance. Two kinds of behavior are pitted against each other: the impersonal one of the social machinery, and the cherishing, responsible one, based on love of mankind. But even here, determinism pushes in. The mother's bitterness is a result of her marriage; Vilander has had unfortunate experiences in trusting girls like Berit.

*Port of Call* deals with two persons, for whom no one wants to be responsible. This element of irresponsibility also touches Gösta in the beginning. He hesitates whether or not to see Berit again. He comes late to their meeting. And when she tells of her hard past, he asks, "Why didn't you keep your mouth shut?" Albert Johansson in *The Naked Night* also regrets that he has forced Anne to confess her unfaithfulness. But B shows plainly that he still does not prefer a lie. He seems to believe that people can live more happily if they are conscious of each other's weakness. It is natural doctrine for an artist who succeeds in turning man's abasement to its opposite, to victory and truth. What is a moment of humiliation other than a second of bitter truth?

The sequences of the second meeting of Gösta and Berit portend the story of Monika and Harry, the physical community which is a spiritual one. A manuscript commentary tells of this: "All the locked-up frozen emotions, all the defiance, all the taut watchfulness with which Berit, always prepared to be attacked, daily and hourly surrounds herself, the mask that is her only protection, all this suddenly lets go before the amusing events that take place on the screen, and her feeling of joy at being together with Gösta. She becomes herself, as she is deep inside, but never has dared to show herself. All her repressed joy and need of spontaneity now find an outlet, and the hard daily discipline she submits herself to makes the reaction uncontrollable. Here is Berit, beautiful, healthy, open."

Berit's girl friend Gertrud asks her man friend to help her get an abortion. It fails, and Berit takes the sick Gertrud to Gösta. Here the last scenes of the film unfold. Against a promise that she may keep her freedom, Berit at last divulges the address of the abortionist. She and Gösta decide to stow away on a ship. They walk through the harbor. Suddenly a decision ripens within them to stay and meet life's difficulties. This is the film's climax and meaning.

The unsentimental tone of the story and the uniformity of the style make *Port of Call* B's most important film before *The Devil's Wanton*. The outdoor scenes possess a scope and power that presage the influence of Sjöström and Stiller. Landscape and authentic environs are utilized in a creative manner. In *The Devil's Wanton*, *Monika* and *To Joy*, B shows city scenes, but he has not even hinted at the urbanization process that is going on in Sweden, the social changes that occur daily. Therefore it may be said that he is constantly working with a social image that is antiquated, that belongs to the past. This does not lessen the value of his contribution, but indicates the possibility of a quite different kind of film drama with the Swedish milieu as a point of departure.

Gösta is a de-romanticized hero. Neither is there anything ingratiating about Berit. The romantic gives way to realism.

### Night is my Future

Compared with *Port of Call*, *Night is my Future* seems to be an almost completely commercial film. It still has some very strong scenes and a suggestive effect in details, although the direction seems awkward, uninterested, and amateurish.

Bengt Vyldeke is blinded when he tries to save a puppy during a rifle drill in the army. The blindness forces him to adjust himself to a new world. His tortures are described in a dream sequence, which in its vividness foreshadows the dream of terror in *The Devil's Wanton*. A young woman saves Bengt's life. She is Ingrid, whose father has died. She becomes a servant in Bengt's home. After many defeats and disappointments, Bengt is finally united with her. This, in bold strokes, is the plot of the story. I will show some single groups of scenes.

1. Bengt plays the organ at the funeral of Ingrid's father. Outdoors it is cold winter, without any snow on the ground. The funeral procession enters the church. We see Ingrid look up. After a long wait, Bengt begins to play. He does not know her as yet, but there seems to exist a secret contact between them. The scene is especially skillful because of its timing. This vignette precedes a similar one in *Winter Light*.

2. Bengt is refused entrance to the Academy of Music. He begins to play in a tavern, where his life becomes a real hell, a *No Exit*. A boy steals money from him. The restaurateur is a boor. There is an atmosphere of hate in the place that makes him unhappy. The aura of the social environment becomes metaphysical.

3. Ingrid associates with Ebbe, who studies and is reported to be a Left Socialist. (The political beliefs of B's characters are seldom mentioned.) Ebbe beats Bengt in a contest of bending arms, and hits him when he discovers Ingrid's deeper feelings. Bengt is grateful for this. He feels that he is treated like a real, normal person. Defeat and humility turn into victory.

The film ends on a light chord. Bengt and Ingrid get the minister's permission to marry. They go away, perhaps to a better life. We do not, however, get the impression that the picture has been a story of blindness. The blindness seems a commercial pretext to arouse our sympathy. There is not much of B's personality in this film.

## While the City Sleeps and Divorced

*Night is my Future* belongs to a group of pictures in which the trace of B's hand is not very clear. *While the City Sleeps* is a tale of juvenile delinquency, built on an original idea by B, but not directed by him. *Frånskild* (Divorced) is a marriage drama, in which B's contribution appears to weigh more, especially in the central description of the woman's loneliness. Much more interesting is *This Can't Happen Here.*

## This Can't Happen Here

This film has been characterized as a Swedish contribution to the anti-Red pictures now in vogue.[19] It was made to order, completed in a few weeks. With equal speed, during the so-called film shutdown in 1951, when the studios, for tax reasons, stopped making features, B finished nine commercial shorts advertising a soap called Bris. These pieces are also very charming. It cannot be denied that B has the ability to create something personal and valuable within the framework of cinematographic improvisation.

The story and the direction of *This Can't Happen Here* are rather in opposition to each other. The story itself is a spy thriller. The mysterious engineer Atkä Natas comes to Stockholm via Helsinki on a trip from the dictator state Liquidatzia. It proves that he is an agent for L, but had intended to present himself at the American embassy. After a long series of adventures, complications, and amusing incidents, Natas is hunted by agents of the foreign power, who have discovered his treachery. Rather than give himself up, he commits suicide.

The plot is worth nothing. The interesting part is B's direction. It underlines the unreal character of the story. This has never happened and could never happen. The serious scenes are exaggerated, and become comical instead. Excitement is whipped up by farcical pursuits and ridiculous complications. Thereby, even death becomes a divertissement. B drives the spy thriller *ad absurdum*, in the same way that Douglas Sirk drove the true-blue American romantic film to the ultimate in twaddle, when it ceased to become twaddle and turned into art.

The film contains an appeal to a Sweden which is unaware. The Swedes have no idea of what goes on behind their backs. The contrast between the wickedness of the world and the Swedes' lack of suspicion never becomes a message one can believe in, because of the absurdity of the framework. B himself does not count *This Can't Happen Here* as his film. The strange thing, though, is that he masters also the conventions of an out-and-out commercial film plot. That is a faculty he did not have when he made *Crisis*.

Except for *Torment*, none of B's films from the forties became a great public success. B worked for several companies. His pictures revealed a much stronger talent and a greater self-willed creative power than those of any other Swedish director during the same time. And it is still unusual, in any country, for a director like B to have a chance to seek his own way. The period of tests and trials in different directions was the foundation and the prerequisite for the know-how that B attained. But the key film remains in all respects *The Devil's Wanton*. As someone has said: "It is possible to judge B without having seen the films that preceded *The Devil's Wanton*. It is impossible to judge him without having seen *The Devil's Wanton*."

Above: IT RAINS ON OUR LOVE.
Birger Malmsten (*David*) and
Barbro Kollberg (*Maggi*).

Left: WOMAN WITHOUT A FACE.
Alf Kjellin (*Martin*) and
Gunn Wållgren (*Rut*).

Below: PORT OF CALL.
Nine-Christine Jönsson (*Berit*).

Below Left: NIGHT IS MY FUTURE. Birger Malmsten (*Bengt*), Mai
Zetterling (*Ingrid*), and Bengt Eklund (*Ebbe*).

Right: A SHIP TO INDIA. Gertrud Fridh (*Sally*) and Birger Malmsten (*Johannes*).

A scene from EVA.

TORMENT. Mai
Zetterling (*Bertha*) and
Stig Järrel (*Caligula*).

# 3

## THE DEVIL'S WANTON

"What is *her* guilt, that she has to live this nauseating life? What is mine, and the other people's guilt? Why can we not intervene and prevent? Why do we stand so foolishly powerless against evil, inwardly attacked by an annihilating fifth column?

"Why must a person sooner or later arrive at a point where he for a moment awakes to a painful and unendurable knowledge of himself and his situation, and why is there, in that moment, no help to summon? Is earth hell, and is there in that case also a God, and where is he, and where are the dead?

". . . why must we distrust our innermost convictions, and why is it so difficult to be faithful to oneself?

"I want to make a film about this. I want to pose questions, in a manner simple and to the point, as I conceive them in my heart. I do not want to end my film with an explanation or with "something positive," as the producers say.

"I want to be just as agitated and inquiring as I am, and I want to make other people agitated and inquiring."[1]

These questions were asked by B at the premiere of *The Devil's Wanton*, the first picture in which he had a completely free hand, in which he, within the frame of a tight budget, succeeded in telling about his world as he understood it. Both *A Ship to India* and *Port of Call* foreshadow *The Devil's Wanton*. Sally in *A Ship to India* and Berit in *Port of Call* are preliminary studies for Birgitta-Carolina in *The Devil's Wanton*. Sally and Berit both achieve freedom, the former through Johannes, who does her the same service as she has done him, Berit because she has by her side Gösta, a man made of other stuff than the hesitant, weak characters in *The Devil's Wanton*.

The loneliness that surrounds the leading participants in B's earlier films is expanded in *The Devil's Wanton* to take in everything and everybody. Beyond the atomistic world shown in the picture, are certain contemporary phenomena in Swedish society, a sharpened feeling that man cannot or does not want to help his fellow man. From its private, personal implications, loneliness can be expanded in scope to have the same experimental strength as in *The Devil's Wanton*, in which Sweden "for the first time in twenty-five years . . . is in the lead of the international development of the film."[2]

The idea for the picture is contained in a seventy-page short story called "True Story."[3] It is openly autobiographical. The fate of the characters is not exactly the same as in the finished film. Especially Birgitta-Carolina's part attains an entirely different stature. Even while the picture was being shot, the interpretation of her role underwent changes. Her death received the present, grandiose rendering. This only proves that B struggled long with the material of the picture. The final product achieves a part of its strength from the fact that it is unfinished, that it bears the stamp of the uncompleted.

In the introductory scenes a man is shown walking to a film studio. Once inside, he appears confused. Through the clutter of scenery and stage decor he makes his way to Martin, the director, rehearsing a scene. The old man is Martin's former mathematics teacher, Paul. In the lunch room he has a chance to expound on what he wants. He has been in an insane asylum, and now he wants to do a film about hell. It is to begin with a proclamation by the Devil: "As I from this day on will assume power over all the peoples and countries in the world, I want to announce the following: I command that everything shall continue as before." The Devil shall forbid the use of the atom bomb, and shall hold those who dropped the bomb on Hiroshima responsible. Mankind is not going to get away with the bombs' putting a quick end to its misery. Paul insists that the Devil is not at all wicked, he wishes mankind well. "He will support man's interest in religion and the church, which have worked so long and hard for the Devil's success."

Paul's statement at first evokes merriment. But Martin and his actors gradually become stirred and serious.

The story now turns to the home of Tomas, an author of the 1940's. Martin has referred Paul's idea to Tomas and Sofi. Tomas finds a connection in an article he has never been able to finish. He begins to read. The action is visualized. Tomas, who has met Birgitta-Carolina, goes up to her and tries to interview her. In these scenes he is a serious young man with glasses. Her answer is evasive and nettling. This takes place six months earlier. The camera then makes a long sweep to Västerlång Street, in Stockholm's Old City. A voice reads the production notices. The action begins. It tells of Birgitta-Carolina—a story "instead of" Paul's project. But it deals with the same subject, hell on earth. This is B's *No Exit*. After the sweep of Västerlång Street, we see Birgitta-Carolina drag herself painfully up some stairs, savagely beaten. Next she is in bed, with a child beside her. Her fiancé Peter, the procurer, and her hard sister Linnea manage to convince Birgitta-Carolina that they should take care of the child. She surmises, but she does not know with certainty, the fate they have in readiness: death. Her surrender to the persuasion is the beginning of her tragedy.

Tomas's and Birgitta-Carolina's paths join again after a parallel action. In his despair, Tomas decides that he and Sofi should commit suicide. Instead it is she who takes the initiative: she hits him over the head with a bottle. When he wakes up, he believes he has murdered her. He runs to the police to confess. Meanwhile, the police are searching for Birgitta-Carolina. She flees to the basement, the same place where she later takes her own life, and hides behind some furniture. A little boy, dressed like an Indian, comes up to her. He shows her a hiding place; he keeps a knife there. She may borrow it, if she wishes. Then the boy's mother descends into the cellar, calling for him. He is hungry, and has achieved his purpose: that his mother should look for him. He leaves. Now the police arrive and find Birgitta-Carolina.

Peter talks her out of her trouble. She is set free. They walk out of the basement and find Tomas, shivering and alone. Peter leaves for a moment. Then Birgitta-Carolina begs Tomas to come with her, to get away from Peter. They leave. Tomas looks up Bohlin's boarding house, where the decisive scenes between the two take place. They are assigned a weird attic room.

1. Birgitta-Carolina sits in the kitchen with Mrs. Bohlin and her daughter, a woebegone teen-ager. When Mrs. Bohlin has left, a young man enters. Like Peter, he is employed by the post office. Birgitta-Carolina observes this scene, first in the same room, later surreptitiously through the door chink, just as Isak Borg studies his childhood in *Wild Strawberries* or the lawyer Egerman witnesses the flight of his son and wife in *Smiles of a Summer Night*. The scene is of decisive importance to Birgitta-Carolina. The girl is pregnant. The young man is happy because of this; the two are going to marry. The parallels to Birgitta-Carolina are obvious: happiness is possible then, *for the others*.

2. A cut-out scene sheds light on Birgitta-Carolina. She carries shaving water to a preacher. He thanks her, and says: "Peace

be with you." Birgitta-Carolina asks what peace is. She does not believe in God. He claims he does. Since the Devil exists, God also must exist. At last the preacher confesses that deep in his heart he is "convinced that God is dead and that the Devil is the absolute ruler of the world. I receive no answer to my prayers, and I am mute inside. But you see, that is just why I must believe!" Tomas Eriksson in *Winter Light* has the same feeling. The preacher in *The Devil's Wanton* cannot help Birgitta-Carolina.

3. Tomas and Birgitta-Carolina experience the romance of childhood in the attic room. He finds a projector he once used to play with as a child.

"That little unsteady movie apparatus, which rattled forth its jumpy and striped pictures, became a magician's box, the many film squares with their small, small moving creatures achieved reality and dimension. I remember situations and pictures, bit by bit, detail by detail. It is strange, really. The toy was a mechanical one, of course, there were always the same men doing the same things, the whole operation was nothing but a mechanical procedure. I have often wondered what it was that fascinated me so completely, and what it is in this thing that still fascinates me (deep inside in exactly the same way)."[4]

B wrote this in 1948 or 1949. Tomas and Birgitta-Carolina experience the pictures in precisely the same way. He starts the projector. We are shown a farce from the days of the silent films, especially staged by B for the occasion, with a crook, a cop, and horror effects. Death emerges from a coffin. The farce ends when three actors, after a wild chase, jump out of the window at the same time.

Tomas and Brigitta-Carolina experience a lost childhood, perhaps a childhood that has never existed. The attic room is a home, a refuge, unfortunately a temporary one, away from "the world."

4. The two sink into sleep. For her, it becomes a nightmare. She is walking through a forest of people. She finds Tomas. He is sad because somebody has thrown out his hobbyhorse. She dreams of belonging to him, but is driven away from happiness. Then she comes upon a bathtub, in which a doll bobs on the water. A hand lifts up the doll. Next the hand picks up a pike, wrings its neck and replaces it in the water. Then she awakens. Tomas perceives her fright and urges her to remember consciously what it is that torments her.

The action that follows causes Birgitta-Carolina to leave Tomas. When she gets to Peter and Linnea, she asks how it felt to kill the infant: "Like killing a kitten." But Birgitta-Carolina must walk the path to the final test, since she lacks the power of resistance to conquer the misfortunes that others have created, but which also are self-inflicted.

The final sequence begins with Tomas's wandering through the desolate harbor. We see him as a vague mirror image. He meets the same boy, in his Indian suit, he who placed the knife in the cellar. Tomas goes out on a float. His moving feet are seen. On the float lies a dead bird. He kicks it into the water. Then he goes ashore. On the shore he sees a placard advertising a weekly magazine. It reads: "Why did you go?" Silence and emptiness. The film cuts directly to Birgitta-Carolina. Peter comes home with Alf, one of her former lovers. She sits in a rocking chair. The camera catches Alf from below first, as a menace. But she does not want to. He insults her. Then her shrieks are heard. Alf runs out. She is moaning on the floor, burnt on the wrist by Alf's cigarette butt. She breaks loose from Peter and Linnea and dashes down the stairs to the cellar.

Her face is turned toward the basement window. She takes the knife. The lighting here, as also later, is expressively stylized, with diagonals that break the picture. From a close-up of her face, the camera moves to the window bars, again approaches her face, moves past her toward Tomas, who is seen behind the bars. She speaks his name. By then she has already used the knife. She bleeds to death on the floor. Once more the camera moves toward her, past her. A woman in veils approaches her, and we see the hand from the dream sequence. She yawns, one hears a child cry. At the same moment her head falls down. She says, "I don't want to." Then Peter enters; the camera catches him in a close-up. He begins to cry and scream. He carries her upstairs, an action which parallels her struggling up the stairs after the sweep of Västerlång Street.

We see the light over the city. Tomas returns to Sofi. He wants to begin anew with her. Martin is at work in the studio. At the end of the day he is visited by Paul. Martin can only say that Paul's project about the film dealing with hell cannot be carried out. It would end in a question, just as *The Devil's Wanton* ends in a question. *The Devil's Wanton* realizes the purposes that Martin declares are impossible to realize. The picture ends with the sound of a gong. If God exists, there is somebody one can ask, otherwise not.

But *The Devil's Wanton* is not, as has often been asserted, primarily a religious film. B's characters do not move in "self-created prisons, but in spiritual concentration camps, brought about by the world around us. These persons are marked by a desperate seeking after meaning and clarity, security and aspiration, healing tenderness and fellowship."[5] *The Devil's Wanton* is a total world vision, the manifesto of a life philosophy. But this would lack interest if B were not able to conjure up his vision. For that reason I first want to treat the picture's cinematographic structure.

The mood of doomsday is all-pervading, but it is often broken by a macabre black humor, as in the contrast between Tomas's interview visit and what happened later to Birgitta-Carolina. With her, everything is seen in a tragic light, while the relations of Tomas-Sofi-Martin are told in a lighter vein. It is only Birgitta-Carolina's fate that really concerns us and becomes all-deciding.

The introductory sequences, with Paul's entry into the studio, give the picture the overall feeling of unreality. This is not a naturalistic tale that is being shown, although the story as such has the character of a story in a tabloid.[6] The scenario is loosely constructed, which underscores the thesis that this is a matter of a morality, a series of burning philosophical questions. B makes use of a symbolic realism, his style is "visionary, projectile-like, it carries us to the starting point, to the future, to background, to a flight of thoughts, to whim and fancy, and all the time it follows a system and a pattern of something thought through: We meet new ways to bring forth Eisenstein's intellectual montage, new ways of projecting the synthetic form of film art."[7]

The logical parallels in the story are skillfully executed: the comparison between Peter and the boy at the post office, the boy in the Indian costume who shows where the knife is hidden and meets the lonely Tomas, the dead bird that forshadows Birgitta-Carolina's death. This logic gathers added material from the contrasts, for instance, between the false and artificial world of the film in the scenes Martin is directing, and the harsh reality illustrated by Birgitta-Carolina's life. The associative effects are stressed particularly in the sound treatment, as when the radio plays "När lillan kom till jorden" (When Baby Arrived in the World), while the sadist Alf is insulting Birgitta-Carolina.[8] In this film B proves to be a masterly creator of sound. When Paul visits the studio, a man somewhere is experimenting with sound effects, hellish sounds that give the appropriate background to Martin and Paul's conversation.

In *The Devil's Wanton* B manages to use camera movement as a creative method, rich in associations. The final scenes, to be sure, possess a strongly melodramatic expansion, but they can be explained by the mounting anguish. B appears here to be completely free from the two dangers that earlier threatened his work: namely, the dependence of the Swedish film on theater-like staging, and on the other hand on a pictorial harmony, the ultimate goal of which is to render the individual shot autonomous, which is against the purposes of film art. In the restless camera movement that characterizes *The Devil's Wanton*, the personal vision is realized. This holds together the mutual contrasts of the sequences, as for instance, between the static full-size pictures of the conversation of Sofi-Martin-Tomas, and the camera's searching movement in Tomas's interview. Here already, close-ups are used with the greatest restraint, evidently because B never wishes to separate the detail from its dramatic context.

In *The Devil's Wanton*, B is an earthly, not to say an anti-Christian, artist. Birgitta-Carolina is looking for a moment of happiness. She is a prostitute, but this is described by B as "a situation, and nothing else. Birgitta-Carolina is mainly a question."[9] Almost all her encounters with reality end in defeat or despair. It is not happiness in the metaphysical sense that she is looking for. She is looking for happiness in the form of staunch fellowship. She lets herself be prevailed upon to be separated from her child because Peter promises her marriage and a changed future. She leaves Tomas because he does not love her, but is only devoted to her. She gives him much, without receiving anything in return. She gives him the courage to find his way back to Sofi. The light of mysticism, a light of grace and mercy, that falls on Birgitta-Carolina, shut up in the cellar, closed in her own death, is a portent that she is, in spite of all, pure of heart and one of the chosen ones. She is pardoned, but there is still no answer to the question why just she had to suffer.

The never-mentioned key word of the film, therefore, is fellowship. To be sure, Birgitta-Carolina lives in a kind of fellowship with Peter and Linnea, but it is one-sided, because they make use of her without her receiving anything in return. In her private situation, suicide is the logical ultimate solution, but the questions remain. Still, hopelessness is not the film's conclusion. Although it happens in a world where the exits are closed, it is still possible to seek solace. *The Devil's Wanton* dismisses the road to art. Tomas and Martin are depicted as helpless or full of lies. The only remaining happiness is that of fellowship, of sexuality. People live with the certainty that life ends, with the certainty of death. This only serves to strengthen their feeling that action must take place in this life.

The choice of persons and surroundings is hackneyed. The circle of people around Birgitta-Carolina is a remnant, less from reality than from popular imagination of a certain segment of Swedish literature. *The Devil's Wanton* does not mirror a social reality existing at the time the picture was made, but a private world of make-believe. This gives strength to the film's ability to observe. The anguish and loneliness that surround the characters seem like a crippling strait jacket. Nobody can break out, physically or psychically. These two manifestations, the feeling that action has been paralyzed and that freedom of choice has been destroyed belong to the decadent inheritance in twentieth-century European literature. One only has to think of the description in Kafka's *The Castle* or of the string of novels where no attempt is made to break the paralyzing feeling of predestination. What places B outside this tradition is his ability to imply another reality, other paths, other ways of existence. These are shown in *The Devil's Wanton*, but the characters have not the power to grasp them.

Seen against the background of *The Devil's Wanton*, with which he made a break-through, B's films appear as constant variations on a group of recurring themes. Now one, now another gets a prominent place in the story. In *The Devil's Wanton* motifs are hinted at which later are treated thoroughly. Birgitta-Carolina and Tomas undertake a desperate escape, but fail. Martin is perhaps a hack, but inside he is tired of creating the lie-studded clichés that make up his films. Paul's statements about the atom bomb portend the moral discussion about man's place in an existence threatened by total destruction.

*The Devil's Wanton* can be viewed as an often very banal film. The very consistency of B's artistic development is made up of this banality, which is that of the true romanticist. B's opposition to society appears to be romantic-reactionary, since he seems to dream of a bygone state of happiness, a perpetual past. Characteristic of *The Devil's Wanton* is Peter's argument when he persuades Birgitta-Carolina to give up her child. He claims that it must be registered and that the authorities will ask about the father. Not a single person in the picture seems to live in circumstances of an orderly society. But the protest that their lives imply is still not without effect, though it must be called by its right name: social anarchism.

At times, the dialogue lacks support in the dramatic situation. However, the problem of B's banality is insoluble, since the courage to stand in opposition implies the taking of a banal stand. The film, as B has often emphasized, appeals to the emotions. It therefore penetrates strata which literature in the first place cannot do. When looking at an abstract painting, one does not ask oneself if the feeling expressed is banal. Faith in life is always banal. One asks whether the feeling is true for the artist behind the work, for the person who views the work. The truth about B's feeling in *The Devil's Wanton* can be analyzed only if one accepts or rejects the committed tone of the film, where the movement of the camera, the cutting, the attention to details are always in line with the narrative material. It may be said that later on, in *Wild Strawberries* and *Illicit Interlude*, B is able to create more convincing film drama. But the danger is that he forsakes the cinematographic mobility of *The Devil's Wanton*, that he moves away from this unique visionary ability. *The Devil's Wanton* is not more important than *Port of Call* because Berit's way leads to the light, Birgitta-Carolina's toward darkness and death, but because B here discovers his "camérastylo," because one of the story's leading characters is the camera itself, present in the room as a commentator, as a comforter.

## Three Strange Loves

*Three Strange Loves* is more slick, more superficial than *The Devil's Wanton* but almost as impressive.

The picture builds on Birgit Tengroth's short stories, which are very skillfully woven into the action. There are four of them. The main story in the film is "Journey with Arethusa," in which Tengroth tells of a train ride from Basle, which constitutes the picture's connecting plot. The first of the stories, "Thirst," is a grotesquely comic episode between cavalry captain Raoul, his wife, and his mistress Rut, which in the picture is a flashback in Rut's consciousness. The second story, "The Faith Healer," contains the material which in the film is used in Viola's scenes with the psychiatrist. The difference is that in the book Viola and Rut are one person called Ingrid. Finally, "Avant de Mourir" narrates the parts which in the film make up Viola's meeting with a friend of her youth, the Lesbian Valborg. All this is combined into one story, in which the transitions are completely natural. The manuscript was written entirely by Herbert Grevenius. It is his most skillful work for films.

The picture starts in a hotel room in Basle in 1946. Rut and Bertil are homeward bound from a trip to the south. They are married; he is a scholar, an art historian. The introductory sequence shows her awakening, busying herself with small tasks in the room, the loneliness that separates them from each other. It is a tragicomic description of disgust and boredom, which ten years later finds its counterpart in Antonioni's scenes of Claudia's loneliness in a hotel room in Palermo, in *L'Avventura*. Rut has once been a ballet dancer. She has lost both her ability to dance and her ability to have children. She is doomed. The film's other feminine leading part is Viola, Bertil's former wife, of whom the parallel story tells. The picture's meaning and movement are the difference between Rut's and Viola's fate and action.

They are both tragically doomed. One can agree with Erik Ulrichsen[10] that the stories in *Three Strange Loves* seem to have been written for B. Many of their characteristics, to which I refer here, are found in the short stories. The balance in the introduction between comedy and tragedy is typical of B. The dialogue concerns rather trivial matters, but these acquire a deeper meaning because of the actors', especially Rut's, inclination to conflict and hysteria. Bertil brings a lunch basket along for the train trip to Stockholm, and does not consider himself able to afford breakfast at the hotel. Still he buys a newspaper, for which he pays a whole Swiss franc. Then he forgets the paper in the room.

Rut's two flashbacks concern love and work. In the first a glimpse is offered of her summer with the captain. He tells her he is returning to his wife and children. She has known nothing of them. They are out in the archipelago, in bathing suits. Still she continues the relationship. One day the captain's wife, Astrid, visits Rut's home and looks her over. Then the captain enters. He upbraids both the wife and the mistress. The wife's place is in the home, the mistress has her place, and what he does concerns neither of them. The scene ends with Rut's tears and despair. She is pregnant, but the captain does not believe it is his child. He leaves her. We are to believe that her sterility is a result of this. In another flashback is shown her life at the ballet school. She and her friends did not "have time for love." Her friend is Valborg, who in the following sequence (the present) meets up with Viola. This is an example of the film's virtuosity in scenario construction.

Rut and Bertil travel homeward while Viola's fate is unfolding to its tragic climax. Shut in the compartment traveling through Europe, devastated by war, Rut and Bertil experience their own inner conflicts, the evil that surrounds them. Rut is a taut spiral, hysterically encased in a spinning of words and thoughts. The flashbacks and Viola's fate show the sad way out that is possible for her, too. The shaping of the scenes on the train is similar to, and foreshadows, the train comedy in *A Lesson in Love*, but is visually more effective. The famous elevator scene in *Secrets of Women* already is found as a nucleus, incorporated in this manuscript. In pursuit of Viola Dr. Rosengren gets stuck in the elevator.

The film tries different possibilities. Viola's path is the same trod by Birgitta-Carolina. Viola has been driven to loneliness. The psychiatrist decides she is incurably ill, but he does not wish to cure her, he wants to seduce her. When she runs out into the empty summer streets of Stockholm (it is Midsummer Eve), she meets another lonely person, Valborg, who also wants to make use of her. It has become late evening. She moves away from the young dancing couples, down to the water, there to drown herself.

The train sequence continues motifs in *The Devil's Wanton*. Bertil and Rut correspond to Tomas and Sofi. The same actors play the roles. Rut is an intellectual woman. She describes herself and Bertil as prisoners in chains. Bertil's attitude is stamped by irony and a certain fatigue. The bonds between them are beginning to wear thin. An ironical vignette shows them distributing food to German children at a station. Of the Germans, he says, "They are so busy trying to keep body and soul together that they have no time to think about any inner life. I can't deny I rather envy them." The misery around Bertil and Rut still cannot make them forget their own egos, their eternally recurring inner questions. Rut describes Bertil as the correct academician, who always finds the right words but says them in the wrong place.

The director himself is seen briefly in a scene in the train corridor, when he passes two conversing Swedish ministers. The priests' words have a certain ironic meaning for Rut and Bertil's relationship, while at the same time, it is one of the many scenes in B's films where the clergy are presented as a group in total absence of spiritual experience.

"At home we have had, speaking confidentially, our storms. I don't like it when they move things about on my writing desk, and my wife is very sensitive when I examine the household accounts in detail. We have now had it out! She promises not to touch my papers, and I don't demand an explanation of amounts under 1.50 kroner."

The brief appearance of B in the corridor reminds one that he, in the Hitchcock manner, appeared in short scenes in most of his pictures from *Night is my Future* to *Dreams*. In *To Joy* he sits in the waiting room at the lying-in hospital, while Stig says farewell to Martha. In *Secrets of Women* he is glimpsed in Paris, in *A Lesson in Love* on the train, and in *Dreams* in a hotel corridor with a dog. However, the scene with B as a bookkeeper in *Smiles of a Summer Night* was eliminated.

While the train with Rut and Bertil approaches Scandinavia, the two plots draw closer together. Viola is driven to her final end. Bertil and Rut's relations reach a sharp crisis. Bertil dreams he has murdered Rut. He feels satisfied that "that tongue isn't going to wag any more." It is Rut's desire to comment on everything, to talk incessantly, that drives Bertil to desperation. When he awakes in a cold sweat he finds Rut alive (compare Tomas's "murder" in *The Devil's Wanton*). The upshot is that both decide to continue.

Bertil: I don't want to be alone and independent. That's worse.

Rut: Than what?

Bertil: Than the hell we are living in. After all, we have each other.

The picture ends with their embrace. The train begins to move homeward.

*Three Strange Loves* concerns fear of old age and sterility, which in the last analysis is fear of loneliness. It elucidates certain motifs in *The Devil's Wanton*, among them the wholly material, physical element in the solutions that are sought. *Three Strange Loves* is staged with a cold, professional clarity. It deals with people who never have time for love—they are too busy suffering, as Siclier says in his book about B. The possibility of death is always present. The characters in the film lack understanding of their own possibilities. They are, in a transferred meaning, too adult. This state of being grownup, in contrast to a child's openness and sensuality, is the central element in B's artistic world. To be an adult and an intellectual is to lose something of the contact with the world, the strength of intuition. At the same time, the yearning for the child is typically romantic, impossible to realize. In *The Devil's Wanton* the scenes in the attic have a trait of childlike play. But it is also the child who, unwittingly, gives Birgitta-Carolina the weapon with which to destroy herself.

A prerequisite to happiness is man's love for woman. According to this ideal picture, woman should not be a seeker, a thinker, like man. The ideal woman is one who lives enclosed in her own happiness in a sphere where only the man can be the intermediary with the outside world. One may regard this interpretation, which appears with greater or lesser force in many succeeding pictures, as a relic of a patriarchal, middle-class phase in the development of Swedish society, an era which B seems to both long for and despise.

*Three Strange Loves* could be called a commercial version of *The Devil's Wanton*. Its visual treatment, however, is perfectly adapted to the nature of the story.

# 4

## SUMMER AND DEATH

Summer as enticement, summer as threat is a central motif in several of B's films.

Foreign critics have interpreted this in a more than necessarily complicated manner. They have sought the symbolic meaning of the summer theme and forgotten its actual one. They have not known what a summer in Scandinavia implies. It is evident that the surroundings and the time, either negatively or positively, are mirrored in art, influence art. It is equally evident that the contrasts in nature between light and darkness, warmth and cold, are reflected in Nordic art and literature. These contrasts are mirrored in the lives of the people, in the dream of freedom, which is almost always a summer dream. One can fashion many different pictures of summer. One may choose sun-drenched rocks or windless coves, the silence of the lake or the deep forests, or open glades with warmth and wild strawberries. These pictures serve as memory's meeting places. They recall moments of festival or rejoicing, or of pain. Summer, always threatened and short, always a surprising season, plays a role in the community life. The Nordic artist who chooses this subject is not original, finds no new symbols. But this does not mean that his creation necessarily lacks strength. All the mean-

ings of the summer are condensed into Midsummer Night. Then
life is most intense, darkness is far in the distance. Life and death
touch each other. Summer means not only a return to the time
of childhood and the games of childhood, but also sexual liberation.

The summer dream takes many forms and expressions with B,
even in his films of the late 1950's. *A Lesson in Love* delineates in
a flashback the highest moment of married happiness. The scene
between husband and wife takes place outdoors, in the summer,
in a forest. *Smiles of a Summer Night* has a theme built entirely
on the release which is thought to take place in people's emotions during a night of summer. Both in *The Seventh Seal* and
*Wild Strawberries*, strawberries play a part as symbols of paradise. In *The Virgin Spring* a hesitant Swedish early summer is
contrasted with the deed of violence that takes place. Violence
becomes violence, not only in itself but also as violence against
summer. After the maiden's death it begins to snow. The hap-
piest scenes in *To Joy*, so far as emotional content is concerned,
are set in the summer by the sea. They are moments of loftiness
and peace.

In Swedish literature the feeling for nature, for summer nature, is a longing for the promised land, the lost land, for the
paradise one never finds. Traditionally, summer means freedom
of movement, in contrast to the shut-in atmosphere of winter.
In his description of summer B shows how Swedish, how national he is. The power of his cinematography comes from his
ability to lift these symbols from a personal experience to uni-
versality.

As self-evident as the summer picture is the picture of death.
It is the might of autumn, of menace and destruction. The
reckoning comes after pleasure. Death is present in the moment
of happiness. Happiness is a way of dying. Evil snares are constantly set for the dreams of happiness. Death is the power that

rules *To Joy*, as if B could not believe in a deliverance in freedom without death.

## To Joy

Swedish critics did not receive this film with special kindness. It was said that "a period of rest for spiritual renewal seems to be necessary to re-establish the contact between his [B's] world of problems and reality."[1] Today one can clearly see that *To Joy* is an important step toward the restraint and freedom of *Illicit Interlude*. It is an uneven film, but important in the same way as certain of Renoir's and Ford's lesser works. None of the films B made around the beginning of the fifties was wholly successful. He tries different approaches.

The film is told in a single flashback, set within a vignette-like framework consisting of the rehearsals of Beethoven's Ninth Symphony at the Hälsingborn Orchestra Society. "Hymn to Joy" has given the film its name. In *Illicit Interlude* the dramatic technique of the flashback is pushed much further. The flashback pictures influence and change the characters acting in the present. In *Illicit Interlude* the flashback is dramatically motivated. The picture cannot, apparently, be told in any other way. *Secrets of Women* is done entirely in flashbacks, while there are none in *Monika*. The flashback is a dramatic convention which B gradually abandons in favor of letting the past be mirrored in the dialogue, in the characters' present actions.

*To Joy* begins brilliantly. During rehearsals, the young violinist Stig Eriksson is called to the telephone. The music follows him as he hastens to the booth. His wife has been killed in an accident in the country. A kerosene stove has exploded.

Stig arrives home. When alone, he sits down in the empty apartment. He considers himself and the world. One sees the doll he gave his wife when they first became friends. Like any other actor with B, Stig does not turn directly to the audience. He looks past us, out into a space we all share, perhaps a void. Such scenes of an inner trial (which also becomes our trial) are found everywhere in B's films, even when two or more persons are in the picture. They do not seem to speak to each other. Their solitude prevents them. They stand before a god, a conscience, an eternity without an answer. Faced with this, they are forced to answer, or at least temporarily solve, their life problems.

A similar scene is found in *Illicit Interlude* at the end of the last flashback. Marie comes from the hospital after Henrik's death, in the company of Uncle Erland. They walk down a corridor. Erland's threatening shadow becomes supernatural. They arrive at Erland's middle-class home. We see Marie turn toward the window and the darkness. Her contempt finds an outlet, contempt for herself and hatred for the unknown:

"I do not believe that God exists. And if He exists I hate Him. And I will not end there. If He stood before me, I would spit in His face. I shall hate Him every day, and I shall never forget it. I shall hate Him until I die."

God is a personal, private God to whom Marie turns. The problem of living becomes a matter between Marie and this unknown figure.

The big central flashback in *To Joy* tells the story of Stig and Martha's meeting, their marriage, discord, and reunion. The story begins seven years earlier, when they are the only new recruits of the orchestra. They get together, marry, and have children. Stig cherishes great dreams of success as a soloist. But he fails at his debut. He turns his bitterness on Martha and deserts her. The road to a reconciliation is long and difficult. Just at the time when a new life seems to be starting, Martha's life is cut off.

The problems posed here are those of artists, but they concern others also. According to conductor Sönderby, Stig is an egoist, who in music sees a means, but not a goal. This is what provokes the dissensions in his married life. It has been said that the reason for B finding his solution in death is that he cannot believe in a union in happiness. It can also be said that Stig does not relinquish the last remnants of his egoism. An often-quoted statement by B himself, the closing words in his lecture, "To Make a Film," show that these questions have been real to him, even theoretically. He says that "the individual has become the highest form and the greatest curse of artistic creation." He salutes the anonymous host of men who built the cathedral of Chartres. He wants to be one of the nameless:

"I never have to worry about the judgment of my own times, nor the opinion of posterity. I consist of a Christian name and a family name, which are engraved nowhere and will disappear when I myself disappear. But a small part of myself will survive in the triumphant, anonymous entirety. A dragon or a devil or perhaps a saint, it doesn't matter which."

Many of B's critics have attacked this statement and confronted it with the ruthless subjectivity of his art. But subjectivity and anonymity are obviously compatible. It is criticism that transgresses when it points to a connubial situation in one of B's films as a parallel to an imagined connubial or sexual situation in his life. The analysis of a work of art becomes meaningless if the truth of the work is equated with the truth about the artist's private life. B has, as we know, gradually arrived at the ideal of artistic objectivity, a sublimation of problems that earlier were offered in a more uncertain (perhaps therefore "subjective") form. We may place *To Joy* and *Illicit Interlude* side by side and find that the greater truth in the latter film is simply the greater ability to create visually a dramatic unity.

At the party where Stig becomes more closely acquainted with Martha, he also gets to know a discarded old actor, Mikael Bro, who in the story represents the power of evil. Stig lies drunk in a bathtub, and Bro leans over him:

"Have you met my wife Nelly? I assure you it is an acquaintance to make. A merry little animal with a mouth like a red flower. I'll take you home and leave you as a present for her. She would appreciate that."

Nelly is the Devil's deputy. In a sequence in Mikael Bro's home, after Stig's failure, the actor Hägerström gives a recitation. He is a nihilist. Therefore he believes in nothing but bodily sensations. Nelly and Mikael, however, are improbable second-string, hackneyed characters taken from a morality play. But B's naturalistic approach cannot be combined with the black and white stylization of a morality play. Bro and Nelly do not have the same realistic quality as Uncle Erland in *Illicit Love*.

Stig's marriage begins to cave in from the moment Martha sees that for him ambition is everything. It is built up anew when he appears to accept his mediocrity. But in between the scenes that create the picture's philosophic motion, there are moments of significant film art, for instance, their meeting among the rocks or the short moment when their hands touch on the window, later their faces in silhouette. There is much sentimentality in *To Joy*, but there is much genuineness, too. It is least good in the documentary transition sequences. In those, B holds to a faded and lifeless photographic tradition. Neither does he quite master the relationships between full pictures and close-ups, or the film's rhythmic outline. It is in the intimate action that he is most skillful, where the camera, from being a penetrating observer, becomes a listener.

The film reveals as its happy theme journeys into summer. A short sequence, told by Sönderby shows Stig's and Martha's married bliss. It is a moment of rest, out in the grass. Sönderby is dozing. The light in the looks that Stig and Martha exchange tells of their love. Sönderby is relieved that he is not a creative artist, not an author: "Think of filling page after page in a book with these daily and hourly happenings, of determining the values of a thousand intonations, of trying to interpret this complicated secret language which two lovers fashion and use freely as a shield for their most secret and finest perceptions."

The reconciliation between Stig and Martha takes place in the summer. After a romantic correspondence he returns to her. In his wordless monologue on the train he thinks of their happiness together: to hear her speak, to sit together at the movies, to sit in the kitchen after a concert, to talk jokingly and not say a serious word. But this reconciliation and the end of the film, Sönderby's final words to the orchestra, reveal a chasm between form and content, or rather between the intentions and the instruments B at that time had at his disposal. The sentimentality of adolescence prevails. Sönderby speaks of joy, "not a joy that expresses itself in laughter or even a joy that says: I am happy." He means a joy beyond pain and despair.

The meaning is that Stig, having returned to the present after Martha's death, shall feel this happiness, too. His son enters the empty concert hall, and finds a seat in a corner. The attempt at harmony lacks visual form. Or: it is staged in a too obvious visual form, which lacks a basis in the dramatic material. Stig is pictured as a much too one-tracked person.

### Illicit Interlude

To look in the mirror is natural for people of the stage. But more than that, mirrors play a dramatic part in *Illicit Interlude*, as revealers of the flight of time, of the melancholy that is the film's background. Marie looks at herself in the mirror, and returns to the past. Through the mirror she returns to the present.

As early as 1945, B told in an interview[2] that after *Crisis* he wanted to do *Sentimental Journey*, one of the many titles of what was to become *Illicit Interlude*. In 1946 he announced that the script was ready.[3] As a matter of fact, *Illicit Interlude* seems to belong to his earliest film plans:

"The first draft lies very far back in the past. It was during a summer, shortly after my matriculation examination. I was ill and amused myself by writing, just for fun and entirely intended for the desk drawer. War was brewing, and fear of a most uncertain future probably made me, deep inside, concentrate all my forces of brightness on a powerful offensive against the uncertainty and a not particularly bright future. The plot had to do with the best there is: Summer vacation in the archipelago and The First Great Love, two manifestations rather fresh in my memory, but already seeming incredibly far away—yes, experienced in another and happier life."[4]

The story was rewritten several times, until Herbert Grevenius helped B return it to its original purity. The picture went before the cameras in the spring and summer of 1950.

The manuscript differs to some extent from the completed film. In the manuscript Henrik's death is described as occurring while he repairs the leaky roof of Marie's cottage. In the film he jumps into the water, hurts himself on a jagged rock, and crawls ashore, bloody and crushed. The picture uses the flashback technique in the most finished way. Marie has forgotten Henrik's life and death when Uncle Erland many years later sends her his diary. Her forgetfulness has been a contraction, a conscious act of will. When she has made her sentimental journey to the archipelago and the memories, to the scene of her love, when she has relived everything, she can both forget and remember in the right way, that is, to go on living. This bitterness of hers influences her relation to David. She gives him the diary to read, so that he, too, will understand.

The picture begins and ends at the Opera in Stockholm. At the stage entrance, a book is delivered to Marie. David Nyström, a journalist, means to give it to her, but is stopped by the doorman and goes his way. It is a dress rehearsal of *Swan Lake*. The atmosphere is saturated with menace. The lights do not function, and the rehearsal is put off until the evening. Marie has received the diary. A picture shows half of her face in the mirror. She looks at the diary, turns its pages, and says: "There are so many that die." Out of the darkness emerges Henrik's face. In the same room at the Opera with Marie is Kaj, of the same age as her, conscious of how quickly age takes possession of them. When Marie leaves, David waits outside. But they quarrel and separate. Marie sets out alone on a trip. She sees a small coastal steamer, a clergyman on his bicycle pedals aboard across the gangplank. She, too, goes aboard.

B often uses a journey as a revealer of truths. It is a catalyst for the conflict between the present and the past, between imagined and real values. This motif is important to Nelly and Aunt Ingeborg in *Crisis*, to Bo in *Eva*, to the sailors in *A Ship to India* and *Port of Call*, to the couple in *Three Strange Loves*, to the young people in *Monika*. Isak Borg's self-analysis is a journey; the Knight and his squire are returning from a journey. Many of B's scenes take place in train compartments, in automobiles, on a journey afoot enroute to somewhere. B finds it difficult to capture an elementary situation of social crisis, a living dramatic conflict. The conflict exists within the persons themselves. The result of the introspection determines whether the person can continue to live his life. B's films therefore become a series of analyses of persons who live in a thought vacuum. The arguments do not come from others, but are created in the persons' own drama.

B himself has compared *Illicit Interlude* to *Torment*.[5] In both cases the starting point is romantic, but *Illicit Interlude* broadens itself beyond this to a drama of quite different dimensions. Marie's trip to the archipelago revives the chain of memories which the diary has induced. She goes ashore somewhere among the islands, in an autumnal landscape, wanders alone, but meets a woman in black, marked by old age and death. She follows the woman for a while, then walks up to a cottage, and looks out over the water. She enters the cottage, which is empty. There is water on the floor. She sits down on the bare bed. Then her memory begins to function, in pictures as well as in her narration.

The first memory picture is seen partly in Henrik's perspective. She is a pupil at the Opera, dancing in *Swan Lake*. Henrik seeks her out, is stopped, only to see Marie being taken care of by Uncle Erland. Next time they meet on the steamer. He tells her she is the loveliest thing there is.

The second memory picture (separated from the first one by Marie sitting on the bed in the cottage), is the summer and purity motif. Marie awakens in her little cottage. It lies in a sun-drenched archipelago landscape. In these sequences, the landscape lives as never before in B's films. It is captured in large, romantic pictures, a lovingly factual reproduction of the settings of happiness. Marie and Henrik meet. She guides him to her secret wild strawberry patch on a hillside by the sea. Henrik's parents are divorced, nobody bothers about him. He is afraid of death. He is a child; she is grown-up. She finds him comic.

The film contains many forebodings of death. The first is the black-clad woman, Aunt Elisabeth, whom Marie meets when she returns to the islands. The trees are autumn black, the landscape naked. The pictures tie into a sequence that is enacted in the last flashback (the third). Marie is rehearsing in the big villa. Henrik merely waits. Annoyed, he runs away. In the evening— it is a Saturday—she goes to the house where he lives. In an arbor an old lady is playing chess with the minister, the same clergyman who took the boat with Marie. The old lady has breast cancer and knows she is soon to die. The minister uses her as a study object: "However absurd it may sound, I have a strange feeling that I am sitting here in the company of death itself. And it is very rewarding, from a professional point of view." The air is chill, "for both the corpse and the undertaker," as the old lady says.

Henrik's and Marie's happiness is described with a rapture of words and pictures rare in modern film. In one scene she pushes Henrik into the water—another omen of death. But after this they experience the night together; we see their hands meet. The two make excursions in the moonlight, dance together, watch the strange luminousness of the summer twilight, the stillness and the freshness. The forest is "full of morning mists and noon-day chiaroscuro, bringing back the hopes and loves of youth."[6]

One of the shadows on the idyl is Uncle Erland. He suggests to Marie that they go away together and "get the most out of life." Uncle Erland is the dislocated man, marked by life. One summer evening Marie and Henrik enter the big drawing room in the villa where Erland and Aunt Elisabeth live. Uncle Erland is sitting by the grand piano, playing. He is slightly drunk. To him, Marie is the incarnation of her mother, whom he has known and loved. Her father is dead. The uncle, in other words, was not able to marry the mother, but lives his life in bitterness. In *Wild Strawberries* we meet a man who was robbed of the happiness of his youth by his brother, who married Sara. The brother is dead. Isak Borg's own marriage has been unhappy. As early as *Illicit Interlude* the theme is perfected that is used with variations in *Wild Strawberries*: the search for a long since lost summer, a youth that has slipped away.

Uncle Erland tries to open the door to the room where Marie and Henrik meet in love. In the scenes of the present, between the second and third flashbacks, Marie finds her way up to the villa, in to the rehearsal room. She hears the piano from below, music by Chopin, but nobody is playing, the furniture is covered, all is darkness and menace. In the kitchen she finds Uncle Erland, who has come out to shoot woodgrouse. She tells him he is nauseating, and leaves. She goes aboard the steamer. In the dining saloon her memory again begins to function. She is alone.

Marie's relationship with Henrik is completed with the promises they give each other one Saturday night. When in the

morning he makes his fateful leap, they have sworn to be true
to each other. Now autumn is here; they will soon move back
to town. It is this tragedy, Henrik's death, all that is meaningless
in life, that Marie tries to kill with bitterness. She travels far
away from Erland, buries herself in work, grows hardened, and
forgets.

The film's outer and inner elements come together. The end
of summer means the end of Henrik's life. The darkness, the
closed-in feeling, in a physical sense, dominates the scenes in
which Marie confesses her sorrow. Contrasted with this is the
light and movement of the finale. Again *Swan Lake*, again liberation through the dance. When Marie has returned from her
trip, and the rehearsal has ended, she meets in her dressing room
a new incarnation of death, the ballet master, dressed as Cop-
pelius. He knows that she has clearly analyzed her own life. He
knows she has eight years left as a ballet dancer. His professional philosophy is: "You are dancing. Period. That is your
formula. Stick to that, or things will turn out badly." David, too,
comes to the dressing room, and she gives him the diary. In these
scenes there is much of what Jacques Rivette has called a
"blessed mixture of the decorative, sentimental, erotic, poetic,
for which the prescription has obviously been concocted in the
1930's in all the Pabst and Sternberg films."[7] Still, this is subordinated to the intentions of the work and receives a freshness and
clarity that leads up to the picture's grand climax, Marie's premiere, the white, dancing, luminous forms on the stage. David
is waiting in the wings. Marie comes up to him. They embrace:

"Marie at last recognizes herself as the person she is, with her
faults and merits, recognizes her mistakes and possibilities, the
sacredness of memory, and the dead man and the living one
finally form a synthesis, that of feeling, and Marie is saved and
can go on living. The end has a harsh, nonromantic tone, which
ties up with the bantering tenderness in *It Rains on our Love*."[8]

*Illicit Interlude* is the first of B's films that has unity and a formal balance. Every sequence seems to be perfectly adjusted to the purpose of the story, even when B makes use of an old-fashioned style. In the summer sequences he permits "the picture outlines of two scenes to remain simultaneously on the screen, clearer and longer than we are accustomed to. It gives the film a retarding melancholy (which suits the subject) and an absorbing, almost hypnotically expository continuity."[9] All the attributes of the Northern summer are used in the film, without being given a too intrusive symbolism. *Illicit Interlude* is enacted in sunshine, in twilight, and contains dance and play, Midsummer bonfires, tranquil water and island scenery.

Since Marie's journey to the past makes it possible for her to renew her relationship with David, the determinism that threatens to destroy the dramatic construction is broken. In the flashbacks she represents all the carefree liberty that belongs to summer, while Henrik is weighed down with problems. In the present, Henrik's questions have been transferred to her. But in both cases she is an independent woman. The entire story turns about her. The questions she asks about God's death, her bitterness toward an unanswering heaven are the continuation of Stig's questions in *To Joy*. Here, as well as in that film, there is no other answer than to go on living. In this Marie succeeds.

The film has many clichés such as, for instance, the picture of Henrik as a Swedish university student, the picture of the relationship between Aunt Elisabeth and Uncle Erland, in fact, the summer motif itself. Still, *Illicit Interlude* is a great work in spite of its imperfections. B has embodied elements from the national tradition in Swedish literature and film. But *Illicit Interlude* is above all a profound intellectual analysis. Without this development from romantic love to the realistic understanding of daily life the film would lack heightening intensity and be played in a static landscape of either idyl or tragedy. Jean-Luc Godard declares his love for it in a piece in which he fulminated against the "patented technicians" who regard the film as a profession and not an art form.[10] But the film is not a profession; "it is art. It is not teamwork. One is always alone, on the stage and before the unwritten page. And to be alone—that, for Bergman, means to ask questions. And to make films means to answer them. More traditionally romantic than that it is impossible to be." To Visconti a film is a question of good taste. He makes good films, and *White Nights* is better staged than *The Seventh Seal*. The difficulty lies in "advancing across unknown ground, being aware of the danger, taking risks, and knowing fear."

That is exactly what B does in *Illicit Interlude*. He dares to complete his purpose and create his own imagined (yet clearly seen) world.

## Monika

This film was followed by *Secrets of Women*, a sort of notebook,[11] with themes pointing forward and back. *Monika* is an independent film, a synthesis of the motifs in *Port of Call* and *Illicit Interlude*. Here, too, love is described as a liberation. Here, too, the nature of the archipelago is employed, its rocks and sheltered coves, the dance motif, and the boat trips. But the roles are interchanged. Nobody dies in the film, some one has said, but love dies. Here the development of the leading male part corresponds to Marie's in *Illicit Interlude*. Harry and Monika, the young couple in the film, escape from an intruding reality out to the archipelago. The strongest sequences describe their experiences out there, the gradually emerging conflict. When autumn approaches, they return to Stockholm and are again confronted with reality. Monika is expecting a child, and they marry. But only Harry can bear his responsibility. Without the film's directly condemning Monika, she drifts back to her former life. For Harry a way out is provided, a freedom and a loneliness. He will live with his father and take care of his daughter and continue his education.

To understand the picture is first of all to understand the motives that caused the decision to run away. Harry and Monika both have about the same external presuppositions for life. P. A. Fogelström's manuscript emphasizes the fundamental difference between them, the difference in will power. The original version of the film is a short story by Fogelström, in which the main characters are named Britt and Harry. He is seventeen years old and goes to school; his father is a painter. The script was gradually molded, and was changed considerably while the picture was being filmed. Monika works for a wholesale fruit and vegetable dealer, Harry in a retail store selling glass and china. They meet in a café. The surroundings in their places of work are repulsive to both of them. Monika is exposed to continual advances. Harry is bullied by his superiors, often without any reason. Monika detests her work, but sees no way out. Harry dreams of another future; Monika of film stars. She lives in a crowded home with her parents and brothers and sisters. Her father drinks. The atmosphere is marked by constant irritation. This B describes by virtuoso sound effects. The people's voices become piercing discords, contrasting with the beauty of silence.

Harry's home life is not completely harmonious either. When Monika visits Harry, his father comes home. He says he is willing to sit and wait in the kitchen. "I have my troubles to carry, little lady. But that's the way it is, so don't let me disturb you. I'll go out and sit in the kitchen in the meantime." Monika leaves.

She eggs Harry on to escape. She gives up her job, disappears from her home, and looks up Harry. They spend the night together in his father's motorboat, tied up by the Väster Bridge. He comes too late to work and is fired. They start off. The description of the boat ride out from Stockholm has often been compared with their autumnal journey home. This is where B shows his ability to narrate in suggestive picture language. The trip out is a song to freedom, a definitive farewell. The images are dominated by the sky, by open space. The return, with its dark views of bridges and silhouettes, gives the heavy feeling of unhappiness and strife which governs both Harry and Monika.

The description of the summer does not have the same idyllic, timeless purity as *Illicit Interlude*. The earlier film takes place beyond time and space, in tale and memory. Monika and Harry are lower on the social scale. They are not subtle, like Marie and Henrik. *Illicit Interlude* is the summer vacation of an undergraduate; *Monika*, that of the anonymous citizen of a metropolis. Harry and Monika seem more adult. They create their freedom in defiance. They have fled from the world, and believe that thereby they have conquered it. The longer they remain among the islands, the harder it is for them to preserve the idyl. In a full picture we see Monika teaching Harry to dance. A gramophone is playing in the grass. Harry is awkward. While they are practicing, Lelle, Monika's former boy friend, who has put up his tent on the island, sneaks down to the motorboat. He pulls some clothing from the cabin, pours on gasoline, and sets it afire. Harry discovers the danger and dashes to the scene, and has a fight with Lelle, whom he beats up with Monika's help. In the final picture of the sequence Harry and Monika stand pressed to each other, look past the camera: two free savages who have conquered the enemy.

There are many dreams in the film. But there is only one that the story seems to accept: namely, the dream of fleeing. But he who flees must know that there will come a day when he will be forced to return. Monika is too far sunk in cheap dreams, irresponsible dreams, to be able to picture the return and the homecoming. Harry can obey the advice that is the key to the film, given by B in a program note: "Run! But come back." When the food begins to give out, the conflicts increase. Monika steals food from the cellar of a summer resident's villa, but is caught. She is taken to the house. The owner calls the police. The situation there is typical of B's way of showing a closed, middle-class world. He is on the side of Monika and freedom against the snug, safe existence.

Monika is geared to life only when the resistance is not strong. She represents an almost pure eroticism.[12] She is not interested in her child. She regards the daughter as an impediment. The divorce is pictured as inevitable. The crisis is the fault of both:

Harry: We'll have to get a divorce, Monika. We can't go on like this.

Monika: You think it's all my fault, but it isn't.

Harry: Doesn't matter whose fault it is.

Monika: You haven't cared for me. You've only ground away at your studies, and kept your finger on me.

Harry: I suppose I have.

The film's technique is very restrained. Nowhere can one discover an especially original picture sequence. Close-ups are used only in the showdown scenes. But the man behind the camera has felt with the picture. He has let his feeling dominate reflection. He possesses his objects. B is extremely easy to unmask, since he seldom sacrifices anything to superficial brilliance. The trouble with *Monika* is not its similarity to *Illicit Interlude* but its dissimilarity. The characters are seen in one dimension only. It is correct to compare this film with *Port of Call*. In both cases the influence of Italian neorealism is felt: in *Port of Call*, Rossellini's; in *Monika*, most sharply de Santis' almost commercial sensualism.

## Secrets of Women

The film is a kaleidoscope: three tales from the past, another one that is never told, and a fifth that is the result of the other three, a story in the present. In its theme, the picture is similar to *Illicit Interlude* and *Monika*. The action in the present takes place at a summer cottage in the archipelago. It is, however, almost entirely a studio film. But B gathers here suggestions and ideas that neither can nor should be given a wider frame than that of a short story. At that time, at the beginning of the fifties, it was the fashion to make episodic films. B approaches his task with a certain abandon.

All of the three main stories have a comic element; the last is almost pure farce. Film comedy demands a perfect sense of rhythm, and an awareness of the relative lengths of scenes and sequences. The director of a comedy must be able to surprise and disarm the spectator. B masters this art in *Secrets of Women*, without, however, being far from the tragic element which, after all, is the foundation and strength of his art.

The first episode (but indirectly the construction of the entire film) is based on a play by B, produced in 1946.[13] Of the play's metaphysical questions almost nothing remains in the episode. Rakel and the cinema doorman do not sustain the questions that are discussed. Certain snatches of dialogue, almost directly lifted from the play, are excellent, but the drama contains nothing that would have made the reader guess at B's formal skill in the film version.

*Secrets of Women* begins with four wives waiting for their husbands. They put their children to bed. In order to pass the time until the arrival of their husbands, each is to tell a story. Rakel begins. One day in the summer cottage her former lover, Kaj, comes to visit. He surprises her, wants to seduce her. She is attracted by the adventure and by him. Pain is reflected in her face. At last they go down to the bath house, and lie down there, far apart. The light is unreal, the air quiet. The water casts dancing reflections on the walls. Something dark and large is glimpsed in the water, a pike. Kaj laughs, and thinks of Freud.

These scenes interpret adequately Rakel's loneliness and longing. It is the consciousness of the distance between the world of men and women, vast expanses that only an occasional physical union can break. When her husband, Eugen, comes home, Rakel confesses that she has deceived him. This gives B another opportunity to unmask the middle-class quality, to which he seems neither able nor willing to be reconciled. Eugen immediately is convinced that they must be divorced. The lawyer takes care of the division of property, support, and other formalities. Finally Eugen hides himself in a shack by the shore, desperate, theatrical, with a rifle in his hand. *Three Strange Loves* is brought to mind: being together is perhaps hell, but loneliness is even worse. Now it is not Rakel's deceit that tortures him, but shame and loneliness. The humiliation reaches out in all directions. Kaj can satisfy only the temporary lust. Rakel's life with Eugen is doomed to eternal restlessness so long as it is childless. Otherwise, the marriage has no meaning.

The second episode, Märta-Martin, some of which takes place in Paris, is a cheaply conceived love story, in part silent. She deserts an American fiancé for him. He is the black sheep of the family, a painter in Paris. She becomes pregnant. She is not yet married when her child is about to be born. From a purely technical viewpoint, this scene is interesting, including a flashback with effects that bring to mind the play of sound in *Dreams*. Both the visual solutions and the general construction, however, are entirely conventional. The same objection concerns the famous elevator episode between Karin and Fredrik Lobelius. B works successfully within the narrow compass. On their way home from a jubilee dinner of the family concern, they get stuck in an elevator. They open their hearts to each other: confessions that otherwise might be called tragic are here turned into farce. In the same narrow compass are set the love scenes between Henrik and Marie in *Illicit Interlude*. When isolated, people are forced to openness, to anonymity.

The most interesting episode is short and takes place in the present. The sister of one of the wives has listened to the others' stories. She has an appointment with a young man. About this time, the husbands return. The two young people decide to escape. This journey away, perhaps without a goal, is the film's final impression. One sees the boat in the dusk out on the water. The journey is toward maturity, responsibility, self-knowledge. This is one more variation of B's analysis of summer, which is lost but constantly regained.

THE DEVIL'S WANTON. Doris Svedlund (*Birgitta-Carolina*).

MONIKA. Harriet Andersson (*Monika*).

ILLICIT INTERLUDE.
Birger Malmsten
(*Henrik*) and Maj-
Britt Nilsson (*Marie*).

To Joy. Victor Sjöström (*Sönderby*), Maj-Britt Nilsson
(*Martha*), and Stig Olin (*Stig*).

THREE STRANGE LOVES. Eva Henning (*Rut*), Mimi Nelson (*Valborg*), and Naima Wifstrand (*Miss Henriksson*).

# 5

## THE NAKED NIGHT

Out of a single vision was born *The Naked Night*. "Some circus wagons were rolling along in the early dawn on a spring-winter day somewhere in the neighborhood of Gimo. The Upland landscape there, in all its gloom, has a strange demoniacal quality that captivates me."[1] Night is on its way toward morning. A string of wagons moves across the plain. Cart wheels plow their way over bridges, through puddles. All the time there is heard a plaintive, singsong voice. The camera is pointed upwards, toward the trees.

This is the beginning of the film.

*The Naked Night* marks a crossroad in B's production. He has never driven the naturalistic observation of details farther, never so close to a gospel about filth and depravity.

B's inspiration always seems to function in such a way that from "very vague, indiscriminate embryonic movements," from "lightning-quick impressions" he succeeds in "transferring rhythms, moods, atmospheres, tensions, sequences, tones, and fragrances into words and meanings in a readable, or at least an interpretable manuscript."[2] The sources of the inspiration are found in the dream, in feeling, in the irrational. No wonder, then, that B's films are so free in their richness of invention, in their

95

inner, spiritual consistency. Still they retain, in their grand moments, the severity of classic architecture. This applies also to *The Naked Night*, the first of B's films that convinced me that he was not only a significant artist from a Swedish or Nordic point of view, but a renewer of the film's descriptive language.

One reason why the film was made was that the producer, Rune Waldecrantz, staked his prestige and determination on the undertaking. The film was received without understanding by many critics in Sweden. In one of Stockholm's largest papers this could be read: "I refuse to view the vomit that Ingmar Bergman has left behind him this time."[3] *The Naked Night* became a failure. It led to a crisis in B's work. With some exaggeration, he described his situation thus: "The criticism was universally devastating, the audience stayed away, the producer is counting his losses, and I myself have to wait ten years for my next try in this genre. In other words, if I do one or two more pictures that result in an economic loss, the producer rightly feels that he doesn't dare to bet gold on my talents any more."[4]

It did not take long before B had regained the freedom of which he, with this reversal, considered himself deprived. He achieved a freedom unique not only in Sweden but also in the whole world. It was in the name of B's freedom, partly inspired by him, that the French film achieved its rebirth.

*The Naked Night* has been called a penny print on film. Behind the introductory texts is the picture of a hand organ. The same shot ends the film. As the picture starts, the monotonous, melancholy melody of the hand organ is heard. It returns often in the film. B brings the penny print to life again, as Nils Ferlin has done in poetry:

"Behind the penny print's eloquent text, with its stamp of cheap popular reading matter and stereotyped action, are often hidden bitter tragedies, catastrophes, which the sellers dramatized and simplified in order to satisfy the taste of the simple customers and their intellectual need. The fact that Ingmar

Bergman has provided the film with the subheading 'A Penny Print' implies primarily an assurance that the characters and the pattern of action externally reflect this world of plain folk literature, but his personal and artistic fashioning of the material naturally possesses a much more many-faceted and deep tone than that of the direct prototype."[5]

The wagons on the road in the early dawn belong to Circus Alberti, owned by Albert Johansson. He is a big, broad man with a mustache. He wakes up in his wagon, dresses laboriously, throws a glance at his young mistress Anne, covers her up, and walks out. He climbs up on the driver's seat beside Jens, who hands him a wooden bowl to drink from. It is cold. Then comes Jens' story, the only flashback in the picture, the tale about the clown Frost and his wife Alma. When Jens asks Albert if he plans to see his wife—it is seven years since the last time and she lives in the city they are coming to—he continues the story about Frost, which took place seven years earlier in the same part of the country.

This flashback is among the most remarkable that B has made. The story is intended to throw a light on Albert's fate, teach him, interpret his situation, in the same manner as the many elements of the theater within the theater that B uses. But Albert does not seem to listen; he sleeps. Jens tells the story to himself, and to us, with slight pedagogic benefit to Albert Johansson.

The clown Frost and his wife Alma worked at another circus at that time. It is summer. "It is like sitting on the shore of a placid lake, where suddenly poisonous springs bubble up."[6] On the shore, the artillery is having fire practice; the officers are bellowing orders. The guns boom out. It is a hot day, and the officers are bored. They play cards. Alma comes walking along, and switches her skirts challengingly. She is still beautiful, although, as Jens says, "a bit on the wrong side of the flower month." The officers collect money in a cap to make her take her clothes off. One officer whispers something in the ear of a boy.

He laughs, and runs away to the circus. Frost is laughing with the circus people, comes out of the tent, dressed in his clown suit. At first he thinks the boy's message is a joke. He repeats the boy's words. Then he stops, there comes the certainty that Alma is bathing naked with the officers. He grabs the boy and rushes off.

The firing has ceased. Frost runs past groups of laughing officers and soldiers. The cannon point down toward the water. Frost stretches out his hands in supplication to the water, where Alma is splashing about with the officers. He pulls off his clown suit. He is afraid of the water. He stumbles over the stones, slips. The boy scoops up Alma's and Frost's clothes, hides them. When Frost reaches Alma, she kisses him and pulls him down under the water. Finally, he drags her ashore. But he is forced to carry her, across the sharp stones, in a revealing white sun, toward the circus. He falls down exhausted, as if dead. When they have lifted him up and carried him into the tent, the boy comes with the white clown suit, and spreads it before the tent. The circus people have followed the procession. The laughter has stopped.

This sequence is done in the jerky technique of the silent film, but only seemingly so. The shots from the shore are overexposed, with a blinding whiteness. The contrasts between white and black are sharp. The transitions in time and place are marked by glimpses of a pale, milk-like sun. The sequences are done in a nightmarish atmosphere, unreal, timeless.

*The Naked Night* is the only one of B's films for which Karl-Birger Blomdahl has composed the music. In this sequence the sound consists of Jens' squeaky, self-righteous voice, narrating, commenting on the story, and a series of rhythmic noises that accents the painful character and its tale of suffering: cannon shots and drums. In answer to a questionnaire in 1949, Blomdahl said:

"If there is to be music in a film, it must, from its presuppositions correspond in its dimension to the idea-content of the picture, otherwise it has no business there. Should the film be so designed, or of such a structure, that it is not suitable for a musical accompaniment, sound effects alone are to be preferred. I am convinced that a feature film that omitted the prevalent musical hodgepodge and worked only with speech and sound effects would have a strong and surprisingly fresh impact on contemporary music."[7]

Blomdahl's opinion is entirely in accordance with the one suggested by Hanns Eisler in his book *Composing for the Films*, and perhaps also with the Soviet sound manifesto, written by Eisenstein, Pudovkin, and Alexandrov. Unfortunately, film music has followed this line in very few cases. It has been satisfied with underscoring the emotional effects of the scenes, and has seldom worked contrapuntally. In Swedish film, even in B's pictures, a conventional musical form is very common. Since *The Seventh Seal* B has used musical effects very sparingly, trying to achieve the greatest possible power of expression with naturalistic sound effects. *The Naked Night* is throughout, not only in the flashback, a successful result of creative cooperation between two important artists who have understood the dramatic possibilities of film sound. Even if the music in some of B's films is conventionally treated, he is unsurpassed in the use of effects.

The acting in the flashback is exaggeratedly distinct, pantomimic. The scenes acquire a grotesque enlargement. The flashback, even in its form, reminds us of the nightmares that plague Isak Borg in *Wild Strawberries*. There are the same black-and-white pictures. The cannon shots are replaced in *Wild Strawberries* by the beating of the heart and the ticking of the pocket watch. The sequence with Frost and Alma has the same effect as a nightmare.[8] The whole sequence possesses a striking realism of detail, an expressionistic enlargement of the essential elements of the action. Frost undresses, both literally and symbolically. He must tread on sharp stones. This increases the impression of torment. The sequence becomes a Calvary, in the same way as

the father and Martin in *Through a Glass Darkly* run to the ship-
wreck where Karin is waiting for them.

The narrative content of the sequence is very slight. Frost is
humiliated, Alma is humiliated and accuses the circus people of
getting her into trouble. The officers and the soldiers are the
perpetrators of the joke, but through her challenging behavior
Alma has provoked it. The circus people remain ironical and indifferent. They look upon the incident as a spectacle. They have
lost the capacity to differentiate between tragedy in jest and
tragedy in earnest. After all, Frost is a clown. This is just one of
his roles, they reason.

Evil is seldom a part of man's intentions. For those who act
evil is, as here, a result of blindness. But Albert, who sleeps his
time away, is also blind. His circus is in the same state of degradation as Frost and Alma. It is raining when they get to the fairgrounds outside the city. When the tent has been raised, the
circus people gather inside. Frost voices their complaints. They
have no money, no food, no clothes. The only thing they have in
abundance is fleas. Albert dreams about America, where circus
people are honored, where they roll in procession through the
streets. It is then he gets the idea of calling on the Sjuberg tour-
ing theater company, which is visiting the city, to try to borrow
some costumes and devise an American publicity stunt.

The humiliation theme, which is the central one in the film,
and perhaps the nucleus of B's artistic philosophy, is intimately
bound up with the feeling of physical exhaustion, the smell of
sweat and stable, dampness, cold, and cheap perfume that per-
meates the story. The circus is dilapidated, everything stinks.
When Albert visits his wife, he reluctantly removes his coat. All
he has underneath is a knitted undershirt. When Anne comes to
Frans he says that she "smells of the stable, bad perfume, and
sweat . . ." Shame on you, how you are made up. I'll teach
you. . . ." He gives her a bottle of perfume. Mr. Sjuberg at the
theater describes the circus artists as dirty; the costumes might

get full of vermin if he were to lend them out. Nobody escapes the circus's own creeping dirt. When Albert is conquered in the film's climax, we experience the smell of the tanbark, the sawdust, and the blood. And yet, because of its character of a penny print, the film keeps its epic distance; we know that the blood is tomato juice. But the film manages to make the horror of the experiences real. It is this mixture of elements regarded as uncombinable that caused the critics to hesitate. In *The Naked Night* we find a ruthless naturalism, simplifications of morality, psychology, and anti-psychology. This makes the final result differ completely from the sources from which B drew his inspiration: the nineteenth-century melodrama, Strindberg, and film expressionism of the twenties.

After the discussion in the circus tent, Albert and Anne set out for the theater. They are dressed up. He tries to talk her into behaving well. But he is afraid; she is not. He is one of those men who in an analysis have been described as characterized by "a sort of smile that perhaps has its roots in the exaggerated naturalism of Nordic culture, which in its cold equality has rendered commonplace the mysterious trait in persons who ought not to live separate but are created to complement each other."[9] Albert and Anne are entering backstage. The poster outside the theater announces the evening's program: *Treason, or The Mad Countess*. Albert is giving Anne some advice:

"You sit still and listen and smile your most beguiling smile. Sjuberg is very much attracted by pretty girls. You may breathe deeply so that your bosom bulges. If he wants to look at your legs, don't be unwilling, I'll not desert you. Should he make indecent proposals, I'll punch him in the jaw. Let's go in."

Mr. Sjuberg is seated far in the back of the dark auditorium. Anne pushes Albert toward the footlights, after Sjuberg has asked them to step forward. Her presence saves the situation. After Albert's halting, unsure request for costumes, Sjuberg gets fun out of humiliating him. The pictures are shot from below. Sjuberg is enormous, imposing, quiet. Why shouldn't he insult the circus director:

"You put up with it—don't hit me on the jaw. We despise you because you live in wagons and we in dirty hotel rooms; we produce art, and you offer stunts and tricks. The plainest and least gifted of us can spit on the best of you. Why? Because you stake your lives and we our vanity. I think you look silly and patched, sir, and your little lady would surely be much more fun without her gaudy rags. If you only dared you would realize that we look even more foolish with our fake elegance, our made-up faces, our studied accents. Why shouldn't I insult you?"

At last, Albert is permitted to borrow some costumes. Anne is wandering around among the masks, the mirrors, and the wardrobe in the storeroom. The actor Frans, a handsome young man, who has glimpsed her as she entered, follows her and declares his love to her. The scene has a masochistic character. She wants him to touch his head to the floor. When he does that she kisses him, but only once.

What Sjuberg has said about the circus people is confirmed during their parade through the city. The wagon is halted by the police, who order them to keep to the fairgrounds, where they belong. The horses are taken as security, the posters ripped off, and the circus people have to pull the wagon themselves, while the people roar with laughter.

The central conflict of the film is developed in a parallel action, the only one in the story. It is Albert's visit to his wife, which causes Anne, after having threatened not to be home when he returns, to go to the theater to look up Frans. Both Albert's and Anne's actions express the same frame of mind, the same desire for escape, betrayal. The visit to the wife Agda is in two parts, and between these is placed the story of Anne.

Albert opens the door to a tobacconist shop. The bell jingles. Behind the counter is glimpsed a small boy, who greets the stranger coolly, telling him that his mother is eating. Albert sits down, and wipes the sweat from his face. The boy asks: "Are you Father?" Albert walks into the apartment. It is neat and cosy, a middle-class interior from the turn of the century: lace, bureaus, flowers, curtains, the lonely chiming of clocks. Albert and the wife almost immediately start a quarrel. Albert is sensitive to questions regarding his health. When she asks him if he wants something to eat, he takes it as an insult. When she wants to mend his jacket, he becomes embarrassed. He has once deserted her, but she is grateful:

"My life became my own, and I escaped from that horrible circus that I always hated and was afraid of. All those shouting, dirty people, your whole world of rush and push and misery and lice and disease and I don't know what. No, I am satisfied. And grateful."

He tries to tell her that he has really never left her. He just continued on his journeys, and she didn't come along. The transition to the parallel action is significant. He is waiting for Agda to finish her sewing. Everything is quiet. He describes the silence in the city, which at this moment also imposes itself upon the spectator. Agda says: "To me it means maturity." Albert retorts immediately: "To me it means emptiness." We shall soon see that he lies. We see Agda in a close-up. She closes her eyes, as if in pain. B then cuts directly to a close-up of Anne, dressed up, in the wings of the theater, watching Frans perform a suicide monologue on the stage. He bids the world farewell, and stabs himself with the prop knife. She shivers with fright at his realistic performance.

When the rehearsal is over, she remains on the stage alone, in a white circle of light. She finds her way to his dressing room, stops at the door to observe him. He wears a robe, reaches for a cigarette, and suddenly stiffens at her words: "You don't have to marry me at all, but you can take care of me, can't you?" He laughs abruptly, gets up and meets her. He locks the door. Having offered to help her make up, he pulls her down on the floor. But suddenly she does not want him. She wants to be free. He offers her a piece of jewelry that he has worn around his neck. He asserts that he has received it from a woman. Anne will be able to live on it for a year. She repeats his phrase and promises to sleep with him.

From here B cuts direct to the end of Albert's conversation with the wife. She gives him the coat. The other son enters and asks for a coin: there is an organ grinder outside the theater. Albert digs in his empty purse. But before he leaves he wants to say something to Agda. He asks her not to get angry:

"I want to stay here, I don't want to continue with the circus. I am getting old, I can't go on any longer. I want to be here with you in this quietness, live with you and watch my boys grow up. I can help you in the shop, I have rather polished manners if I try, you know that. Can't you let me stay, Agda, you will not regret it, I promise you I'll never fail you again."

We can see on her face that this request is impossible to fulfill, even if he sells his share of the circus as he has promised. He is ready to betray Anne for the emptiness and the silence, for the material security Agda can provide, for the spiritual death she radiates. But Anne is ready to betray him. Both are again thrown at each other, with no prospect of freedom. When Albert reaches the street certain that there is no return, he sees Anne emerge from the theater and enter a jewelry shop. Soon she comes out again. "The jewel is worthless, but the price is real, for the jewel is Illusion."[10]

Albert returns to the circus wagon. Anne is lying on the bed, playing solitaire. Slowly, by degrees, his anger rises, while he squeezes the truth (which he already surmises) out of her. Drumbeats—a link with the Alma-Frost episode—have, even as Albert sees Anne come from the theater, foreshadowed this new theme, the gradual destruction of all illusions. During their argument, he is in a close-up in the beginning, she in the background. With this B underscores the fact that reality is seen from Albert's point of view, not hers. He, too, has betrayed her. Frost enters with a bottle in his hand. The two begin to drink. Albert digs up his pistol and urges Frost to commit suicide. Somebody has to die, as a deputy. But in the midst of this great despair, there is a sudden reversal. Albert tumbles from the house wagon, out into the sun. He stumbles and falls. Like Gösta in *Port of Call* he regrets the truth he is forced to live in. No other escape is possible.

As payment for the costumes, the Sjuberg company is invited to the performance. The group has arrived as Anne is riding around the tanbark as a Spanish equestrienne. On the edge of the ring sits Frans with an actress; he glances at Anne, whispers in the ear of his companion. Somebody throws a firecracker and frightens Anne's horse. She falls to the ground. Albert paces around the ring like a caged animal. With his long riding whip he flips the hat off Frans. As he retrieves his hat, Albert kicks him in the behind so that he falls. The fight can begin.

In the film, the fight does not take more than a minute and a half. The parallel with Unrath in *The Blue Angel* is justified here.[11] Albert is seeking his Lola-Lola. The ninety seconds of the fight seem very long. Pitted against Albert's unreasoning anger is the ironic, feminine elegance of Frans. He is a fencer. Albert begins to bleed after the first blow, but grapples with Frans. But when they fall to the ground, Frans takes an unfair grip on Albert, who lets out a frightful, bestial shriek. After this the fight is decided. Frans blinds Albert with sawdust and hits him. Albert sees nothing, wants only to fight, but is unable. Frans brushes the sawdust off his clothes. Frost announces that the performance is over. Anne rushes in and scratches Frans. Albert is carried away.

He drives Anne out of his wagon, is seen in silhouette inside. He takes out his pistol again, and aims it at his temple. This time it is serious, not a game as it had been during the day. During the day desperation had turned into joy of living. But the shot is not fired. His face is seen in the mirror, he turns his pistol toward the glass. Now the shot goes off. His death is symbolic, almost the real thing. To be avenged and restore balance he walks to the cage where Alma's bear is kept, and shoots the animal, as Frost once suggested. Alone he goes to the horses in the stable, sinks down on the straw, and pulls the horse's muzzle toward him.

The circus starts up again, on to the unknown. Albert walks beside Frost, who tells of a dream he had during the day. This was included in *The Fish*, B's film story from the forties.

"I dreamed that Alma came to me and said: 'Poor Frost, you look tired and sad. Don't you think you need some rest?' 'Yes,' I replied. 'Then I'm going to make you as small as a fetus,' she said, 'and let you crawl into my stomach and there you'll have a real good sleep.' I did as she told me, and snuggled down in her stomach and there I fell asleep so beautifully, so sweetly, rocked to rest as in a cradle. Then I got smaller and smaller until at last I was only a little plant seed, and then I was gone."

Alma calls him from the door of their wagon. With a strange, almost frightened smile he explains that she cannot sleep without him. He goes away.

The picture's final scene is not in the original manuscript.

The story's contrasts are equalized. The lonely Albert meets the lonely Anne. There is a light on her face, and on his. She almost smiles. Together they wander into the night, united and lonely. Siclier feels that the end, and the film as a whole, is B's darkest. I cannot share that opinion. Even though despair is great in the film, there is a dramatically acceptable answer to this. To be sure, the film says that "everybody carries his fate within himself. Every one makes his choice, alone."[12] The film's doctrine about man is hard and heavy. But B is not a pessimist. One would like to answer, with one of his French critics, that he is none of the things he has been called. He is all these attributes at the same time. His films are similar because they seek, and often find, a possibility of consolation. The most convincing of B's films is the one in which the whole is fashioned most convincingly. This happens in *The Naked Night*, in which the inner and outer levels of the story achieve a perfect balance.

What is the film about?

One may say that it is the contrast between the free, adventurous life and the fettered, empty one.[13] Freedom is represented by the artists and half-artists of the circus, forced to keep on moving in order to exist, shut out from normal, middle-class society. Their privations become a symbol for all people who, by desire or compulsion, choose departure and journey, the uncertain points of view in preference to the certain and the safe ones. He who lives in the world of adventure obviously feels a longing for security and peace. That it is not realized does not depend entirely on the person himself. Anne permits herself for a moment to be intoxicated by the imagined freedom that Frans offers. For Albert, however, a return flight would mean death. Let us repeat: people do not seek tenable moral concepts; they seek a state of happiness. They seek no guiding principle in the presence of eternity. They do not seek action. Since they live according to earthly, material standards, they must choose their action each time. There is no guiding principle; therefore there is no security.

Seen from this perspective, the majority of the persons in the film become representative of the static. That applies to the officers, who humiliate Alma and show no regard for anybody else. It applies to the town police, anxious about public order. It applies to Agda, even if her security is pictured with a certain understanding. It applies to Sjuberg and his troupe. It applies to Frans, who is an immeasurably cynical person, incapable of loving. He can love only himself, and for that reason he gets nowhere.

B's films from *The Naked Night* onward are a running monologue about the position of art and the artist in the world. Of course, Anne and Albert are not great artists, but we do not find such persons with B. We find the failures, worm-eaten by their doubts. We find the unknown, the thwarted ones, entangled in their questions. If they can bear their failure, they can also bear life. With some limitations it is true of B's later important characters that the condition of happiness is their only ideal. They regularly pose great life questions. The answer never comes. The answer is to stop asking and begin to live. Henrik Egerman in *Smiles of a Summer Night* is the romantic hero. As long as he holds on to morals, he cannot live. The same is the case with Henrik in *Illicit Interlude*. His love affair finds no obstacles once it has begun. *The Naked Night* is more truthful, more honest, because it shows how rugged is the road that leads to harmony, and how few the chances of success.

*The Naked Night* is a declaration, an artistic credo. The belief in a state of happiness is faltering. B appears to be able to believe in persons who have endured everything, who stand close to death, but are able to overcome it. Only through dirt and destruction can the new life begin. It is an artistic vision that builds on the apocalyptic visions evoked by the experiences of World War II, even for artists who lived outside the actual sphere of tension.

On a formal plane the thought is confirmed that the film is a movement toward pain, perhaps from it. These painful conditions are given a frightening reality. One might at the same time read pessimism from the fact that the picture shows only a moment's union between the two main characters. Nobody can be quite sure that Albert and Anne will continue together. To me the question appears irrelevant. Through their experiences Albert and Anne have become richer, in other words, happier. The very fact that they are capable of appreciating the beauty of the night, that they are alive, breathing, is a gain. Life is not a series of defeats or a series of victories. Life can be lived by him who sees the greatness of the moment, who manages to reshape existence into something dramatic and full of meaning. This struggle has no purpose beyond life. Beyond life there is only one certainty, that of death.

It may seem strange to praise *The Naked Night* as B's hitherto best film—a wholly subjective evaluation—if one at the same time is conscious of the prototypes in film and literature which have been advanced by different critics. Thus Dupont's film from the twenties, *Variété*, has been mentioned, as well as Murnau's *The Last Laugh* and Elia Kazan's *Man on a Tightrope*. The last one is the story of a Czech circus which flees through the Iron Curtain to West Germany. It is a political film, in the spirit of the cold war, with Fredric March in the leading role. But all it has in common with B is the circus motif. Other sources that have been mentioned are Schnitzler, Ophuls, Wilde, Strindberg, Sartre, Stig Dagerman (*Burnt Child*).

It is evident that a diligent researcher will probably establish that almost nothing in B's films is absolutely new, absolutely B's own. Quite rightly, B himself seems not to be disturbed because the motifs are not new to one who knows the literature and film of our time. B's importance does not lie in his having introduced new surroundings, new characters in film art. It is better to compare *The Naked Night* with an essay, a series of questions that emerge from the dramatic form. In its structure, the picture is open, free, and subject to many interpretations.

Here is told the contrast between security and insecurity, between the safe middle way and the bold attempt, the balance act on a tightrope. Is it perhaps sufficient to see the artist as a collecting symbol of man in our time? The artist constantly experiences the insecurity which today is a reality everywhere. This is tied up with the philosophy of art which dominates the West, that the limited, personal experience becomes the ultimate testimony in the creative process. *That* is true, as I myself have experienced. *The Naked Night* takes place in the year 1900, but the decor is quite accidental. It gives B an opportunity to use a bombastic baroque style. The remarkable thing about B, as Eric Rohmer points out, is that he works here *as if* he did not know the history of the film—in other words, creates *The Naked Night* in conscious provincialism: "His conception of the camera angle, cutting, montage, of the acting itself is, on the whole, that of the directors of the years between the wars. We are often reminded of Sternberg, sometimes of Vigo. Furthermore this archaism is here all the more evident—but all the less troublesome—in that it is conscious. In the beginning, done practically in silent-film technique, there is a short and strange dream sequence, before which even Buñuel pales. But this total isolation of Sweden both in time and in space has its advantages as well as its disadvantages. It is better calmly to go one's own way than, like so many small nations, to run oneself breathless after an ancient technique."[14]

It is pertinent here once again to point out the contrast with Stiller-Sjöström. In the classic Swedish film there existed, on the one hand, the will to give the film prestige among the art forms by means of valuable, literarily accepted material, and on the other hand the striving to reach the autonomous means of artistic expression which were unique with the film. None of these pioneers went the whole way, tied down as they were by the imperfect technical possibilities of the silent film; but B did.

Costumes and props, as well as the very molding of the picture, bear throughout the stamp of baroque. The characters and the action are seen indirectly, by means of an intricate system of mirrors and reflections. The scene with Frans and Anne in his dressing room is a typical example of this. It is a style that contains something dissolved, dissolving, that justifies the criticism that baroque is femininity, weakness.[15] The stylistic analysis suggests that the structure, too, of *The Naked Night* reminds one of *The Blue Angel* in von Sternberg's version. The pictorial banalities are many, but serve the purpose of the story, if we bear in mind the fact that this is a penny print. As early as the introductory sequence there are water reflections, static observations underscoring the cold neutrality with which B often treats his medium. On the other hand, neither does this film permit any creative work on the cutting table. The movement of the camera is never too rapid or too abrupt: "Consequently, the camera tracks a great deal, weaving around the sets to encircle the players and center the observer's attention upon the matter of greatest interest, the actors' faces and their dialogue."[16] B never omits a careful description of the milieu, which is particularly important in *The Naked Night*. He shows us the open field where the circus puts up its tent. He sketches the streets of the town, Agda's home in full screen picture, also the theater, outside, inside, the auditorium, the wardrobe. He never lets the spectator remain unconscious of where he is. Still, he does not resort to the banal method of first presenting the surroundings. He often switches in time and place, from close-ups to close-ups (as above in the parallel action Albert-Anne): "Bergman tracks more than he cuts, and the cuts he employs are not for violent emphasis but for a contrasting purpose, to mute effects before they are completed."[17]

What is revolutionary is that B is able in a creative fashion to realize the theories about an intellectual sound-picture montage in the direction Eisenstein prophesied. The picture-narration in B's case demands, as Archer has said, a "critical evaluation according to literary standards as well as by the purely visual and symbolic criteria normally applied to the motion picture."[18] The sound effects portend and recall an event, bring together meaningful fragments. The combination of naturalistic effects with a very plain musical structure creates a rich symphonic interaction. The rhythmic adjustment is perfect, in a harmonic synthesis with the film's predominantly dark graphic scale.

The hint of a compromise appears almost as a *deus ex machina*. It has happened earlier that optimistic conclusions in B's films have seemed unnatural, having little to do with the film drama itself, with an added pinch of romanticism. *The Naked Night* has traces of romanticism, too, in that the narrator seems almost enamored of suffering. Life begins beyond despair, as with Orestes in Sartre's *The Flies*.[19] A deeper humiliation than this can hardly be imagined. As Frost in the flashback undresses, so does Albert, before his fight with Frans, remove his coat and hat. He is no longer a circus manager with borrowed finery. The form of the film is in sympathy with the content because the motion, esthetic as well as ethical, strives at throwing down the masks and draperies before people. On the stage Frans is a seducer with grandiloquent monologues. In his dressing room he is a cheap country actor with exactly the same studied intonations that Sjuberg described to Albert.

In interpreting *The Naked Night*, I have used as my point of departure the possibility of pessimism or of confidence to which the film leads. The interpretation and the point of departure may be wrong. In all respects the drama has a construction that excludes the accidental, despite its freedom of form. The people in the film are freed from a part of their living lie. They have not found the answer, but they are living. Perhaps it is a matter of complete indifference what the answer to their lives will be. They all live under the same cold, unanswering sky. In the legitimate drama one road leads from expressionism to Brecht. In the film, the same road takes us to *The Naked Night*. The epic grasp reminds us of Brecht's. The actors are exhibitors of roles in the marketplace. Their masks indicate certain traits of character. Agda's blank face reveals the emptiness within her. Albert's sweating and heaviness show that he lives a life of the flesh. The drama has a few exalted, intense moments of life. That is the meaning of the picture, not the philosophies, the explanations.

In sheer competence, B has not advanced from *The Naked*

*Night*. His film language has become much more subtle. What he expresses in this picture he has learned to say in another way. At the same time, perhaps something of the spontaneous inspiration has been lost. *The Naked Night* belongs among the rare films that continue to grow, to live with the spectator.

DREAMS. Harriet Andersson (*Doris*) and Gunnar Björnstrand (*The consul*).

A LESSON IN LOVE. Harriet Andersson (*Nix*) and Gunnar Björnstrand (*Dr. David Erneman*).

SMILES OF A SUMMER NIGHT. This scene with Ingmar Bergman, in the background, as a bookkeeper was not used. THE NAKED NIGHT. Åke Grönberg (*Albert*) and Hasse Ekman (*Frans*).

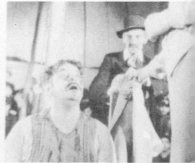

# 6

## INTERLUDE

These words by Shaw stand as a motto for the manuscript of
*Smiles of a Summer Night*: "Life does not cease to be comic
because somebody dies. Neither does it cease to be tragic because
somebody laughs." The words could also stand as a motto for
*A Lesson in Love* and *Dreams*, in which the comic and the tragic
are blended. In these three films the surface is polished. The
danger of perfection is obvious. That B has nevertheless been
able to overcome this danger to a great extent is due to his assurance. He has the ability to put together the pictures of a film. *A
Lesson in Love* is a complicated and skillful game between past
and present. Situations of the present support those of the past,
and vice versa.

Infusions of comedy have earlier been found in B's work.
*Crisis* was "almost" a comedy. The laughter in *The Devil's
Wanton* and *The Naked Night* is dark, but it is there, in Tomas's
ignominious murder, or in the confrontation of the circus artists
with law and order. B has ever criticized power and its execu-
tors. The personnel in Harry's place of employment is conceived
of as completely ludicrous. The restaurateur in *Night is my Future* is a fat pig. B uses both verbal and visual means. He has the
same sense of the grotesque and the aberrant as Hjalmar Berg-

man. If *The Naked Night* is the height of bitterness, balance is restored in the almost-comedies.

In the series of interludes that began with *A Lesson in Love*, B won the audience to his side. He succeeded in accomplishing the magic act of seduction which is the subject of the mesmerist Albert Emanuel Vogel's confessions in *The Magician*. B knows that *A Lesson in Love* does not belong among his best films. But as a French critic expressed it: "Perhaps the best criticism of a film is another film." The best criticism of *A Lesson in Love* is, surprisingly enough, *Wild Strawberries*.

The situation, so far as Swedish criticism is concerned, was rather strange after the comedies were released. With few exceptions, B's greatness in *The Devil's Wanton* was not acknowledged. But his fame in Sweden rested on the unspoken opinion that he was not a conformist, that he rejected the conceptions of the majority. His comedies break with this view. Here, middle-class virtues which B earlier had rejected are praised. *A Lesson in Love* ends with everything being as it used to be. In *Dreams* the dreams are dismissed. *Smiles of a Summer Night* introduces a constellation of love in which age seeks age, and one social group seeks another. The characters pass through a landscape of compromises and defeats, as always with B. They find a way of living in this landscape. The comedies (if they may so be called) present a spirit of conformity. They attract the public with their unconcealed eroticism, a love of the body and of contact, which reaches its climax in *Smiles of a Summer Night*. All the rules of the game in that picture are aimed at conquering or reconquering a man. The comedies are an expression of a bourgeois patriarchalism. The world is viewed through the eyes of men. Behind their backs, the women pursue their shameless erotic intrigues. The men are children and puppets.

On the basis of the image that had been created of B, the opinion of his "real" way that had been presented, it was now possible to dismiss the comedies. One critic asked: "Do you make pornography on purpose or have you only failed in making something else?" Another said: "The evil imagination of a pimply boy, the shameless dreams of an immature heart, a boundless contempt for artistic and human truth are the forces that have created this 'comedy.' "[1]

More deeply analyzed, these films of B's are not so surprising as might be imagined. Erotic comedy was introduced into Sweden by Mauritz Stiller, The wrestling with moral-metaphysical questions in B's earlier pictures led to an acceptance of the moment, of its happiness. The comedies advocate the small solutions that remain. They turn upside down the rhetorical content of B's *Sturm und Drang*. They are a deflector. Had B continued along this line he would undoubtedly have landed in a sterile landscape. But the continuation is called *The Seventh Seal* and restores the balance.

Those who reject the comedies believe perhaps that B must always remain the same, immobile in his attitude toward life. Without sharing this opinion, it is of course possible to dismiss these three films because one's appreciation of B is founded on the awareness that he is important precisely because he rejects bourgeois conformity. His art, however, is vacillating in its relation to the Swedish community and to the middle-class milieu. One nuance on his path is obviously the attempt to know what is valuable, what is bad, in his own tradition. Therefore he must test and query. His development may be compared with that of Thomas Mann, so far as the bourgeois element is concerned.

In a remarkably keen analysis of B's comedies, Jouko Tyyri[2] points out that their foundation is a crisis of values in man's social status. Agreeing with Yrjö Hirn, he shows that man, who always tries to exceed his limitations, is a more suitable and common comedy figure than woman. The crisis of values has, in the end, social roots. Don Juan and Tristan, the victor and the hero, are

disappearing: "Man's value becomes democratized, man's protecting attributes are socialized, so to speak, and the entire ideology of love is shaken to its foundation during a period of social
crisis." In B's comedies, the women are usually satisfied with the
role traditionally allotted them, and try to keep it. The men are
dreamers or professional people—in other words, living in various worlds: those of the home, of work, and sometimes of free
eroticism. None of these worlds can entirely satisfy them. The
key scene here is the confrontation of the lawyer Fredrik Egerman and Captain Count Malcolm in *Smiles of a Summer Night*.
One is attired in a dressing gown, the other in military panoply.
One is a former lover, the other is the current one. Between
them stands the woman, who finds them both ridiculous.

In the comedies B finds an opportunity to sketch the contrast
between man's and woman's world, which has concerned him
previously. If he sides with emotion and the free life as opposed
to reason and aridity of feeling, then it is quite natural that he
chooses woman as a symbol of this freedom. He does not want
to solve the riddles. The nature of the comedy is that contradictions become united. Obviously, the surroundings in all the three
films are middle-class, or artistic. On a lower social plane there
is not the freedom from worry about the material tomorrow
which is prerequisite for the sport and play in these comedies.

## A Lesson In Love

The blend of the banal and the important is splendidly demonstrated in *A Lesson in Love*. The first spoken lines strike the
note of retreat which is that of the film. The scene takes place
between a physician and a young, beautiful woman in his consultation room. She says, among other things:

"You are a wretch. You are spoiled and brutal and cynical.
And you are supposed to be a woman's doctor, you who have

never understood a woman in your whole life. If I could, I would laugh at the whole thing. You are so incredibly naïve."

He answers in part:

"I admit that my retreat is inglorious, but I am not a passionate superman, I am only a tired and bored fellow with headaches and remorse. Can anything be more dismal? I am a little old, a little, little old, a little, little, little old."

He is the gynecologist Dr. David Erneman, married for sixteen years, the father of two children, a daughter and a son. She is his mistress up to now, Susanne, with whom he became acquainted at a consultation, in the same room. He tells her he is through.

She leaves in anger. The rest of the action shows the consequences of this, partly in that David tries to win his wife back again, partly in that both he and she relive the past. What has happened is most often seen through his eyes, though sometimes by both of them together in a flashback through her eyes. The surface action is that he, after having turned Susanne away, drives south and catches up with the train to Malmö, where he finds a seat in the same compartment as his wife—without the spectator knowing who she is. Even during the motor trip David begins to remember. As in *Wild Strawberries* the important thing here is the flashbacks, the light they shed on the present. *A Lesson in Love*, too, is a self-analysis, but in the spirit of play.[3]

As a film story, *A Lesson in Love* is schematic, free, and with a touch of vaudeville. The material is very funny, elegantly presented; but in spite of the flashback technique the actual movement is mainly in the words. In order to free himself from Susanne, David has to humiliate himself—that is, to represent himself as older, more tired and set in his ways than he actually is. In three flashbacks we see the development of his relationship with Susanne, their summer together and the farcical sequence in which David's wife, Marianne, surprises him on the bed with Susanne in a tourist inn. David has looked up Susanne, or been driven to her, from boredom with his marriage and a frenetic desire for youth. It is in an attempt to find his former self that he tries to return to Marianne.

The contemporary part of the play adheres to the rules of elegant drawing-room comedy. The dialogue is well written, the lines often consisting of general aphorisms about love: "The marriage bed is the death of love. I believe that love needs a slap now and then, or else it dies by itself." In reply to this, we may say with Marianne: "You are playing with words." The scenes follow the laws of the theater, its immobility and relatively static compositions. During the trip to Malmö the struggle between David and Marianne begins. It ends in Copenhagen, where it becomes a triangle drama with Susanne's former lover, the sculptor Carl-Adam, as the third party.

The most interesting parts of the film occur in two of the flashbacks. One begins with David alone in the railroad compartment, picking up a learned book. (In *Three Strange Loves* the art critic Bertil tries in the same manner to become distracted from reality.) A picture of David's fifteen-year-old daughter Jacqueline, called Nix, falls out. We see his face in the train window; we see the landscape behind. By means of the flashback out into empty space we arrive at the event of the past, when David one rainy day finds Nix walking her dachshund on the seaside road. He stops his car. She distrusts his assurance that he has plenty of time (for he never has). They walk to a cafe, and later to some relatives who run a pottery.

Nix does not want to be a woman, does not feel like one. She dresses like a boy. She feels disgusted by the erotic activities of her contemporary girl friends. She feels sorry for her mother, who has been deserted by David. She tells as if it were something self-evident that her mother has resumed her acquaintanceship with Carl-Adam. She is bitter, in a childish, defiant way. But David, too, is bitter. He describes eroticism as an occupation for baboons. But it is exactly this that he has sought in his relation with Susanne. He despises himself, and finds everything enormously unimportant. It is on the same shore—symbolically viewed—that the meeting between the husband and wife in *Wild Strawberries* takes place. There they reach an agreement about a child that she wants to bear but which he does not desire.

The construction of the scenes between Nix and David is loose and self-evident. The two other flashbacks are seen through both Marianne's and David's eyes, and indicate the possibility of a reconciliation between them. The first one tells how Carl-Adam in Copenhagen is waiting in vain for his bride (Marianne), and sends his best friend, David, to fetch her, whereupon it becomes apparent that in actuality it is they who love each other. A classic farcical situation, with smashed china, threatening fist fights, and the spiritually impotent minister, who vainly tries to mediate. It is the powerless clergyman, the preacher who cannot change or transform life.

The flashback that shows the direct road to *Wild Strawberries* is the last one. It is occasioned by David's and Marianne's conversation on the train, the fact that only a year ago they had, after all, enjoyed married bliss. The memory picture begins very early on a summer morning in the country at the home of David's parents, Professor Henrik Erneman and his wife, Svea. It is the professor's seventy-third birthday. His children and grandchildren serve him morning coffee in bed. Later in the day an automobile excursion is planned. The professor abhors the traditional outing, but is not able to have it stopped, although he, in conspiracy with David and the chauffeur Sam, creates the impression that something is wrong with the car.

Henrik Erneman is a smiling opposite to Isak Borg, perhaps because his wife is still living. Nix is too shy to offer her gift to the professor in the presence of the family. They are alone in his room. She asks him about death. She is afraid; he is not. His feeling is that one lives to die, that this gives life a meaning, and that one therefore must completely possess the moment.

"Death is only a little part of life. Think how dreary it would be if everything were the same, always, always. Therefore there is death, so that there may come new life for all eternity. Think only how tiresome it would be for me to wear long underdrawers a hundred thousand years."

The picture of Henrik Erneman is a subtle study of tolerant middle-class respectability. In the evening there is a dance. Henrik and Svea Erneman seem to have grown together, in mutual understanding of each other's weaknesses. The Ernemans are like Philemon and Baucis, with a friendly irony, a dignity that the young characters in B's films all too seldom achieve. These two prove that man's fate need not be just to grow old in solitude. He can meet the unavoidable with someone else. Into this realization, perhaps, there also enters the belief that man must first be ground and beaten by life before he becomes sufficiently resigned, before he has reduced his demands to such an extent that he can continue to live with someone else. Erneman is a study of free, middle-class good manners, to which B really has never taken exception.

The picnic outdoors becomes for David and Marianne a reminder of their own happiness. They stroll through the forest. The light among the trees is enchanted. They feel a tenderness for each other. Their hands touch, like Henrik's and Marie's in *Illicit Interlude*. They reveal their secret wishes: hers, to have one more child; his, to have a diving bell to go down into the depths of the sea "and look for sunken treasures and fight with sharks and cuttlefish." She laughs at him. In this moment he is the child the mother always dreams about, the irresponsible one, possessed by his spirit of play. We must remember that David has earlier been described as obsessed by his work, tired, and aware of the fact that his marriage has been killed by boredom.

*A Lesson in Love* does not lack style, but it lacks a unity of style. It oscillates between farce and seriousness, poetry and realism. The separate bits become independent little essays. But perhaps one may say with Jean Wagner[4] that a mistake by B is worth much more than an anonymous perfection. Underlying the film there is a bitterness and a hardness, which is even more plainly expressed in *Dreams*.

## Dreams

Paradoxically, *Dreams* reminds one in part of a silent picture with sound added. At the same time, an analysis of these sounds is important to demonstrate the film's enduring qualities. *Dreams* approaches serious comedy, approaches tragedy. The film lacks unified strength. Still it remains one of B's most interesting failures.

The opening is almost entirely silent. It takes place in a fashion photographer's studio. In a chair sits the head of the establishment, Susanne; at a table the genial fashion director Magnus. He drums with his fingers on the top of the table. Busy people are attending the model Doris. No words are spoken. Still the scene is pregnant with secret tension. The same strength is found in the train sequences, when Doris and Susanne travel to Gothenburg. Susanne is fighting a lonely battle against the fear of death and her sudden impulse to commit suicide. Her face jerks about in the wind and the rain, mirroring her inward struggle.

The text in the film, as Jean Collet[5] has pointed out, is more music and effect than direct communication. The sounds distill the anguish of the scenes, in the studio, on the train, and in the telephone conversation between Susanne and her lover, Henrik. The sound effects describe emotions. They interpret a theme that is constantly recurring with B, people's inability to draw near to each other, the truth of the statement that they speak past each other. The sound effects as such have a naturalistic background, but they are not used naturalistically. The sound effects shut the actors up in their prisons. When the words no more serve the need to convey something, they become reports from a world where man in vain tries to surround himself with protective covering.

Two women, two dreams, are placed opposite each other. Susanne is the older. She has long had an affair with acting manager Henrik Lobelius, who is married and has children. During the visit to Gothenburg, she tries to arrange a meeting. She walks in the woods, near his home, sees his wife go out with the children; a very ordinary view, filled with Susanne's longing. She telephones Henrik, makes him promise to call on her at the hotel. She is so tormented that she is willing to humiliate herself to any extent to win him back. Their relationship has been over for seven months. Like David in *A Lesson in Love*, he is tired, but the drama this time is seen primarily from her point of view. Henrik admits his fatigue. More important, however, is the likelihood that his business faces bankruptcy. He is economically dependent on his wife. This is humiliating.

It is a tragic mistake for the two in the hotel room at last to let their feeling master them. Marta Lobelius, the most intelligent, clear-sighted, and dreary of all the women in the film, looks them up at the hotel. She unmasks them all, her own narrowness and cold-bloodedness, their lack of prospects. Her fortune remains intact if Henrik becomes bankrupt. She understands them all: Susanne's longing for love, Henrik's for adventure. But she yields not an inch. Her comprehension has the same touch of cruelty as Agda's in *The Naked Night*. She lives safely in the world that spells children and her own home. Henrik needs her, but she does not need Henrik.

Strangely enough, she is a synthesis of the evil figure we have found in B's films, and of the clear observer who produces crystal-clear, necessary, perhaps unpleasant solutions. Being together with Susanne is for Henrik, in Marta's words, "full of life, violent emotions, and demands of every kind," while being together with Marta means "quietness, clarity, and calm sleep."

Marta is not jealous—does not, perhaps, love her husband—but
can tend home and children. She succeeds in producing a change
in Susanne. When Susanne in the final sequence (which is repeated under the same conditions as in the beginning) receives
a letter from Henrik, in which he offers her the tormenting and
tempting condition of an adventurous liaison, she tears the letter
to bits. Mr. Magnus believes it is a dunning note, a request for
money, or favors. Susanne does not deny this.

Like the mannequin Doris, she returns to her profession, to the
opiate and the satisfaction of work. Susanne's dreams are those
of approaching middle age. Doris's dreams are girl dreams, like
Monika's in *Monika*. The action develops parallel with Susanne's
and reaches its disillusionment at the same moment. Doris has a
fiancé, Palle, a typical Swedish university student. She prefers
to go to Gothenburg rather than to spend the evening with him.
When she travels, she is lonely in her soul, like Susanne.

In Gothenburg she strolls about, looking into shop windows.
An old gentleman, Consul Sönderby, speaks to her in the street.
The outline of the story is classic. He buys her clothes and shoes,
he offers her jewelry. B contrasts his age with her youth, his
weariness and convulsive vitality with her matter-of-factness.
Cinematographically, he does this brilliantly. He takes them to
the amusement park of Liseberg. The violent rides in swings and
merry-go-rounds, on dizzying roller coasters make the consul
more and more afraid, Doris more and more exhilerated. A
dreary, long-range shot of the exit of the amusement park shows
the consul falling. He scrapes his hand. Doris tries to support
him. He manages by himself, anxious to preserve his dignity.

B's technique here is that of the light suggestion. In contrast to
Antonioni, he does not wish to break his discreet camera movement by placing persons in clearly indicated space relations. His
technique emerges from the situation. In the consul's home,
Doris gets drunk on champagne. She tells him her dreams. These
dreams humiliate him, since they are only aimed at herself, and

emphasize that this whole world is inaccessible to him. She has a crooked tooth, and wants to have it capped. She wants to play the leading role in a film that he will finance. She wants a sports car and a bungalow in the country. During these scenes the consul grows older, Doris becomes younger, for dreams make one younger. The consul is dignified, amused by her performance. She enjoys her new clothes, the borrowed elegance.

The play is here interrupted by the consul's daughter, who comes to beg for money. She humiliates Doris, just as Doris humiliated the consul. When Doris leaves, without her new dress, without her shoes or jewelry, she feels sorry for the old man. He is doomed, set in a pose, in his quest for a youth he does not possess. Like Isak Borg, the consul has been sentenced to loneliness. They both seek their youth, in images of reality, in figures which they see. "Call me Otto," he says. "Nobody has done that since I was ten years old." He is seeking his childhood. As she leaves, we see his face in the dark castle that is his prison and his home.

The extreme view of *Dreams* is that B's Devil has experienced the same fate as the pigs in Orwell's *Animal Farm*. "Everything disturbing, shocking and restless has disappeared and been replaced by a perfect unity of thought and action. And the thinner, and, from a bourgeois point of view, more meritorious his films become, the more perfect become the technique and the polished action."[6]

For sheer technical virtuosity, *Dreams* is one of B's foremost achievements. It has often an effectiveness of narration that brings to mind commercial American comedies. Nothing is unnecessary, yet nothing is really urgent. I should still like to designate *Dreams* as a significant in-between film. It works consciously with strong visual and sound contrasts. It does not build up a running montage, but transmits broken fragments of reality. The outer elements of the plot are commonplace; its inner power in some scenes is considerable.

*Dreams* is a repository for ideas which have not achieved definite form.


## Smiles of a Summer Night

*Smiles of a Summer Night*, on the other hand, lies complete and closed within itself, to some extent impossible to reach. Of its kind it is perfect. But the picture has a strange, perfumed, ingratiating atmosphere which scarcely harmonizes with the predominant line in B's production. Still, the tragic element exists, based on the characters presented. The laughter is bitter.

The picture's threads of action are brought together in a big final complex which is the nucleus of the story, a week-end visit arranged by old Mrs. Armfeldt at Ryarp manor house in Skåne. Before the action becomes concentrated in the events of the summer night, B has developed a remarkable erotic strategy.

1. The lawyer Fredrik Egerman attends the theater with his young wife, Anne. Anne begins to weep; the two walk home. On the stage stands Desirée Armfeldt, Fredrik's former mistress. His first wife is dead.

2. Fredrik visits Desirée after the performance. Finally he exits ingloriously in a white nightshirt as her current lover, Carl Magnus Malcolm, makes a stormy entrance.

3. Early the next morning Desirée calls on her old mother and persuades her to arrange the party. Invited are: the Count and his wife, the lawyer with his wife and son, and Desirée herself.

4. Carl Magnus hints to his wife that he has found the lawyer with his mistress.

5. Mrs. Malcolm visits Anne, reveals to her the escapade of her husband, of which Anne declares she is informed.

6. The lawyer's grown son, Henrik, a student of theology, is exposed to bold temptations by the servant girl, Petra, but wards

her off and defends himself halfheartedly with quotations from Scripture.

According to the manuscript, the film takes place in 1901. *Smiles of a Summer Night* is a love film with an ancient motif, also touched upon in Renoir's *La règle du jeu*. Compared with B's, the Renoir picture is a direct satire on capitalism and the bourgeoisie.[7] B's film has no such ambitions. Nor is there any of the Central European nostalgia that characterizes another closely related work, Ophuls' film version of Schnitzler's *Der Reigen*. The eroticism in *Smiles of a Summer Night* is not subtle. It expresses an unrestrained sensuality, a manic desire, beyond the difference in time and clothing, to expose the human beings concerned. They move like marionettes in the game of love. Hence the comparison with *The Naked Night* is perhaps meaningful.

The spirit of social and artistic compromise dominates the film. The story follows the social conventions strictly. When Petra has challenged Henrik with her charms, the cook says: "Petra only wants to get up in the world, but I'll tell you that a flirt is a flirt, even if she flirts with His Majesty the King." Quite logically, Petra is united with the coachman Frid during the summer night of truth that ends the film. The union of the others also takes place within the framework of social convention. Henrik is of the same age as his father's wife Anne. She is a virgin. He is united with her.

B describes a world still untouched by a new social thinking, a world tied up in conventions. Like Schnitzler, he is both fascinated and nauseated by this. It has been said that *Smiles of a Summer Night*, like others of B's period pictures, delineates modern people dressed up in the costumes of the turn of the century, of the past. This is only half true. I have the impression that B retains a certain romantic love for the past. It is a nostalgia for "the good old days," when class privileges were regarded as obvious and the work of social renewal had not yet begun. The comic effect arises also from the absolute unreality of the world of the turn of the century, seen with our eyes.

B hardly believes in the possibility of reconstructing the past naturalistically. He produces a masque insofar as he seems to know that if the camera moved outside the picture frame, it would discover a modern reality.[8] Irony and distance are better indicated in this way. The unmasking unmercifully exposes both ourselves and the persons in the play. The middle-class man of the turn of the century was just as much possessed by erotic dreams as people today. The stench of eroticism expresses indirectly the criticism of a form of living in which nobody dares to be quite open. It is against this life that Henrik protests.

The key word is man's dignity.[9] It is spoken by Desirée Armfeldt in the wedged-in theater sequence which causes Anne's tears and the couple's premature return to their home:

"We women have the right to commit many offences against our husbands, our lovers, our sons, so long as it does not wound them in their Dignity. If we do that, we are foolish and have to bear the consequences. We ought instead to make the Dignity of our men our ally and caress it, sing lullabies to it, speak tenderly to it, and treat it as our dearest plaything."

When Fredrik walks with Desirée, to her home, he falls into a puddle of water and has to change his clothes. He is forced to put on his rival's nightshirt. The action aims at destroying the last of Fredrik's dignity. During his conversation with Desirée, a boy strolls through the room, Desirée's child, but she refuses to say whether this Fredrik is the son of the lawyer. He is later forced to escape ignominiously from her home. The party at Ryarp B carries off with great strategy, in order to complete the theme. Fredrik is beaten at croquet by the dashing Malcolm. During the dinner he sees that his son Henrik is observed with peculiar tenderness by Anne. Countess Malcolm makes a bet with her husband that she can quickly seduce the lawyer. After dinner she succeeds in this, at least theoretically. When the

Count finally challenges the lawyer at Russian roulette, he has nothing to defend. His wife Anne has betrayed him.

The short scene demonstrates B's masterly situation analysis. Anne hastens to Petra and Frid, who are making love outdoors. Frid runs to the stable and hitches up the horses. The scene is played in the dusk of Midsummer Night. Far in the background stands the lawyer. He takes a step to stop what is going on, but checks himself instead, realizing the futility of such an action. He is a passive, conquered observer. As the carriage rolls by at high speed, Anne's white veil falls to the ground. He picks it up. B here puts the spectator in the actor's place. In spite of the restraint of the camera movement, the viewer becomes a subjective, sympathetic witness.

The Russian roulette, the clash between the Count and the lawyer, ends with the lawyer's shooting himself. The pistol, however, is loaded only with soot. B manipulates the elements of surprise with extreme skill. As a matter of fact, the lawyer is the more courageous of the two. He does not know that the engagement is a matter of life and death. Count Malcolm does not think it necessary to risk his life for the sake of a lawyer. He is concerned only with his own welfare and pride.

The picture includes one more suicide attempt, Henrik's. Offended by the others' cynical conversation at dinner, he goes up to his room where he appeals to his Lord: "If Thy world is sinful, I want to sin; let the birds build nests in my hair, take my miserable virtue from me, for I cannot stand it any more." He tries to hang himself from the damper of the tile stove. He falls, and happens to touch off a mechanism on the wall. Bells begin to chime. The bed in the next room comes rolling into his own. In it lies Anne, untouched, innocent, sleeping.

Henrik has been described as a serious young man with a fanatically dark outlook. Frivolity in all its forms is alien to him. In a scene in the home, Anne takes his pipe and dressing gown from him, and calls him dirty. He has not wanted to be con-

soled by anybody, by Petra, Anne, or his cynical father. His
outer appearance corresponds to the conception of him as a
demoniacal, romantic character. In contrast to the sensuality of
the others, his is a spiritual quality. He has some of the same
abruptness that one imagines was found in the artist who wrote
*Torment* and created *The Devil's Wanton*.

The suicide scene is very short. It shows how the constant
modulation and reformulation of identical problems is one basis
of B's cinematographic richness. *A Lesson in Love* has a similar
parody-like suicide scene, in the flashback of Marianne's youth.
Desperate at having to marry Carl-Adam, she tries to hang herself from a hook in the ceiling. The suicides, the attempts at
suicide, the threat to commit suicide seldom lack in B's pictures
a dramatic motivation. This does not mean that "real" life offers
so many acts of desperation, but that B has a hypersensitive
understanding of the crises of man and of moral values. The
trait of hysteria is not alien to his characters. Therefore they are
driven to extreme acts. Suicide becomes the only way out for a
person who sees no chance of living with dignity or of solving
the great questions he asks. It is also a matter of a lack of power
to resist.

For B's purposes, however, the unfinished suicide is most
typical, for it corresponds to his tenets of constant humiliation.
The persons who fail in their suicide attempts receive from this
the courage to change the direction of their lives. Theirs becomes the understanding that the only value there is, is life itself. Berit in *Port of Call* tries to drown herself, but is rescued.
Gradually she experiences the hope of a better life. Eugen in
*Secrets of Women* comes to his senses after having stood in a
shack and threatened to commit suicide. The author in *Through
a Glass Darkly* tries to commit suicide in Switzerland but does
not succeed and thereafter regards his life and surroundings
with other eyes. In this case, though, the motive has an almost
parody-like touch. The author is obviously a man who lives a

lie, possessed by self-deception. Albert in *The Naked Night* has nothing to hope for after his abortive suicide attempt. He can therefore face tomorrow without illusions.

It is not necessary to present Henrik and his kind as cheats only because their attempts at suicide are so amateurish. In *Dreams* Susanne tosses her head in the rain and the wind outside the door. One seems to understand that she does not really contemplate throwing herself out. She is testing, testing the possibility of death, in order to recover herself for the only task that remains hers.

Sudden and evil death often meets the persons in B's films, for instance Bertha in *Torment* or Marthe in *Eva*. The aim of the Christian thought is to reconcile man with his death. B does not seem influenced by this doctrine. On the contrary, death is viewed as a frightening executioner. Against its power there is no propitiation. Death is the terrifying possibility of existence, the trapdoor that opens. In *Smiles of a Summer Night* it is vanquished, and turns into romantic harmony, because the meaning of the comedy is reconciliation. The parody-like is blended with adolescent seriousness.

The idea of the summer night as an hour of truth makes us first of all think of *Miss Julie*. But even the heathen customs in the North laid great stress on summer. Perhaps one can give a heathen significance also to the motifs in B's art that make use of this night of truth.

Fredrik is humiliated, but in the end regains Desirée. Her wish has been to return the Count to his marriage, to recover the lawyer, to have everything the way it used to be. In all his vain manliness, the Count dispises life. He hides a bitterness that nothing can eradicate. By promising his wife not to deceive her, he shows his own weakness, dooms both himself and her. They are both willing to go on living defiled:

"I will remain faithful to you for at least seven eternities of pleasure, eighteen false smiles, and fifty-seven enamored whisperings without meaning. I will be faithful to you until the big yawn separates us. In short, I will be faithful to you after my fashion."

*Smiles of a Summer Night* is a mating game, not any more shameless or cheap than the characters B describes. Roughly expressed, there are only two worlds in it. Men are the object of ridicule, women of sympathy. It has been suggested that the scene in which Petra and Anne throw themselves down on the bed and embrace each other is Lesbian, but Juoko Tyyri[10] maintains, probably with greater plausibility, that their embrace is a demonstration of a secret communion and their superiority to men. They are too easy to bring to a fall.

The key scene of the picture does not take place in any of the sequences mentioned here, but during a conversation between Desirée and her mother, when the daughter has come to ask the old lady to arrange the party. In the beginning, the dialogue is very light. The interior is as baroque as in *The Naked Night*. The mood is gay and intimate. The old lady confesses that she received the estate against a promise not to write her memoirs. The two women are playing with words, as often with B, an art that he masters, but drives to absurdity and surfeit.

The two are very much dressed up, the old lady in a big bed, Desirée in a tailored suit. As a matter of fact, they are very much undressed, very lovely and truthful to each other. Like other bits, this has a lingering fragrance of sickly sweetness. "Certain pictures," says Béranger,[11] "with swans floating across a mirror-like pond by a small wooden bridge remind one of the lids of those little pill boxes our grandmothers still have in their bureau drawers."

The scene ends with a full view of the old lady's room. The frail little woman lies immobile in her bed. It has the effect of words: "One can never protect a single person from a single suffering. That is what makes one so terribly tired." That is the picture's key line. Man cannot help his neighbor to live. He must go through his trials alone. The deeper implication is that man is always alone. The barriers can temporarily be broken down by love and a sense of fellowship. It is a pessimistic doctrine, in the most hedonistic film B has created. But just as firm is the conviction that fellowship is necessary.[12]

The formal problems in *Smiles of a Summer Night* are on the whole those of the theater. The solutions are perfect, but empty. What is important is the poetic observation of nature, in Fredrik's and Desirée's brief nocturnal stroll, in the love play between Petra and Frid, the twilight that envelops everything in the forgiving light of compromise.

# 7

## THE SEVENTH SEAL

Of B's films, *The Seventh Seal* is the least immediate, the most rhetorical. It is therefore understandable that the critics who dismiss B's art use this very picture as an object lesson. A characteristic essay about B is written by Caroline Blackwood,[1] who is of the opinion that instead of Cecil B. de Mille's "Religion and Sex" B has given the public the "Supernatural and Sex, decked out with Symbols." The impact of B's brilliant, skillful fragments and vignettes is often lost, according to this critic, in "all the messy smörgasbord of his hysterical whimsical ideas." *The Seventh Seal* can indeed appear to be overloaded with scenes in which the symbolic meaning, the many-faceted ornamental function, prevents the narrative, analytical material from coming into its own. This arises from the nature of B's inspiration, on the long and difficult road from original artistic vision to finished film. B has often wished for "a sort of notation which would give me a chance to translate all the nuances of the vision, the product's innermost structure, into distinct mnemonic symbols."[2] Something of the spontaneous inspiration that seems to characterize *The Naked Night* has been lost in *The Seventh Seal*. The film's single images may appear as too calculated, too beautiful, too harmonious an impression which makes one re-

135

gard as almost a parody the caption on a laudatory Swedish review: "A New Swedish Film Classicist."[3]

In B's amazing ability to adjust himself there lies a danger. It is possible that he makes himself the interpreter of his manuscript to the extent of self-immolation. But such a criticism of the style of *The Seventh Seal* can concern only certain sequences. One must remember that this film poses the greatest of questions, and that among B's films it is the one that perhaps most exactly formulates something akin to a philosophical credo.

Since the end of World War II there has been a strange transformation in the willingness of the Western cultural world to accept works of art of this kind, as Andrew Sarris points out in a brilliant analysis of the film's structure and philosophy.[4] "The individual's situation in an indifferent universe would have struck an artist as a meaningless subject a generation ago, when man's striving hardly extended farther than the next bread line." During the years between the wars, social illusions lived on in undisturbed peace, whether their stamp was Liberal, Marxist, or Christian. To be sure, the break-through in modern art and literature had taken place under the shadow of a disillusionment with the belief in man's chance of a future as a collective creature. Time, however, was not yet ripe for an art which, like *The Seventh Seal*, was modern in its conception of man, while at the same time posing the central questions about the purpose of life and death. The second World War, nuclear weapons, anxiety about a continued life on earth, and the self-destroying development of technology have made people wonder about the meaning of progress, the meaning of the future. In this situation of crisis, *The Seventh Seal* appears as a mature philosophic declaration.

The film has been described as a morality play, a designation which has been used, with more or less justice, in several of B's works. "Moralities" was the title of three plays by B which were published in book form in 1948. One of them. *The Day Ends*

*Early*, tells of a Mrs. Åström, a patient in an insane asylum. She manages to escape. She visits a number of people, telling them that they are to die at a certain hour. One of the persons is a Pastor Broms. His faith is too weak to allay his fears. Prayer is the only help. He pictures "God and the Devil wrestling in a life-and-death struggle. We like to imagine that God is the stronger. Unfortunately, that is wrong. God is about to be killed. And it depends on each and every one of us, however unimportant and ridiculous we are."[5] Exactly the same basic feeling is found in *The Seventh Seal*. This feeling, even among people who call themselves Christians, that they have lost their direction-giving moral and spiritual center, is probably more common today than in the fourteenth century, in spite of the fact that the Black Death was ravaging the province in which the Knight and Jöns find themselves. But to the Knight, the great fatigue after the crusade, combined with what he has experienced of plague and spiritual intolerance, are a counterpart to the feeling of meaninglessness that has met modern man because of the depths of human bestiality he has witnessed. The Knight is a symbol of modern Western man. Not all of the bestialities of modern times can be traced to something evil, to a will that lays evil plans, to a Hitler, a Hoess, or a Himmler. One can also experience evil as ever present, as a ferment in the life we are living. In that case, the interest turns from the outside inward, from the community to the individual, from the individual's condition to his soul. These are the questions posed in *The Seventh Seal*. The accusations against others die away in those who utter them. The feeling of powerlessness is paralyzing. But, as the film demonstrates, there is an escape from these troubles, too. The trouble with the analyses that have been made of the film's structure is that attention has been too one-sidedly concentrated on the Knight, without suspecting that the Knight and Jöns complement each other, are parts of the same spectrum, like Vogler and Dr. Vergérus in *The Magician*.

B has told how in his childhood he accompanied his father on preaching trips to country churches. Many of the single bits in the film are echoes of the old church paintings, for instance, the Knight's chess game with Death, the Holy Virgin in the field (in Jof's vision), the dance across the hills into death. While his father preached, B followed these paintings with his eyes. In one of the sequences in the film, the Knight and Jöns enter a church where an artist is busy painting pictures aimed to frighten and edify the congregation. But B, too, wants to emphasize that *The Seventh Seal* is not a realistic description of Sweden in the Middle Ages: "It is a modern poem, presented with medieval material that has been very freely handled. The Knight of the film returns from a crusade as a soldier in our times returns from a war."[6]

This shows how pregnant B's world of imagination is with Christian ideas. The film also builds on the Book of Revelation, on the selection the Knight's wife Karin reads to her returned husband and his entourage. The action is thought to take place during the half hour of silence that occurred when the Lamb has opened the seventh seal: "Woe, woe, woe, to the inhabiters of the earth by reason of the other voices of the trumpet of the three angels, which are yet to sound!" It is easy to draw the parallels between this vision of destruction and the threat of destruction that today seems to hover over humanity. The religious criticism of the film's success in rewriting the Apocalypse has swung between unreserved approval and clear rejection. According to one critic, Revelation finds its grandeur "in the colossal perspective, which reaches all the way to the throne of God and the Lamb, and where the individual torments have their place in God's cosmic system. If these torments are eliminated, the result is in every sense terrible."[7] For a criticism that only looks at the film, it is difficult to accept this conclusion. The question that has to be answered is this: Has B succeeded in giving the drama of the Knight and Jöns an artistically convincing form? Is *The Seventh Seal* tenable as cinema? It is not theological discussion that can answer this question, but an analysis of the film's structure.

*The Seventh Seal* is built on a one-act play by B, *Painting on Wood*. The action in this short piece is more taut, more concentrated than in the film. Many critics have regarded it as B's foremost dramatic work. Strindberg has earlier treated similar subjects, especially in *The Tale of the Folkungs*, regarded by some as a prototype.

The film's action is very simple. The Knight Antonius Block returns, after a long crusade, to the Sweden of the fourteenth century, devastated by the Black Death. He is accompanied by his squire, Jöns. On a desolate shore, he engages in a game of chess with Death. The prize for the Knight's victory is to be his life. While the game is in progress, the Knight manages to perform a meaningful act. He saves a couple of traveling jugglers, Jof and Mia, from death. The Knight arrives home and finds his wife. Then enters Death. All present are compelled to join in his dance, while the jugglers look on.

The most interesting figure is Jöns, a refutation of the often advanced statement that "The only villains in any of his films are always men of science and intellect."[8] It has been maintained that B has one-sidedly presented an irrational philosophy. It has been said that his penetration into the world of women is an expression of this, since to live seems more important to women than to think, to act. I cannot entirely accept this theory, because that would mean to deny the root and origin of B's art: the Swedish community. The questions of society have not been finally settled, to be sure, but in most cases they have been changed into queries that concern the technical application. B emphasizes the irrational in man's nature. He turns attention inward, to the individual. This seems to correspond to a tendency in the community itself, that the Swedish citizen "is able to devote too much spare time on self-reflection, which often leads to confused eschatologies or an abuse of moral freedom."[9]

Perhaps B is seeking a consolation which is too simple for one who, like Freud, wants to heal civilization. But to regard him exclusively as an irrationalist does not correspond to the image his films give us.

In *The Seventh Seal* Jöns acts and lives in conscious opposition to the other persons in the film. The Church is busy with persecutions and witch-burning. The Knight unceasingly asks questions, which rebound against emptiness. When the Knight's game with Death begins, Jöns is asleep. He then "opens his eyes, and grunts pig-like, yawns widely, but rises and saddles his horse, lifts up the heavy pack. The Knight rides slowly away from the sea, through the forest by the shore, up toward the road. He pretends not to hear the squire's morning prayer." This morning prayer is a particularly blasphemous song, which Jöns recites to the Knight's rising indignation. The riders pass a human form. Jöns dismounts. But when he takes hold of it, an empty skull is grinning at him. He wasn't mute, Jöns answers to the Knight's question. He was highly eloquent.

One of the clearest scenes takes place in a church where the Knight is at his prayers. Jöns begins to talk to the painter while he is waiting for his master. He becomes so shaken by the artist's tale of mankind's self-torment and stupidity that he asks to have a little brandy. This is interwoven with the Knight's questions. The parallel action in B's films is always illuminating, as, for instance, in *The Naked Night*. The Knight's questions remind us of the confession the minister Tomas Ericsson delivers in *Winter Light*: "How are we going to believe in the believers, when we ourselves do not believe? What will happen to us who wish to believe but cannot? And what will become of those who neither wish to nor can believe?" The Knight demands an answer, knowledge, not faith. In a moment of fright he discovers that the unknown who stands behind the bars is Death himself. In the meantime Jöns continues his conversation with the painter.

In his description of the crusade, he renders the background to the Knight's questions:

"Ten years we sat in the Holy Land and let the snakes bite us, insects prick us, wild animals nip us, heathen slaughter us, the wine poison us, women give us lice, fleas feed on us, and fevers consume us all to the glory of God. I'll tell you, our crusade was so stupid that only a real idealist could have invented it."

Jöns has not much use for the doctrines of the Church. Outside the church he spies a young woman who has had "fleshly intercourse with the Evil One." She will be burned. Critics have offered the information that no witches were burned in medieval Sweden, and have advanced this as an artistic argument against the film.[10] Strindberg's historical dramas could very well be condemned with the same argument. His portrait of *Master Olof*, which is historically inexact and faulty, has become the prototype for the picture the Swedish people have made for themselves of the great Reformer.

In a shop Jöns runs into Raval, a thief and a grave robber. Raval was the doctor from the theological seminary in Roskilde who ten years earlier convinced the Knight of the "necessity to go to the Holy Land on a splendid crusade." Jöns announces that he has suddenly come to understand the purpose of the wasted years. "We were too well off, we were too satisfied, and the Lord wanted to chastise our contented pride. Therefore he came and spewed his celestial venom and poisoned the Knight." Jöns is a materialist and a skeptic. He doubts that the big questions have a meaning. Still he is not insensible to the sufferings of others. The Knight continues his questioning. But Jöns helps other people.

Juggler Jof has entered the Tavern Embarrassment. Suspected by the smith Plog of having seduced his wife, Jof is forced by Raval to execute a bear dance on the table. These dark pictures are frightfully, nauseatingly cruel. There is a directness there which otherwise is expressed too seldom in the film. The sequence in the tavern is perhaps the best in the film. It brings to mind the exposure and the absence of disguise that we find in *The Naked Night*.[11] Jöns has promised to get Raval if they ever meet again. Jöns enters the tavern and rescues Jof.

Once more Jöns appears as a helper, when he tries to console the smith for the loss of his wife. But Jöns' words are then spoken on a level that would be more justified in some of the cynically tired train-sequences in *A Lesson in Love*. On their way through the nocturnal forest the group meets eight servants who are taking the witch to be burned. The Knight wants to see the face of the Devil to ask him about God. He, if any, should know. Ironic before the servants, Jöns is trying to think up a practical plan to rescue the girl. He is moved in her presence. But he does not want to use his stirred-up emotions as an excuse for propounding his own questions. The person is the main issue, regardless of how much he tries to hide his sympathy behind a mask of cynicism.

The group meets one more person (aside from Death, with whom the Knight finishes his chess game). It is Raval, now infected by the plague. He wants something to drink. Jöns holds back the girl who accompanies him, not because of hatred toward Raval, but because help is futile. Raval is doomed to die in any case. Jöns' actions are practical. The Knight performs his actions as if there were another task beyond that of living. Jöns is prepared to enjoy life as long as possible. He curses his fate. Jöns is no philosopher: to live is to live is to live. Viewed in this perspective, the foolishness is not found in Jof and Mia ("the golden virgin and her idiot husband"[12]) but in the Knight, because he went on a crusade, and because he is still asking his meaningless questions.

Jöns has been called "a modern agnostic, himself not a little cruel, but not indiscriminately so, skeptical toward everything and everybody, not least himself, at the same time candid with his fellow man, aware of his inadequacy passive up to a certain point, but beyond that full of energy and responsibility."[13] The difference between Jöns and the rest finds its clearest expression in the final sequence. The group has reached the home of the Knight. The morning gets lighter. Karin receives her husband. When seated at their breakfast she reads from Revelation, eighth chapter. Death enters. He is the unknown one who has come to take them away. They speak to Death. The Knight continues to call upon the God that *must* exist. Jöns remains sarcastic. All he knows is that his body exists, that he himself is. The girl whom he has saved from Raval, bids him to be silent. And he answers: "I shall be quiet, but under protest."

Jöns is a realist. We are reminded of the ballet master's admonition to Marie in *Illicit Interlude*. The dance is her profession. We remember the laborious and masterly cinematographic strategy that makes possible the final picture in *The Naked Night*. The solution, that of protest and action, that Jöns chooses does not appear as the film's only ideal, but as its most dignified. The persons who remain alive are Jof and Mia and their son Mikael. Their solution is in privacy, in the happiness of marital communion. They find their satisfaction in the knowledge that the family will perpetuate itself. But in any world at all, a Jof and a Mia have the chance to escape. Jöns, on the other hand, is a character who aims at a militant, active relationship with the world around him.

The squire's part is played by Gunnar Björnstrand, who by now has appeared in more than a dozen of B's films. In *Torment* his role was very small, while in *A Lesson in Love* he was one of the dominating figures. The most typical portrait was delineated in *The Magician*, as the medical counselor Vergérus, who proposes to prove the sorcerer's incompetence, but becomes frightened by the unknown powers. With B's conception of the film medium, it is obvious that he has preferred to use the same actors in picture after picture, for instance, the romantic hero Birger

Malmsten during the forties, or Harriet Andersson from *Monika* on. (In *While the City Sleeps* she has a walk-on bit.)

B wants to create an artistic instrument which he can fully master. He has seldom changed cameramen, designer, cutter, composer. He has worked in the same surroundings, with a crew he knows well. This analysis of his films is built on the conception that he is one of few artists who has succeeded in realizing his personal vision. He has achieved this through the intermediary of closely associated artists and technicians. The films are analyzed here as the final result, the completed work. It is evident that a great deal of the credit for this result, for the films' inner richness of meaning, belongs to B's collaborators. They are instruments in his hand, nothing more, nothing less.

"There are many film makers who forget that the human face is the starting point in our work. To be sure, we can become absorbed by the esthetic of the picture montage, we can blend objects and still lifes into wonderful rhythms, we can fashion nature studies of astonishing beauty, but the proximity of the human face is without doubt the film's distinguishing mark and patent of nobility. . . . In order to give the greatest possible power to the actor's expression, the movement of the camera must be simple and uncomplicated, in addition to being carefully synchronized with the action. The camera must appear as a completely objective observer and should only on rare occasions participate in what is going on. We must also consider that the actor's finest means of expression is his eyes."[14]

The choice of actors corresponds to the change and the shading that have taken place in B's films. The romantic heroes were superseded by persons with greater intellectual complications. The idea content in B's pictures achieved a deeper form and was interpreted by such actors as Ingrid Thulin, Max von Sydow, and Gunnar Björnstrand. Still it seems to me a grossly mechanical conception to lump together, for instance, Gunnar Björnstrand's roles and consider that his character remains the same in film after film, as Béranger has done in his book about B. The artist's creative imagination works with the material of reality. A part of the reality that surrounds B is the world of the film, his actors. It is obvious that he creates his characters and writes his parts with a consideration, among other things, of the qualifications he finds among his interpreters. Perhaps the squire Jöns has something of Gunnar Björnstrand, a dignity and a vulnerability found in this actor. This is, however, as irrelevant to the analysis of films as to combine the facts of private life with the fiction of art. It suffices to note the importance of Jöns to the action of *The Seventh Seal*: "Here we perceive the outline of Camus' modern hero, a symbol of man's, of the individual's, integrity. The portrait is not fully rounded. Bergman apparently has not dared to give it the central place it deserves in modern drama. But the fate of the squire intimates in any case modern man's dramatic relationship to the world around him. Man's sluggish hopelessness is contrasted without any religious embellishment with his courage and dignity. This is more than social consciousness: this is the most urgent social message."[15]

The film's main parallel action is between the Knight-Jöns and Jof-Mia. These are the poles around which the action revolves, Jof dreams that his son Mikael will achieve the impossible: that is, to make the juggling balls stand still in the air. Their story begins with the awakening, shown in another light than Albert Johansson's awakening in *The Naked Night*. Albert, too, has sons, but they do not wish to join the circus. While Albert must pass through darkness and suffering before he is freed, Jof slips away from all questions despite the moments of terror he experiences in the tavern.

It is the Knight's meeting with the jugglers that changes his action and gives these characters another meaning. Before this, however, the jugglers' appearance in the market place has been interrupted by the passing procession of the flagellants, a vision of man's folly and the Last Judgment. The scene takes place on a sunny slope. At first, Mia is alone with Mikael. Jof is at the tavern.

The scene, in B's construction, has the simple, magnificent seriousness of a consecration, a religious rite. The play of light in *The Seventh Seal* shows plainly the contrasts between the contemporary patterns of action. In the lighting of the Knight's story, the dark, the black, dominates. Above Jof and Mia there almost always hovers a brightness of grace, as if the action took place in another reality. Jos Burvenich[16] believes that the image B makes for himself of a God represents a higher being to whom one should dedicate himself with pain, like a sacrifice. The dream of paradise and purity in *The Seventh Seal* cannot become dramatically (Catholic) correct before B speaks of evil by its rightful name, which is the sin that lives in the hearts of men. Accordingly, one should not seek a religious interpretation of the film outside of Jof and Mia: their mutual love is God. The Catholic interpretation presupposes that the paradise of innocence cannot be found here on earth in the momentary, but only in God's love, which is the Realm, the Kingdom.

As I look at the film, I find it an exact expression of earthly dreams of paradise, of a philosophical materialism. One may answer Burvenich, with Colin Young, that both the Knight and Jöns are, "by their philosophical positions, unable to dispatch the problems presented by death, but Mary and Joseph never commit themselves to this argument and are, in fact, aloof from it and from the double scourge of pestilence and a reactionary church. Calm and serene, they are the only ones who in the end are saved."[17] If we place Jof's and Mia's fate in a social connection, the solution is unsatisfactory. It is just about as purposeful as to flee to a desert island to escape a nuclear war. Philosophically, however, the solution is the right one. The juggler couple ask only the small questions. Their existence acquires depth from the power of being together.

"Sex, art, and imagination" are, according to Eugene Archer,

the consolation that is offered in B's films for the inescapable
loneliness of existence. He who proceeds further, like the
Knight, is on the wrong track. With Jof and Mia the world is
clearly self-evident—an existence for themselves. "The supreme
value toward which consciousness, by its very nature, is constantly transcending itself is the absolute being of the self, with
its qualities of identity, purity, permanence."[18] This is according to Sartre's philosophy. It is not in the search for meaning
that life is decided, but in the choice of action.

In B's films a mental breakdown is expressed that could be
loosely described thus: The persons imagine a belief in Fate,
History, God, Happiness, or something else. They cannot, however, live according to these premises, since reality constantly
revises their view. In practical, everyday life they discover that
such guidelines cannot be followed. Therefore they are forced
to deny God's existence. They still leave evil and the devil as a
force in life, a power opposed to themselves. Without, however,
throwing the major questions overboard, the question that
possesses them can never be solved—the question of happiness
and fellowship, of practical daily life.

The only certainty that remains is the certainty of death. The
question does not concern Jof and Mia, since it is meaningless
to discuss it. Joachim in the radio play *The City* says that there
is only one thing "that is really true, and that is that I shall die.
Even this, that I live, is doubtful, but death is certain."[19] To this
Burvenich might have objected that the problem of evil is still
not solved. Before one can ask for a settlement with God (de-
pose him), one must search one's own heart. According to this
interpretation, Töre in *The Virgin Spring* is, from a religious
point of view, the most satisfactory of B's characters. He confesses his sin.

Jof and Mia just live. In the evening, the Knight finds his way
to Mia, who is alone, playing with her child. A while later Jof
appears, limping and hurt from the ill treatment at the tavern.

Finally he is joined by his rescuer, Jöns. Mia offers wild strawberries from a big bowl, and milk for the berries. The berries,
here as before and later, symbolize "the warmth of life, the human values, undamaged by metaphysical fear."[20] The Knight
asks to be informed about the plans of the juggler couple. He
dissuades them from continuing on to Helsingör, and suggests
they accompany him through the forest. He warns them about
the plague. This scene with the wild strawberries is the nucleus
of the Knight's impulse to sacrifice himself in order to save them.
During the night, when the chess game is to be finished, the
Knight sweeps the chessmen from the board, and succeeds in
detaining Death so long that the jugglers escape safely.

Mia has described their existence to the Knight: "One day is
like the other. There's nothing strange about that. Summer is
better than winter, of course, for then we don't have to freeze.
But spring is best of all."

The core of the dialogue comes at the end:

The Knight: Faith is a heavy suffering, do you know that? It
is like loving somebody who is out there in the darkness and
who never reveals himself, however loudly we call.

Mia: I don't understand what you mean.

The questions asked by the Knight do not exist for Mia.

The Knight: How meaningless and unreal everything seems
to me when I sit here with you and your husband. How unimportant it suddenly is. . . I shall remember this moment. The
stillness, the dusk, the bowl with strawberries, the bowl with
milk, your faces in the evening light. Mikael asleep, Jof with
his fiddle. I shall carry this in my memory between my hands,
as carefully as if it were a bowl, filled to the brim with fresh
milk. . . And this shall be for me a sign and a great sufficiency.

The scene has been subjected to completely opposite analyses.
The visual content corresponds to the one the Knight voices in
his final words. Harry Schein[21] emphasizes the contrast between

literary and narrative dialogue. The literary dialogue must "in literature and the theater suggest the visions and moods which the film interprets by its own means." He seems to find a great deal of narrative power in *The Seventh Seal.* Important bits, however, are spoiled because the words too obviously underscore the meaning of the pictures.

This opinion seems to be based on a certain cinematographic purism, related to that of Arnheim and Kracauer.[22] Arnheim dismisses as a corruption the development of the film art after the advent of sound. The sequence with the strawberries is, of course, double. The literary mood-creating does not carry the action forward. It means instead that B lets the picture appeal directly to the emotion, to the viewing, while the words communicate the philosophic debate which is the idea of the story. The scene with the strawberries is one of the moments that "man has at his disposal to manifest his moral center."[23] It comprises the center around which the entire film revolves.

We know that the picture ends in the death of everybody except the juggler family. The first one to succumb is the actor Skat, who in a grotesquely comical scene manages to do away with his tormentor, the smith Plog. Skat has eloped with Plog's wife. This happens in the forest during the night. Skat climbs up in a tree, but Death saws it off. On the stump appears a squirrel, to indicate life's continuity. Skat is a failure, and all except the jugglers have at some time in their lives failed.[24] The Knight has left his wife for a meaningless crusade. He goes with Jöns to the clearing in the woods where the servants have built a pyre for Tyan, the woman we saw outside the church. He interrogates Tyan. Since the Devil is with her, perhaps he knows something about God. He sees the emptiness in her eyes, nothing else, and receives no answer. He consoles her; she cannot console him. She goes calmly to her death, for the Devil will protect her from all evil.

"I believe at times that to ask questions is the most important thing," says the Knight in the frightful scene with Tyan. He thereby intimates his faith in intellectual aspiration. But what remains purposeful in his life is still the one action, namely, that he saves Jof and Mia. The Knight, in other words, gets a chance for a creative action. His life has had a meaning.

*The Seventh Seal* opens itself slowly to the viewer. This is partly due to the many planes the story touches on, the polyphonic structure of the work. The framework of the narrative is, of course, the chess game with Death, a threatening vision, underscored by the desolate seashore, where the game begins. *The Seventh Seal* has a plastic effect which few of B's films possess, a harmonious rhythm, in spite of the fact that one may detect such different stylistic sources as German expressionism, the Japanese film (Kurosawa), and the Swedish tradition.

B's greatness lies in the fact that he is able to give to terror and insecurity such a dramatic and urgent molding. That I find Jöns to be the film's most interesting and commanding figure is a subjective evaluation, since *The Seventh Seal* "will continue to be a source of discussion for many years to come and—this concerns all the classics of thought—the interpretations will change with the ideas and the era of the critics."[25] In order to survive, man must be able to conquer death. It is a matter of escaping both the inner death of feeling and the threat that looms from without. The film lets this attempt end in success and failure, but the important element is the salute to human dignity, the longing for justice, for life in peace, which constitute the movement of the film. The picture contains a great wisdom and a great naïveté. However: "it is a naïveté that characterizes the eras in art—here the Middle Ages—the spirit of which Bergman has succeeded in transmitting, without spoiling it with pedantry, thanks to his incomparable artistry when it comes to transferring to the language of the film the motifs in the iconography that has inspired him. The shape and forms he shows us are never insignificant, but the fruit of a constantly original creation. His art is so genuine, so new, that we forget art for the questions' questions and the endless series of conclusions. Seldom has the film managed to aim so high and so completely realize its ambitions."[26]

THE SEVENTH SEAL. Scene with strawberries. Nils Poppe (*Jof*), Bibi Andersson (*Mia*), and Max von Sydow (*The Knight*).

WILD STRAWBERRIES. Victor Sjöström as Professor Isak Borg.

THE SEVENTH SEAL. Gunnel Lindblom (*The girl*) and Gunnar Björnstrand (*Jöns*).

# 8

## WILD STRAWBERRIES

In the introduction to Strindberg's *A Dream Play* we read:
"One consciousness, however, stands above all, and that is the dreamer's. For there are no secrets, no inconsistency, no scruples, no law. He does not judge, does not exonerate, only relates, and since the dream is usually painful, less often joyous, a tone of melancholy, of pity for everything living, runs through the rickety story. Sleep, the liberator, often appears painful, but when the torment is most severe, there comes the awakening and reconciles suffering with reality which, however agonizing it may be, still in this moment is a delight compared to the torturing dream."[1]

*A Dream Play* has inspired *Wild Strawberries* in several scenes, such as the description of the honorary degree award in the Cathedral of Lund, and in the scene where the Officer is being interrogated about the multiplication table and fails the test. In the same manner Isak Borg is examined and found wanting. Like the Strindberg play, *Wild Strawberries* uses the technique of the dream, its free associations. As a matter of fact, the Strindberg inspiration makes itself felt everywhere in B's production. No director has ever come to the film with such a great reliance on literature,[2] with such a pronounced affinity with his country's literary culture. B tells of the relation between man and woman in a manner that reminds one of Strindberg's. He lets the past flow through the experience of the present.

The differences are still great, however, and partially determined by time. Strindberg and B emerged during two separate epochs of crisis in the Swedish community. Strindberg lives and interprets the changes from the break-through of capitalism to the victory of democracy. He remembers and is able to describe Stockholm as it was before its transformation into a modern metropolis with a distinctly urban culture. In his time, the idea of the good old days lives as a reality in the present, and collides with the onrushing popular movements, represented by the nonprivileged classes. The society of class and status has not yet been broken up. In private life there still rule unrestricted the prejudices and inhibitions which in Vienna created the foundation for Freud's psychoanalysis. In Strindberg, the ideological influences are wrestling with each other. He alternates between aristocratic and democratic ideals. In spite of his lack of consistency he remains an entity, a man of revolt. He always wants to place himself on the side of the downtrodden, the wounded, the suffering, whatever class of society they come from.

The crisis epoch B experiences is reflected also in his works. The Social Democrats, in control of the government, create, without appreciable opposition from the bourgeois parties, a many-branched system of social welfare, aimed at safeguarding the weal of the individual. The community strives for collective solutions of wide scope. Work is not slackened by war. Sweden becomes a model society, which on a certain plane stands outside the events of Europe. The feeling of isolation creates difficulties of conscience among the intellectuals. Since, however, the external questions are considered solved, interest turns to the internal ones: to man's adaptability to his environment and to the problems of living together and of growing old. Lutheran Christianity loses its grip, but not entirely its power to set standards. Individuals live in city-like communities; men's outward circumstances become similar. Lutheranism remains as a decoration at baptisms, weddings, and funerals, just as, in B's art, it is an ornament, a memory from childhood. Swedish literature from the 1940's on accentuates the spiritual transformation by leaving behind all the collective philosophies to which the authors of the 1930's still were attracted. As an artist, B becomes extraordinarily representative of the change, a victim of the time, and simultaneously its interpreter.

The journey toward the center of the ego, which is made in *Wild Strawberries* by Eberhard Isak Borg, 78-year-old professor emeritus of bacteriology, is thus an adequate expression of the precariousness of values which touches not only this fictional figure. Isak Borg is afraid of dying, afraid of ultimately drying up, afraid of a horrible doom. He has lost the woman he loved. He has had an unhappy marriage. He has a son who relives the difficulties of his father. Isak Borg lives shut up in his own world. The question of the film is this: Can he get out of it?

As Fereydoun Hoveyda points out, *Wild Strawberries* contains three analyses.[3] They are: Borg's self-analysis, B's analysis of Borg, and, finally, the audience's analysis of these two. Still, there is a uniting bond between them. As a whole, the film can be labeled a psychoanalysis (in the correct sense of the word, a soul analysis). We are presented with Borg's interpretation, B's interpretation, and on this basis we must make our own interpretation. The unpleasant pictures and moods that force themselves upon Isak Borg lead him to test his own words and actions. The memory visions and the dreams touch even upon matters which he has never experienced in the past, but which he now observes as real. They are the reason for the frigidity he has felt all his life. *Wild Strawberries* follows exactly the pattern outlined in a psychoanalytic handbook: "The way we live, eat, work, make love and bring up our children, our attitudes towards politics, economics and international affairs, how we play, our choice of companions, how we dress and sleep, our attitudes towards pain and suffering (both our own and that of others), our tolerance for uncertainty, our proneness to anger or to depression, our tendencies towards dependence or independence, how we react to success and failure, our morals, the balance in us between generosity and selfishness—all of these and many other personality traits are consequences in the adult personality of the residues of the unresolved neurotic problems of childhood. These residues make us what we are as craftsmen, artists, professional men, citizens, husbands, wives, parents, and friends. They determine the peace of mind, serenity, and gaiety with which we are able to live or the veiled tensions, anxieties and angers which discolor our lives. They can be the source, equally, of greatness of spirit or of meanness and crime; and they can cost us much of the happiness which would otherwise be ours for the taking. They lie at the heart of that oldest of human problems, human discontent. They are the veiled and universal neurotic component of 'normal' human nature."[4]

The portrait of Isak Borg is also a portrait of Victor Sjöström. During a crisis in his private life, Sjöström in 1916 made a bicycle trip to the parts of the country where he knew he had lived with his parents as a child.[5] While the picture was being shot, B studied Sjöström's face, spied on its moods, almost as David in *Through A Glass Darkly* studied his daughter Karin.[6] As a film, *Wild Strawberries* is a salute to Sjöström's films. B puts them ahead of Stiller's. Many scenes have a tie-in with Sjöström's work. A smashed watch plays a part in *Karin Ingmarsdotter*.

Most important, however, is the reference to *The Stroke of Midnight*. There is much in the fate of David Holm that reminds us of that of Isak Borg.[7] Both pictures occupy a central position in the film art of their time.

In external time, *Wild Strawberries* is enacted from an early summer morning to the evening of the same day. Dreamlike flashbacks take us backward in time. This does not, however, change the film's concentration on some decisive moments. Both *Illicit Interlude* and *To Joy* are enacted within a short period, but the flashbacks dominate the pictures. In *Wild Strawberries* B has achieved a perfect balance between present and past.

The film has been blamed for being episodic. But every moment has a connection with the present—its visual purpose, its purpose with respect to thought. The film's time concept has its roots in Strindberg, but also in the great storytellers of modern literature, Proust, Joyce, Faulkner. It concerns the inner monologue, "the Bergsonian time concept, surrealism, dreams, the associations and disassociations of thought."[8]

*Wild Strawberries* is a film in novel form. It has certain similarities to Akira Kurosawa's masterly *Ikiru* of 1952, which B had not seen when he was making his picture. In that film, the external action is in the same way almost illogical. Seemingly disparate elements are tied together by means of the path to self-analysis which the central figure treads. B, like Kurosawa, frees the film from dependence on the physical world, for the purpose of describing instead "the infinitely richer and more complex area of the mind."[9] *Wild Strawberries* frees film art from a conventional dramatic structure and a naturalistic development of events. In this development, B meets with Antonioni, Resnais, Rossellini, and other rejuvenators of the film. In different places, the picture presses ahead to insights with which literature has been familiar since the beginning of the century. Today a fruitful interaction exists between the vanguard of the film and of the novel, an exploration toward an ever more subtle analysis of reality. Strindberg was a predecessor in liberating the structure of the drama. B has not had to seek foreign sources.

He has told[10] how, while on a motor trip, he came one summer morning to Uppsala, where he spent a great part of his childhood. The city was empty and silent. He walked up to the house where he had lived as a child. He grasped the door handle: "I thought that if I now open the door, I will walk into the world of childhood." *Wild Strawberries* tells how Isak Borg travels to Lund to receive an honorary doctor's degree. He has decided to fly, but under the impression of a dream he gets up early and takes his car instead. Traveling with him is his daughter-in-law Marianne. During the trip he gains a certain clarity about himself and others. In B's films, travel is often a catalyst for the conflicts of the soul. More than a journey, however, *Wild Strawberries* is a diary, a self-confession. B often uses such a form. The surprising element is the age of the leading character. After having been involved with all ages in his art, B can now concern himself with people for whom certainty "is within reach any day." This is, in fact, exactly what is said in a short scene, cut out from the finished film.

The scene is enacted immediately before the degree-granting ceremony. The three honorary Doctors-to-be are conversing. It is the former Bishop Jacob Hovelius who gives Isak the clue to certainty. The certainty that exists for him, the Christian, is death. Isak's struggle has under these circumstances become identical with the Knight's: to perform one meaningful act of love before death comes. Under the pressure of his own and others' accusations, he discovers that his coldness and his great solitude have cast their annihilating shadows over him. In spite of the fact that he is soon to receive the outward sign of successful achievement in the service of science and mankind, he constantly doubts the truth of his action. It is the picture's great idea that Isak, until he begins the autobiographical story (which is the film's), has lived his life in peace of mind and cynicism, but that he, toward the end, can win peace of mind and still relinquish cynicism.

While the film is told in the first person, it does not use a subjective camera. Here, too, B's dialogue has an ornamental, literary function. It aims at deepening the feeling, reaching double effects. It can therefore be read and listened to as literature. Its true worth, however, is evoked in the pictures that are the origin of the text (or vice versa). Style is subordinated to content. The style, however, imposes its own purpose and meaning, and "meaning demands its own style; the two are interrelated, and both come directly from the creative artist, the director, who is consequently forced to originate his own projects rather than merely interpret. Each film therefore becomes a personal statement by its director, and this principle, inevitably, is the most important of all."[11]

Before the texts we are introduced to the professor's middle-class home, to him, and to the objects that surround his life. We then experience his nightmare, done in the same severe black-and-white, overexposed, silent-film type of pictures as in the flashbacks in *The Naked Night*. It is correct to see the film mainly as a portrait of Isak Borg, and let the other characters become shades in the picture of him. He is writing an auto-biographical story, which is the film. He alternates between joy and the deepest despair. He listens to evidence against and for himself. The answer to the question he asks is of great importance, not only because he is old. The mistakes he has made and makes are, on the whole, very small. They can happen to all of us. The professor's wisdom becomes a lesson for us all.

His dream on Saturday, June 1, expresses his most profound misanthropy. It shows him in effect standing at the brink of the grave. He sets out for a morning stroll in the deserted city. The accustomed and habitual have been rubbed out. The hands of a clock outside a watchmaker's shop have disappeared. When Isak pulls out his own pocket watch to check the time, he finds that his timepiece, too, has lost its hands. He then meets a male figure, but his face is deformed, nonexistent. (This corresponds to Jöns' encounter in *The Seventh Seal*.) Finally, Isak is about to be run down and killed by a hearse. The carriage falls to pieces. A hand reaches out of the coffin. When Isak grasps it, he is pulled toward it. The dead man is himself, with his own face.

He wakes his housekeeper Agda and informs her of his decision to drive his car. Their quarrel wakes up Marianne. She begs him to let her come along. Persons like Agda, seemingly plucked from the middle-class world of the turn of the century, appear rather frequently in B's films. It has been said that they interpret B's dependence on the bourgeois milieu, just as Isak's memories of his youth have a strange touch of nostalgia.

The black automobile resembles a hearse as it moves through the summer-empty streets of Stockholm early in the morning. Isak's travel in the company of Marianne is a death journey (the manuscript intended that the academic procession in Lund should meet a funeral procession). After the full-screen pictures of the landscape and the automobile, we are taken into the car. Isak drives, Marianne sits silent beside him. She prepares to light a cigarette, but Isak asks her not to. Women should not smoke. Smoking is "a vice for men." Isak speaks in a self-satisfied, matter-of-fact tone. Suddenly Marianne begins to upbraid him. She says he is an old egoist. He has lent his son Evald money and he wants it back. This means that she and Evald can never feel free. When Marianne came to Stockholm a month earlier, away from Evald, Isak dismissed her with these words: "Don't try to drag me into your and Evald's marital calamities, for I don't give a damn about them. Everybody must look out for himself."

This introduction is told in immobile, conventional inter-
change pictures between Marianne and Isak. She regards him
often with wonder, perhaps with fright. After her accusations,
he obviously wants to tell her about his dream, but she says she
is not interested in dreams. Isak means something to her because
the son resembles him. Suddenly he turns in on a side road, and
drives into a forest. Here begins his journey to childhood, by a
deserted house. Marianne has gone to the shore to have a swim.
He sees the house, bolted, abandoned. "I don't know how it
happened but the day's clear reality changed into the shapes of
a dream. I don't even know if it was a dream or if it was memories that appeared with the strength of real events." What he
now perceives, he has never seen in reality. It seems that Isak is
out with his father, fishing.

As a spectator he observes the love of his youth, his cousin
Sara. She is picking wild strawberries in the woods to honor her
deaf uncle Aron on his name day. She is accosted by Isak's
brother Sigfrid, who, it develops, married her later. She and
Isak are secretly engaged. Yet she allows herself to be kissed by
Sigfrid, half against her wish. What later follows is a delightful
summer breakfast for uncle Aron, watched by the old Isak Borg,
who stands in the darkness of the entrance hall, listening and
seeing. The scene is not real. It expresses Isak's nostalgia, mixed
with bitterness. It contains a contrast between comic details and
a tragic appreciation of reality, which is common with B. On
the other hand, the scene may appear unnecessary, overbur-
dened, as if the narrator himself were in love with it.

After breakfast, Isak becomes the witness to a conversation
between Sara and Charlotta. It is about him. Sara tells of "how
terribly noble and moral and sensitive" he is. He talks about the
hereafter and "wants to play four-handed piano and he only
cares for kissing when it gets dark and he speaks about sin. I
think he is awfully high-minded, and I feel so wretched and

worthless, and I *am*, too, there's no argument about it." The
trouble is that brother Sigfrid is bold and exciting. As a young
man, Isak is preoccupied with moral and metaphysical questions.
He can never achieve Sigfrid's simplicity. In *Smiles of a Summer Night* Henrik achieves happiness when he gives up the metaphysical meditations. The questions of right and wrong are regarded by the women as an obstacle to love and fellowship.

The strawberries that Sara picks once more symbolize purity
in life. When Sigfrid kisses her, she drops her basket and the
berries scatter on the ground, become unclean. The breakfast
symbolizes a serene existence, before the problems and errors of
adulthood occur. The scenes are sentimental, confusing, encum-
bered, but, as Kenneth Cavander says, "perhaps the very confusion of symbols is a relief, being such a rich source of theoris-
ing for anyone who likes to construct theories. Whether any
of the solutions offered represents Bergman's own intention or
not, or whether that intention is communicable at all, is another
matter."[12]

The technique in *Wild Strawberries* is revolutionary and in
time will gain in importance for film art. The picture's lack of
outer stylistic unity may seem very bewildering before the spectator has become accustomed to the thought that the spiritual
content has "relegated the realistic narrative to second place."[13]
Behind the film lies Proust's conception that "life is composed of
a series of isolated moments, given meaning by their temporal
relationship to the memories of the man who experiences
them."[14] But it is not only a question of a temporal relationship,
but also one of place. Isak visits the scenes of his past, and begins
with the summer villa, the spot where his childhood reached its
highest intensity. He drives through the part of the country
where in his youth he practiced as a physician. He sees again his
mother, now as lonesome as himself. The reunion evokes memories, which in turn automatically drive him farther on the road
to self-knowledge. The end of this occurs late in the evening,

in the dream during the night after the academic event. The way in which to look at Isak is akin to a view which, in the novel, has found its best expression in Durrell's *Alexandria Quartet*. It is a question of a continuous revision of reality. In such a fashion did Kurosawa create *Rashomon*, where different testimonies are pitted against one another. They are not permitted to cancel out one another, but create the shimmering spectrum that remains the truth—the truths—about the film's main characters. This revision of reality began in B's films as early as the 1940's; it is, in other words, not the fruit of filmatic influence. One day in a person's life can be as revealing as his whole life. Gesture and speech betray his attitude. The film has the power to describe such a day. It presents details that can hardly be told in words. Still, in *Wild Strawberries* both verbal and visual experiences set the stone rolling, partly Isak's dream, partly Marianne's charges and his own gnawing self-accusation.

We are to understand his hardness and cynicism as actual. His isolation and his strange emotional aridity stem from the experiences of his childhood and youth. With all the greater zeal he has plunged into his scientific work. This professional victory (the outward token of which is the honorary degree), becomes Isak's defeat as a human being. Devotion to work is put as a contrast to devotion to life, to fellowship. B manages to make this development cinematographically convincing, although he borrows from many different kinds of films, and although he swings between the immobile, tableau-like and the explosively hysterical rhythm.

When Isak walks toward his car, he meets a young woman in shorts and a boy's shirt. Her name, too, is Sara. The part is played by the same actress. She asks for a lift. She tells him that her father owns the ground and the house. She is accompanied by two youths, Anders and Victor, whose roles in the drama correspond approximately to Sigfrid's and Isak's. One wants to be a doctor, the other a theologian. But it is the theologian

who plays Isak. The journey continues. An approaching Volks-
wagen forces Isak to drive into a ditch, while the other car turns
over. Out crawl two persons. The man introduces himself:

"The fault is entirely ours. We can offer no excuse. My wife
was driving. . . . The murderers might as well introduce themselves. My name is Alman, I am an engineer with the Stockholm
Electric Works. There stands my wife Berit. She has indeed
been an actress, and it was just that situation we were discussing
when . . . when . . . when . . ."

The portrait of this dreary pair is the ghastliest in the film.
The two are tied to each other by great hatred. When the
man tries to get the car up, Berit warns him of a cerebral hemor-
rhage. They are destroyed, crushed people. They constantly be-
little and humiliate each other. According to the man's words,
her refuge is hysteria, his Catholicism. "As you can understand,
we are dependent on each other's company. It is sheer selfishness that we haven't killed each other." She hits him, but he contains himself, takes off his glasses, and manages a laugh. The
expected explosion has arrived. Strindberg, too, could describe
marriages in this manner, so that nobody knew whose fault it
was. It just hung suspended in the air, as a cold threat. Alman
and Berit are fates that have a message for everybody in the car.
For Isak, because he could not marry the one he loved; for
Marianne, who is now making a last attempt at a reconciliation
with her husband; for Sara, who is traveling abroad with two
men. But Marianne asks the Almans to get out of the car. They
remain on the road like two shadows, two lonely people who
have been forced together, fragments from a hell. To B, the
Almans are obviously equivalent. They are compelled to endure
in lieu of something better to live for.

The following scene shows the happy side of Isak's past. He
stops for gasoline in the small city of Gränna. Of the scene that
takes place Marianne again is the wondering spectator. The man
who runs the service station, Åkerman, and his wife praise Isak

for his kindness during the fifteen years he was a physician in these parts. Isak says to himself: "I should have stayed here." During the lunch in Gränna, at the Golden Otter, Isak tells stories from the time when he was a district practitioner. Gradually, the religious questions are resumed, with Isak beginning to recite a hymn by Wallin, a pantheistic salute to life. In the conversation between Anders and Victor is repeated in almost parody form the contrast between Jöns and the Knight, between the one who believes that questioning is a result in itself and the one who believes only in matter.

Isak goes to see his mother. The mother believes it is his wife, Karin, who has come into the room. She does not want to see Karin, for she has done the others so much harm. When she is told it is Marianne, she wonders why Marianne is not at home, tending her child, who does not exist. The scenes between the mother and the son are observed by Marianne with a cold, frightened look. In this relationship between the very aged woman and her son, Marianne gets the explanation of her husband's behavior. The mother produces a box of old things, among them a watch without hands. The mother is constantly cold, although it is not cold in her house. She has had many children, many grandchildren, and sends them presents and greetings. Hardly anybody, however, visits her. Everybody is waiting for her to die. She knows it, and revels in it, like Henrik's aunt in *Illicit Interlude*.

When the journey resumes, Isak falls asleep, but is pursued "during his sleep by dreams and visions that appeared to me extremely tangible and humiliating." In the beginning of the dream, the fear of death becomes prominent. Isak again finds himself at the strawberry patch of his youth, with Sara. She gives him a mirror to see his face—one of the many mirrors in B's films that show the human being's double existence. Sara calls him "an old, old anxious man who is soon to die," while she is young and has life before her. She plans to marry Sigfrid.

She walks away from him, up to the house, and lifts her child from the crib. She enters the house. But when he seeks to follow her, he tears his hand on a nail. He is excluded from the warmth of the home. Instead of Sara, he meets a man who asks him in.

The man is Alman. They proceed through a narrow corridor into a lecture hall, where the university students and Sara are in the audience. Alman asks Isak to produce his test papers. Isak has to look into the microscope but sees nothing. He is to read a text that is written on the blackboard, but he understands nothing. Alman asks if Isak knows what a doctor's first duty is, but Isak has forgotten. A doctor's first duty is to ask forgiveness. Isak is "guilty of guilt," he is accused of lack of feeling, selfishness and ruthlessness, exactly the same complaints Marianne has voiced, directly or indirectly. Alman asks Isak to diagnose a patient lying on a stretcher. He says that she is dead, but at that she sits up and gives a ghostly laugh. She is Berit, Alman's wife.

It is Isak's wife who has brought the accusations against him. Isak answers that she is long since dead, but Alman guides him through a magic forest to a moonlit glen where his wife and a strange man are copulating. It is this scene that Alman wants Isak to see:

"Many forget a woman who has been dead thirty years, some cherish a sweet and fading picture, but you can at any time recall this scene to your memory. Strange, isn't it? Tuesday, May 1st, 1917. You stood exactly here, and heard and saw precisely what that woman and that man said and did."

The importance of the scene does not lie in the wife's unfaithfulness, but in her words to the stranger. She plans to go home and confess everything to Isak. She knows what he will answer:

"Poor little girl, I feel so sorry for you. Exactly as if he were God Almighty. And I will weep and say: Have you really some pity for me, and he says: I feel terribly sorry for you and then I will weep even more and ask if he can forgive me, and he will say: You should not ask me to forgive you. I have nothing to forgive you for, but he doesn't mean a word of what he says, for he is completely cold. . . . And I say it's his fault that I am the way I am, and then he looks terribly sad and says it's his fault. But he cares about nothing, for he is completely cold."

Alman metes out the customary penalty: loneliness.

After he wakes up, Isak tries vaguely to recount his dream. He seems to know that there is something he wants to say to himself in the dream: that he is dead, though he is living. At this point the action turns into the only flashback of the film not seen through Isak's eyes. On a rainy day by the seashore, Marianne and Evald are sitting in their car. Marianne tells him that she has received word. She is expecting a child. Evald stiffens. He does not want to have children in this world. He feels like an unsuccessful fruit of an unsuccessful marriage. He knows that she wants to live, but his need is "to be dead, absolutely, immovably dead." It rains all through this scene. The two walk along the shore. There is a great distance between them.

Marianne explains her fear to Isak. First the mother, then Isak, now Evald. She wants this feeling of death to end somewhere. But when Isak asks if he can help, she replies that there is no help.

The central theme of *Wild Strawberries* is loneliness. It surrounds all levels in the story, whether it concerns old or young. Existence seems closed up, unchangeable. Satisfaction and a real joy of living are found only among the intellectually simplest characters: Åkerman and his pregnant wife, Agda, the housekeeper (who is a stickler for form), and Sara, with her two attendant cavaliers, not yet marked by the bitterness of life. The intellectuals in the film knock themselves bloody against the wall of loneliness, in questions that cannot be answered. The very fact that they are intellectuals makes them lonesome.

The Christian alternative has no supporting power. Perhaps it is Christian that Isak verbally forgives his wife's adultery, but it does not correspond to his real views. Alman is a Catholic, but that does not help him. B follows the Christian views. The conversations between the believer Anders and the doubting Victor, the doctor-to-be, go on continually, but without result. It is only words.

In connection with Marianne's story about Evald, Isak permits himself to grant her the favor of smoking a cigarette. He wants to show his magnanimity. The film would be totally static if it remained in the same attitude shown in the introduction. Something has happened to Isak. When he gets to Lund, Agda has already arrived, in spite of her threat to stay away. She takes charge of him. During the ceremony in the church, when the Latin words of homage are pronounced, and the doctoral hat is placed on his head, Isak begins to recall the events of the day. He decides to write them down, as truthfully as he is able. Since the film is the result of this written narrative (and therefore enacted in the past), the analysis has, on a certain plane, liberated Isak.

He returns early to his room at Evald's, and finds Agda. He regrets the events of the morning. But his awkward attempt at calling Agda by her first name is firmly rebuffed. He asks if she always does the right thing. She replies: "Almost always. At our age we must know how to behave. Don't we, professor?" Most touching to Isak is the serenade he hears outside his window. Sara and Victor are singing, accompanied by Anders. They have come to say good-bye; they are going on. As the boys disappear in the darkness, Sara returns and declares that it is Isak she loves, "Today, tomorrow, and every day." When she has gone, he murmurs softly, "Let me hear from you sometime." Nobody hears his words. But the sentence mirrors a transformation.

B's lines of dialogue are tied to each other in a strange fashion across a bridge of many years. In his play *As a Warning to Me...* he describes a similar pastoral. It is lifted from the diary of the author Paul, i.e., Joakim Naken:

"When Joakim had talked himself warm in his childish eagerness to have everything expressed in the right way, the girl smiled and patted him on the cheek and whispered: 'However all that may be, I know that I love you and will always love you.' The sun shone on them and the bay was morning-still. Somewhere a summer bird sang and the grass was damp from soft dew. . . ."[15]

Isak's attempt at changing himself is simply an awakening interest in his surroundings, the problems of others. His loneliness has been the result of his indifference toward others. Sara of his youth was an object of his ideas of sin and the hereafter. He forgave his wife because it didn't matter to him what she did. He could have his daughter-in-law Marianne live with him a month because he never asked her why she had come. He did not want to become involved in anything, and this caused the dreams and the fear gradually to thrust themselves out from his subconscious.

It is already a step forward when Isak ask Evald about his marriage. Evald knows no answer. But he says he cannot be without Marianne. Even the nocturnal farewell words between her and Isak hint at a reconciliation. But in the deeper, artistic development of the film, it is of no consequence whether Isak really changes. The important thing is our analysis, the self-analysis. In this B is again a contemporary and a follower of the literary philosophy that has found its foremost expression in existentialism. The important thing is not to place Isak's suffering against a nonexistent absolute measure, but rather in a clear-thinking way to determine his situation. The important thing is that he realizes the meaning or the meaninglessness of his life, that he looks himself in the face. Ibsen attacked the living lie, regardless of whether it was useful or not. Behind this was the conviction that man was closest to spiritual health if he abandoned his disguises.

During the course of the picture, the father-image is always a vacuum, a nothingness. Evald does not wish to become a father, Isak's relation to his son is not that of a father, and the breakfast for the deaf uncle Aron is dominated by women. In the dream of harmony that ends the film, Isak sees his father sitting by a calm, reflecting water, fishing, in the light-colored clothes of the turn of the century, of a past era. The father and the mother are waving to Isak. He has found the strawberry patch, paradise and happiness.

We notice in this scene how the words and the visions work on different planes with B, evoke related effects, but all the time lend a deep variety to the narrative style. B is on his way toward a new cinematographic method. He abandons all conventional patterns. He leaves behind the apprentice years' strict dependence on the theater. His style and technique signify a dissolution, and at the same time a renewal. Such a technique demands of the creator that each scene be given maximum power, maximum feeling.

Visually, *Wild Strawberries* has not much new to offer. The transitions between the sequences are commonplace and often used, "clouds and leaves moved by the wind, the moon through the trees, twisted branches, etc."[16] This is possibly the price B has had to pay for not devoting enough attention to the expressional function of pictures, except in the cases where the human being and his face take part. He is still strikingly helpless in his documentary scenes, of nature or of objects. But as soon as a person or groups of persons participate in the action, he becomes transformed. To be sure, he uses conventional arguments remarkably often, but the balance within the sequences is perfect, the cutting a shining montage of visual and audible effects. The sequence in which Isak as an old man observes his past belongs among the high points in B's production, in modern film in general.

Viewed superficially, *Wild Strawberries* is static. Still it moves forward on a show path toward self-knowledge with the sureness of dream and sleep. If we say that B might have made a more significant work of art had he permitted the camera to participate more actively in the narrative, it might mean that we wish B to be another artist than the one he is. This film never begins, never ends, but is a short segment of the unceasing stream of consciousness.

THE DEVIL'S EYE. In foreground, Jarl Kulle as Don Juan.

THE LAST COUPLE OUT. Harriet Andersson (*Anita*) and Björn Bjelvenstam (*Bo*).

THE MAGICIAN. Ingrid Thulin (*Manda*) and Max von Sydow (*Vogler*).

# 9

## THE ARTIST'S FACE

I have tried to see the artistic development in B's films as an unceasing battle, in which the participants are at last forced to recognize or even conquer the fundamental humiliation life has in store for them. The same development, with some limitations, can also hold true of the sensitivity of art and of the artist himself, even though the chances of consolation and conciliation are present. Edmund Wilson tells how Dickens, even when he was "famous and caressed and happy," surrounded by children and a devoted wife, harked back in his memory to the time when he was "utterly neglected and hopeless." His bitter childhood experiences created a lasting wound, which time and success could never quite heal.[1]

Dickens could suddenly doubt that he was a man, could be attacked by a feeling of unreality, reminiscent of several scenes in B's films, in which the characters never say or show anything but that they exist, that they have a hand, that blood flows through their veins. The very physical time, its objective existence outside of the persons themselves, is set in doubt. This is the expression of an extreme but fruitful subjectivity. The unsure and hesitant ones embody the crisis of values in B's films,

173

while the secure and earthy embody the answer to the questions of existence: namely, to live.

The theory about the wound and the scar is not the property of Edmund Wilson. It has been developed by modern psychologists to apply to man's existence in general, his need to assert and defend himself. It applies to man's psychic handicaps as well as his physical ones. The man of action strives to restore equilibrium after a defeat. With Dickens, the horrible humiliations of his childhood are turned into a social protest without counterpart in literature. The theory about defeat and abasement can be applied also to B's imagined idea of the artist's position, the image he gives us in *The Magician*. It is one of his most camouflaged pictures, and at the same time one of the most open ones.

### The Magician

The main character is a magician, conjurer, charlatan. B often presents artists of different kinds, authors, actors, musicians, ballet dancers. As persons they interpret the insecurity of values, a crisis of which B's production as a whole is an expression. Some of his key films are set entirely in an artistic (or, rather, semiartistic) milieu. In his films are expressed many thoughts about the conditions of art, its difficulties, about the opposition of art and life. One need not view this one-sidedness as a weakness. Nor need his film style, described by many as unoriginal, signify a real weakness in his equipment.

The literature and film of our century have given us many (probably too many) portraits and self-portraits of artists. As I have earlier pointed out, this results from a refinement of the means of expression. Subtlety in describing detached, separate fragments of reality has forced authors to seek the immediately understandable, the personal experience. At the same time, something has been lost, namely, the attempt to make a social situation understandable. One has consciously pushed to one side important dramatic material. These tendencies, however, the individualistic and the social, do not stand in irreconcilable opposition to each other. If the big questions are dismissed, one also turns away from the big solutions. What remains, though, is the attempt to describe man, his unique experience. It is possible to throw light upon the world with a single gesture. But the emphasis on psychological time has led to a total reevaluation of the rhythmic element in film art. A system of esthetics for film art will be forced to admit the futility of all sweeping answers, just as it is more difficult to see the similarities between Joyce and Kafka in technique than in the psychological perspective.

B's method of resorting to disguises in *The Magician* is the final protection, which in this picture, too, proves to be brittle and useless. The film takes place in Stockholm in July 1846. The introductory vignette shows the silhouette of a vehicle. Horses, people against the sky; otherwise silence. A party makes a halt on its way. Persons are shown, but not introduced. An old woman is collecting herbs and spits on a raven. The group is Vogler's Magnetic Health Theater en route to Stockholm to give performances there. The journey is resumed to the city gates. A bit later the coachman Simson becomes scared by a strangely frightening sound in the forest. The group's central character, Dr. Albert Emanuel Vogler, steps out. In a puddle he discovers a dying man in rags. He is the actor Johan Spegel. He asks Vogler why he wears a false beard and mask: "Are you an impostor who has to hide his real face?" Vogler does not reply; he is mute. At the South Gate the carriage is stopped by police. The party is escorted to Consul Abraham Egerman's big house, where the action of the film takes place.

The final vignette, taken from Brecht's *Threepenny Opera*, tells how defeat turns into victory, rain and storm into sunshine. The crushed, destitute Vogler learns through a message from the King that he has been invited to perform at the royal palace.

Vogler and his troupe leave the house in triumph. True, the chatterbox Tubal, publicity agent and manager, has become lost to Egerman's cook, Sofia Garp. True, "grandma," the herb-collecting old quack, takes her savings and leaves. But one of the maids in the house joins the troupe, because she loves the coachman. The carriage pulls out in triumph, to the accompaniment of merry sounds, and disappears behind a hill. Only a street lamp remains hanging. It stops swinging. The royal letter that releases Vogler from his humiliation is dated July 14, 1846. B was born July 14, 1918.

What has been said about B's other films holds true of *The Magician* to an even greater extent: namely, that the possibilities of interpretation are many, that the story has more than one meaning. The play with symbols and words seems to leave quite open the matter of the direction of B's art. It can be expressed in the words that Gilbert Salachas puts into B's mouth: "Messrs. critics and docile filmophiles, regard my picture carefully. It is 100-per-cent Bergman. I have included a selection of 'profound themes' and 'personal compulsion ideas.' In order to make the interpretation even more interesting, I have mixed them up a bit. Now it is up to you to identify them, to take stock of them, and elucidate them. You have the right to use the dictionary of my collected works. Get started!"[2]

What is important to know is Vogler's adventures during the course of the film and the attitude of the others toward him. When the group is escorted into Consul Egerman's drawing room, it is introduced by the manager Tubal, an eloquent and smiling man. Around Vogler are grouped Aman-Manda, his young assistant (here wearing man's clothing, but in reality his wife), and his grandmother, formerly a celebrated opera singer under the name of Agata de Macopazza. (A marquis in *The Devil's Eye* has the same surname.)

The other side, the bourgeois, consists—aside from Consul Egerman and his wife—of police chief Frans Starbeck and the counselor of medicine Anders Vergérus. Starbeck begins the interrogation by reading the advertisement that Vogler has inserted in the newspapers. The grouping in the room is obvious. The representatives of power are ironic, superior, standing around a big table. Vogler and his company are insecure, waiting. Vergérus sums up his opinion of Vogler in a murderous salvo:

"On the one hand, we have the idealistic *doctor* Vogler, who practices medicine according to Mesmer's rather doubtful methods. On the other hand, we have the somewhat less lofty and pure-thinking *conjurer* Vogler, who arranges all kinds of hocus-pocus, according to entirely homemade recipes. If I have understood the matter correctly, the Vogler activity moves quite unscrupulously between these two extremes."

Vogler remains silent. He has black hair, a black beard. He looks moodily, bitterly, into space, perhaps because he realizes the justification of what is being said about him. Vergérus examines him, but can find no reason for his muteness. Vergérus also tries to have himself hypnotized, but nothing happens. Vergérus says to Vogler: "You believe I hate you. You're mistaken. There's only one thing that interests me: your physiology, Mr. Vogler. I would like to conduct an autopsy on you." After the interrogation the troupe is told that the following morning at ten o'clock they are to show their tricks in Egerman's big drawing room. Supper is being served within an hour. But Vogler's Health Theater are to eat in the kitchen.

The scene in the kitchen may best be described as a divertissement in a style typical of B. Manda and Vogler absent themselves, silent. The scene is at first dominated by the grandmother and Tubal, who together offer love potions for sale. Tubal is attracted by the charms of the cook, Sofia Garp. The maid Sara flirts with the coachman Simson, who tries to appear worldly-wise. At last Sara walks with Simson to the washhouse, and they end up in a laundry basket. B lets loose his wantonness, his comic talent, which seems to be primarily suited to describing sexual relations, the play between the sexes. It begins to thunder. Sara clings to Simson. His necktie gets a hard knot. The dialogue runs like this:

Sara: I'll help you. No, don't look.

Simson: Heavens, does that button have to be opened? This is an awful lot of trouble, this.

Sara: You don't seem so experienced, little Simson.

Simson: I've been mostly abroad, you know.

In the kitchen, Egerman's footman Rustan and the big coachman Antonsson have been left alone and deserted. Antonsson hates Vogler, would love to punch him in the face. Just then the door opens, the lights go out, and a ghost begins to frisk about. It is the actor Spegel, who grabs the brandy bottle and disappears. In the meantime Mrs. Egerman comes over to the Voglers in the drawing room, where they are getting ready for the performance. She wants to console Vogler, ask him to forgive the humiliation her friends have caused him: "They cannot understand, and therefore they hate you." She wants Vogler to explain her daughter's death, and asks that he come to her in the night. Behind a drapery stands Egerman, listening terrorstricken.

Up to this point B has produced only a series of mystifications. Now begins the unveiling, the unmasking, the development that leads to the scenes in the attic, the post-mortem, and the final mortification. The dialogue is realistic, moves between extremes of comedy and bombast. One is reminded more of Almqvist than of Strindberg—Vogler's apparition has been compared to Almqvist's. We think of *The Book of the Briar Rose* and the strange fluctuations from mysticism and sensational reporting to realism which we find with Almqvist. His mysticism, like B's, was Nordic, both childishly pious and cunning. Vogler as a person could have been plucked from Almqvist's works. The time, 1846, was marked by the struggle between rationalism and religion. There were many who held that spiritual experience could be aligned with science. Positivism was the fashion. The European crisis was on the way to its culmination. It occurred two years later, but ended in most of the European countries with a defeat for the forces of progress.

The possibilities of interpreting *The Magician* are many. Georges Sadoul has compared it with the Passion play. Vogler may be Christ. As Carl-Eric Nordberg says: "By his presence he makes everybody strangely disturbed, he exercises an irresistible fascination on his environment, whether it reacts with hatred or with love."[3] The same critic is reminded by Mrs. Egerman of Pilate's wife, who says she has "suffered much in the dream for his sake," for the sake of the Crucified One. Stig Wikander, the historian of religion, has rendered the most thoroughgoing interpretation. He believes that Vogler's history corresponds point by point to the early Christian legend of Simon Magus, Simon the Magician. It is true that Vogler wears a Christ mask. But he is not Christ, neither is he a false savior, but a Gnostic savior: "Early Christian literature has strange things to tell of the meeting between the Apostle Peter and Simon the Magician, with Emperor Nero as referee. It turned out in about the same way as when medical counselor Vergérus and Doctor Vogler in the film meet before police chief Starbeck, a small-time Nero."[4]

The final change to victory receives the following natural explanation: "When the King's Son, the One sent forth, has been as deeply humiliated as is possible, there is a turn in the tide. Then comes, says the Gnostic, the Letter, the Royal Letter from the world outside of our reality, and conveys the King's will: That his son shall be rehabilitated and enter into the glory of his Father."

B's ability to create artistic illusion does not exclude this interpretation. Another one, however, is much closer to hand. The question that constantly recurs in the literature about B ever since 1945 runs: "Have you a face? What happened to your heart?"[5] One may see *The Magician* (in Swedish entitled *The Face*) as an answer to this query. At the same time the film as such is equivocal. Here, too, B is hiding behind masks, becomes ambiguous, and makes use of a difficult symbolism. Here, too, it is hard to see a center in the story. The answer, though, may be that this very ambiguity is B's real face. The knowledge of the uncertainty of values, the difficulty of interpreting man's action have made him what he is. Man appears stripped of ideology, dechristianized. His only consolation is accidental victory and accidental proximity to other people. Vogler is a self-portrait of the fictitious figure who throughout this book has been designated as B; the figure, imagined or real, whom we discover behind Ingmar Bergman's films.

Åke Runnquist points out in an astute essay on *The Magician* (as does also Georges Sadoul) that the arrival of Vogler's troupe creates change and chaos in the Egerman house. In Sadoul's words, "everything becomes confused, the bourgeois see themselves made ridiculous and humiliated, a *danse macabre* turns the established order upside down, without the government functionaries being able to avenge themselves in the end."[6] Egerman's wife pays attention to Vogler while her husband listens. During Vogler's séance the next day, Starbeck is mocked by his wife. And Vergérus panics after having dissected Vogler's corpse. New emotional bonds are tied in the kitchen regions. The Vogler troupe brings with it a whiff of the free world. It reveals "both to the masters and the servants something new about life, makes them see themselves and their existence in a new light."[7]

According to this, in other words, *The Magician* is a self-analysis, in which Vogler and his company represent art, while Egerman's massive house is a symbol of society, power, the critics, and the broad masses (the people below stairs who are taken in by cheap tricks). Criticism of the existing order, of society with its stable habits, gets a nuance which in B's production is entirely new.

After the supper, Vergérus looks up Manda, finds her in woman's clothes, with her hair undone. He confesses that he has been torn between repulsion and sympathy for her and Doctor Vogler. The dialogue between them reveals a mutual fear. In the eyes of Vergérus, Vogler represents what he most detests, "the unexplainable," while Manda says she is not frightened by his intonation and his intellect, but by his smile, his kindliness. He suggests that she look him up when she has tired. Vogler hears this, from behind a door.

He becomes enraged at Vergérus, but calms down at Manda's urging. Manda and he are alone. Vogler begins to divest himself of his protecting masks, the beard and the wig. They go to bed. They are two human beings, beyond time. They are hunted and scorned. Just as Antonsson has said that he hates Vogler, so does Vogler now say, like an echo: "I hate them. I hate their faces, their bodies, their movements, their voices. But I am also afraid, and then I become powerless."

The performance the next day has two high spots. One is Mrs. Starbeck's trance-like revelations about her husband, that he is a carrot, that he eats like a pig, breaks wind at the dinner table, and visits a whore-house every Saturday. After this, coachman Antonsson is tied with the invisible chain. Powerless and fettered, he tries at last to strangle Vogler. A great commotion ensues. Vogler apparently is dead. Antonsson dashes out. Vergérus has now achieved his goal, and decides to perform an autopsy forthwith, while the police chief, who by now has regained his composure, recommends to Mrs. Vogler "an excellent house on Luntmakare Street, where I have some influence."

Vergérus discovers nothing remarkable at the autopsy. The police chief, who has assisted him, leaves. Vogler is a bluffer, not even the corpse reveals any secrets. But in the laundry coachman

Antonsson has hanged himself, and in the attic, where Vergérus has performed the post-mortem, the door slams shut. He is suddenly exposed to some unaccountable experiences: a series of shockers in the dark, which make him more confused by the moment. His glasses are ripped off and stepped on with a horrible crushing noise. He sees a face in a mirror. A hand reaches out from the dark and grasps his throat. At last he falls against a door leading out from the attic. He calls for help. The door opens. Manda says to her husband: "Leave him alone."

Some of the baroque details in this sequence bring to mind *The Naked Night*. But the attitude toward the camera's possibilities is much more restrained in *The Magician*. The scenes in the attic are done in a slow rhythm. The silence and the effective pauses accentuate the rising tension, which at last snaps when Vergérus rolls down the stairway. He is then seen from above, in all his smallness, whereas the scene has introduced him life-sized, conscious of his victory and his power over the secrets of life. The cinematographic method is subtle and difficult to analyze.

Because B uses all the means the sound film has at its disposal, his method has been compared with that of the theater. Still, this is not theater. Etienne Dor[8] observes how the characters are presented in theater-like life-size pictures, as for instance the adversaries in the first confrontation between the artists and the worldly power. Thereafter, the camera moves right up on the actors. The end of the confrontation is told in a brilliant scene. Vogler and his troupe are in the foreground, on their way out. Through the open door we see Egerman and his friends laughing and conversing.

Two stairway scenes emphasize the restraint in B's expression. When Vogler's wife opens the door, she seals her husband's defeat. He moves slowly down the stairs, moving toward humiliation and forlornness. He begs money from Vergérus, who has now calmed down and treats him in a very haughty manner:

Vogler: You are ungrateful, Sir. Haven't I exerted myself way over my ability to give you an experience?

Vergérus: That was a rotten performance, but naturally you will be paid.

He tosses a coin at Vogler. Vergérus says he prefers Vogler when he is masked. Mrs. Egerman claims she does not recognize him. This whole long and painful sequence was added after the manuscript was finished. In the manuscript the construction is more conventional. The contrast to this scene on the stairs is another, very brief one, when the King's people arrive. The pictures are shorter, the cutting quicker. The rhythm is conducive to moods and emotions.

The first effective close-up in the film is Vergérus' examination of Vogler's throat and mouth. Another is the nocturnal dialogue between Vogler and Manda. The film is played mostly in dim light. According to the story's intention B mystifies his spectators. The forest and the silhouettes in the beginning are familiar from earlier films. Since B apparently does not wish directness and explicitness in his narrative, he has removed it to a past era. His discussion concerns mainly all those who stake their will and energy on uncertain cards, people who are as defenseless before the authority as are the artists.

Vogler and his wife are treated with great cruelty in the moment of their defeat. They are forsaken by their own. B puts into his presentation no nuances of social criticism or politics. As early as 1947, his social consciousness was characterized as being "very little developed, not to say shrunken."[9] The pictures of the official community are ironic and hateful, but also show the weakness in those who wield the power. As long as police chief Starbeck feels that he is defending the right cause, he is blown up with complacency, but his wife's confessions and the message from the King deflate his certainty. The reason why Vogler's troupe is taken to the Egerman house is a bet between the Consul and the medical counselor about the existence of supernatural, unexplainable occurrences. Egerman is a weak man, who loses his bet, and discovers that his wife despises him. But the most important person among those who have power is without comparison Vergérus.

The portrait is not entirely negative. To be sure, he is Vogler's adversary. But many characteristics bind them together. Both intensely wish that they could believe. Vogler is forced to continue an existence which he knows is a fraud. Vergérus is forced to act as is expected of him. His coldness is an obstacle to experiencing the world. They stand on either side of a boundary in society. Both are stripped of their protective qualities. The process produces neither victor nor vanquished, since both are imprisoned in anguish.[10] On this basis we may conceive of the leading characters as spectra in a portrait, as parts of one single image.

The official world, with its laws and regulations, its stagnant self-sufficiency, is worm-eaten from within. It tries to check everybody's happiness. What obviously interests B is to show how the equilibrium of self-satisfaction becomes dislocated. Exceptional circumstances, however, are required to create such a situation. In *The Magician* the bourgeois world is regarded not only with disdain but also with pity. It is narrow, closed by solid stone walls. Only for artists is life an adventure, a constant, unsure waiting for new chances.

The person on whom Vergérus actually has performed an autopsy is the actor Johan Spegel, who has accompanied Vogler on the trip to Stockholm. After having stolen the brandy bottle in the kitchen, he reels up to the drawing room. He has never been convincing as an actor, but as a ghost he is. He speaks a key line in the film: "I have said one prayer in my life: Use me. Manipulate me. But God never understood what a strong and devoted slave I had become. So I remained unused. That was a lie, too, by the way. We walk step by step into the darkness. Movement itself is the only truth." He then dies and falls into a box. His whole life has been a failure. But he performs one single meaningful act: he serves as Vogler at the autopsy.

In a short article B has stated that it is permissible "to commit any outrageousness, any artistic violence, tell any dizzy lies one pleases, as long as they are truly seductive; to give the art form an enthusiastic contempt blended with respect for the minority of people who have managed to live while maintaining the relative purity of spirit and body."[11] *The Magician* is the clearest expression of this philosophy. The film corresponds exactly to the conception one may have of B's position as a film artist. As long as Vogler's trick is not revealed he convinces the spectators. When they see through him, he is transformed into the most miserable beggar. He uses a magic lantern to create "annoying and hideous sights." To the police chief Tubal describes the apparatus as "a ridiculous and perfectly harmless toy." Still, B has managed with the aid of this toy to evoke an imagined world which has the unique ambiguity, the humor, and the seriousness of *The Magician*. Out of humiliation, Vogler rises to comply with the King's invitation. He carries a great disillusion but he knows that he can continue. He knows that his trick is still a hit with the audience.

## The Devil's Eye

One of B's least important pictures, made after *The Virgin Spring*, is called *The Devil's Eye*, and is introduced by an Actor, who comments on the goings-on. *The Devil's Eye* may rightly be regarded as one of the scenes Vogler produces with his magic lantern, an interlude, a *rondo capriccioso*, as it is called in the text preamble. Right at the beginning, the Actor apologizes for his commission:

"Please excuse me, the idea is not mine. I am only performing my duty as an actor, in addition I have, of course, my problems of making a living, and—why not—also my ambition. The most important thing, after all, is that one does one's job well."

Satan, the ruler of hell, a well-dressed gentleman in his middle years, has a sty in one eye. He sends Don Juan with the footman Pablo to the earth to seduce a virgin Britt-Marie, the daughter of a country parson. The scenes in hell are a theater-like mixture of opera and bons mots concerning woman's virtue; the scenes of earth an anthology of motifs from B's production.

Still, the comedy is staged with sureness and a great sense of style. Some of the figures become really interesting, such as, for instance, the simple-minded and credulous minister, who awakens to reality when his wife is seduced by Don Juan's servant. As a whole, though, *The Devil's Eye* is an uninteresting film, a commissioned job, done with skilled craftsmanship, nothing more.

## The Last Couple Out

In contrast to certain other directors, B has never concealed the fact that film production has to be geared to often very difficult economic realities. Several of his pictures were done solely with the economic result in mind. In spite of this, there are sections of value also in these works, just as a film by John Ford never can be quite indifferent. How vague the border is between B's commercial and noncommercial works is clearly shown in a comparison between *Torment* and *The Last Couple Out*. Both pictures are written by B and staged by Alf Sjöberg. *The Last Couple Out* emerges as a continuation of *Torment*, but almost everything that in the latter film was searing analysis and subjective truth has, through the intermediary of the manuscript and Sjöberg's in part extremely unsuccessful direction, been made into a cliché in *The Last Couple Out*.

The desire to please, to accommodate, is possibly a part of B's artistic equipment. This desire clashes with the need to be truthful, but these opposites wage a battle that does not always end in victory for truth. The two poles find expression in *The Magician*. Therefore, in its hesitancy and duplicity, it seems to be truthful toward its creator. More we cannot ask.

# 10

## THE VIRGIN SPRING

The final sequence in *The Virgin Spring* takes place on the spot where Töre's daughter Karin has been raped and slain. Karin's stepsister, Ingeri, blames herself for the evil that has happened. Karin's mother Märeta levels the same accusation at herself. Töre has meted out revenge by killing the herdsmen. He is perplexed. After the murder he looks at his hands. We get the impression that his action has been independent of any thought. He has fulfilled something which will and reflection were not able to master. It often happens in B's films that the actions of the hands have a deep dramatic significance. In *Night is my Future* the blind Stig is dependent upon his hands for all contact with the world around him. He can speak, but physical communication is more important. Many of B's characters seem unable to imagine anything as real if they cannot touch it. In the deepest sense of the word, they are materialists, even if they, like Töre, worship a god, offer him sacrifices.

His dead daughter has been found. He walks down to the brook that runs below the scene of the crime. He turns upward in prayer, almost falls to the ground, as if stricken. His words at this moment, uttered with rhetorical emphasis are a summing up of what has been regarded as the film's message:

188

"You see it God, you see it! The death of the innocent child and my vengeance. You permitted it. I don't understand you. I don't understand you. Still I ask you now for forgiveness—I know of no other way to be reconciled with my own hands. I know of no other way to live. I promise you God, here, by the dead body of my only child I promise you that in penance for my sin I will build you a church. I shall build it here. Of lime and stone and with these two hands of mine."

Direct quotations from the dialogue in B's films seldom do full justice to the inner meaning of the lines. The pauses, the rhythmic measure, play an important role in the build-up of a scene. The last sentence in Töre's vow is spoken with special emphasis. If men's consciences, already penetrated by Christianity, stand in contrast to action, Töre's promise means literally that he reconciles his hands with Christianity. He wishes to perform the penance not only of the word, but also of the deed, in order to prove his changed state of mind.

Still I have difficulty in seeing that, as many critics have maintained, B has "given himself up to religiosity"[1] in The Virgin Spring. This would mean that one agreed with Jean Wagner's discouraging opinion, expressed in a comparison between Three Strange Loves and The Virgin Spring: "Bergman has today reached perfection, but at the same time petrifaction. He who so often has wished to converse with Death, has opened the doors of his work wide for it. It has moved in there as a ruler. We are waiting patiently for the resurrection."[2] Many have advanced the view that The Virgin Spring as cinematographic action and spiritual movement is on the way to a silence, an inertness, a lack of tension and debate that is truly repulsive. I cannot join in this opinion. An acceptance would mean that one regarded B as an artist with a ready answer to given questions. In his art, however, "questioning is the most important" (the Knight in The Seventh Seal), but its importance also is the constant shading of a whole series of personal, subjectively conceived problems. This involvement penetrates even through the cool observation and the objectively epic narrative.

In *The Virgin Spring* B strives for an objective coolness. This coolness has been found earlier, in the camera's role as a silent observer. In *The Virgin Spring*, however, objectivity is without a doubt "the only stylistic solution permitting Bergman to tell his story with perfect unity; in this, one cannot discover any message, any concession by the director toward a religious belief, or any faith at all, but only a great, objective narrator's lofty play with his creative imagination."[3] Only through the coldness of great distance can the horrible scenes achieve their gruesome significance, become moving and comprehensible. There was hardly any other solution, unless B wished to immerse himself in a naturalistic description of details.

It is necessary to place Brecht and B against each other, as two of the most important artists of the postwar years.[4] It has been maintained that Brecht's esthetics is the only practicable means to achieve a total vision of society, present or past. The Marxian esthetics, as Brecht uses it, presents the socially significant in an action. The action as such has pedagogic value. Yet the selection of facts about man's life is not limited to only one interpretation, as *The Life of Galileo* shows. Brecht's esthetics implies an historical view, a belief in the meaning of the past, in order that the future may be analyzed and predestined. B's esthetics rejects in Nietzsche's philosophy and that of the following irrationalists, all moral concepts, presenting instead man's, the individual's, responsibility. The artist can, of course, give a picture of a social field. But human beings are regarded not as parts of a series of events with cause-effect, but as isolated entities. The artist thinks he sees in the world around him a confirmation that this theory is correct, that the world is atomistic, meaningless. For such an artist, the interesting thing is not sacrifice for the future, but man's immediate chances of life.

The Christian ethic (as expressed in the manuscript of *The*

*Virgin Spring* leaves the individual alone with his God, his conscience. It is a weakness in this Christianity that God can be entirely omitted. This authority can be replaced by some other,
or can be disregarded. For this reason there is, surprisingly
enough, an extreme point where two world interpretations
meet, Brecht's and B's: namely, in the emphasis on the material,
the temporal. The essential difference, however, is that whereas
Brecht presents man's crass materialism as a result of external
circumstance, B turns all accusations inward, even when the film
shows repulsive persons, bourgeois and representatives of the
existing order of power, as in *The Magician*.

The important thing in *The Virgin Spring* is that B manages
to surmount the weaknesses of the manuscript, create a shatter-
ing drama from something that was intended to be a sermon. In
the shaping of the film he approaches, more clearly than ever
before, the tradition of the classic Swedish film. Most of the
picture's convincing scenes are played out of doors, in settings
that are timeless and not created for the shooting of a movie.
Almost all the weaker scenes are enacted indoors, in the studio.
This difference could often be seen in older films, and not only
the Swedish ones. The interiors seldom had the genuineness of
nature. *The Virgin Spring* is in many ways a drama about
natural forces. Its strength is not that of historic reconstruction.

The manuscript was written by Ulla Isaksson. The idea of
making a film from the medieval legendary material, "Töre's
Daughter in Vänge," came from B. He has stated that he planned
to write a play, later a ballet. For some reason he preferred not
to do the manuscript, perhaps partly to free himself from the
charge often expressed, that he is a remarkably poor writer.
(One has often heard the opposite that he is a good writer, but
a poor director.)

It is possible rather accurately to establish Ulla Isaksson's con-
tributions to *The Virgin Spring* by comparing the literary material (the manuscript) with the final result, the final molding.

The legend as such is completely lacking in psychology. Three herdsmen rape and kill Karin. They take the same road she has come, and call at Töre's farm. They are given room for the night, offer Karin's shift to her mother, after which the father avenges her by killing all three. The material of the legend and the film is such that the spectator-reader is not held by the outer tension. Interest in the plot as such is nonexistent. The spectator knows that ravishment, murder, and revenge are part of the story.

On the spot where Karin was killed, a spring wells up. Töre atones for his crime by building a church. In a commentary on the manuscript Ulla Isaksson says: "The film must in quite another manner make the story of young Karin and her parents realistically understandable, credible as to continuity, psychology, and milieu. However, to recreate the standards and the outlook of such a distant time with full realism and to evoke understanding for them among modern people did not seem possible. What became urgent was to find as great a common denominator as possible and build the film around it, so that the legend could at once be preserved and accepted. Certain additions were therefore unavoidable."

All these additions and new perspectives are not fortunate. It is splendid to let the miracle with the spring form the final climax of the film. But the description of the early morning in Töre's home, before Karin has waked, and her conversation with the mother have justly been compared with interiors of the folk museum of Skansen, in Stockholm. Only the external stage properties seem historically accurate. The dialogue is spoken by people who have read the fairy tale books by Elsa Beskow.[5] When Karin and Ingeri have set out on the ride to the church Ingeri does not dare to venture into the frightening forest (as an alternative she asks Karin to stay). She remains with a bridge guard, a heathen. The scene where he shows the instruments of his cult is surprisingly tasteless claptrap. The psychological explanations for man's behavior disturb the story, do not make it stronger. On the other hand, it is a very good idea for Ulla Isaksson to have a frog symbolize ill omen. The stepsister Ingeri, who is pregnant, is asked to make up the food package for Karin before she leaves for church. On the floor she spies a frog, which she places between two pieces of bread. According to the old folk belief, the frog was the symbol of evil, the Devil's deputy: "When food is turned into frogs and toads, the Devil is frisking around."[6] The frog also appears as a sex symbol. When Karin sits with the herdsmen in the forest glade the frog jumps out of the loaf of bread and scares them all. This becomes a release for Karin's mounting fright. She knows its significance.

It is thanks to B as a director that so much of the objective coolness of the legend has been salvaged, in spite of the manuscript.

We must imagine the film as a latter-day variation of the legend material. The distance from the time described and its morals creates a contrasting effect which gives the story its strong inner tension. But it is unreasonable to interpret the film solely as a faithful re-creation. We do not judge the morality of *The Virgin Spring* with the eyes of the Middle Ages, but with our own eyes. In the legend and the film there is suggested a conception of sin and atonement belonging to a time more cynical than ours, cynical because man's religious conviction, his conversion, is represented as a mechanical act. The film tells of the transitional time between Christianity and paganism of heathen who have adopted the outer forms of Christianity. It is the heathen who are seeking an answer. The moral of the legend becomes something like this: man is full of sin. He pays for this through an act of atonement. When the account is balanced, it is assumed that the question is settled.

We know that this is not true. It would be pleasant indeed to be able to refer judgment and punishment and the torments of conscience to an outside tribunal. We should then be assured that penance has saved us from our sins. We could then really believe that Töre's decision to build a church was sufficient to make him whole. Film can never represent the past; it can only display the past. *The Virgin Spring* shows the customs and the morals of a past time. It achieves grandeur and suspense through the contrast between our consciousness and that of a bygone period.

When the film opens it is early morning; the cock crows. The strong light of early summer penetrates into the house. We are moving in an aura of evil omens. Since this drama, too, has been constructed to take place within approximately twenty-four hours, the opening scenes have a parallel at the end. Töre sits in his big chair waiting for the sun to rise. He has thrust his butcher knife into the table. It is growing lighter. The sun penetrates through the half-open hatch in the roof; the cock crows. The light falls on the knife. This marks the beginning of the vengeance, the slaughter in the house. We have seen the knife before: in *The Devil's Wanton*, where it was used for self-destruction and had come into the basement by chance. Now the murderers shall be killed. This is done as when one cuts the heads off fish, or when children throw to the ground things that have incurred their displeasure, to punish them.

The really evil deed in Töre's action is that he kills the boy. In his way, the lad is, in fact, guiltless. To be sure, he does not intervene against his companions. He covers Karin with a little earth. He is left alone, and looks up into the sky. It begins to snow. He picks up the bread that has been left on the ground and starts to eat. He vomits up the bread. He reacts in the same manner in Töre's house, later, when the herdsmen partake of the evening meal. Töre says the same grace that Karin did when she began to eat with the herdsmen. The boy pushes his plate away and the soup spills over the table. During the night, as a punishment, he is abused by his two comrades. Blood pours from his mouth. When Töre has killed the other two, the boy in panic rushes to the mute witness, mother Märeta. But Töre tears him away from her, and dashes him against the wall.

A visual parallel between the beginning and the end is found in many of B's films, but never in so fatefully mechanical a way as in *The Virgin Spring*. A contemporary narrator would perhaps begin where the film now ends, in the conflict of conscience. B permits us as spectators to take over this discussion. He adds another question to the many posed in his earlier films.

The opening scenes carry evil omens. One of them has already been mentioned: Ingeri's behavior, the frog in the bread. Through the entire story, up to Karin's death, we feel that Ingeri wished that this would happen. She watches the deed. On the other side of the brook she is a witness to rape and murder. She picks up a stone to throw, but it falls from her powerless hand, and rolls into the water.

When Karin in the morning lies in her bed, she is nothing but vain and lovable. This sequence hints at a conflict motif concerning her. Mother and father disagree about how to bring her up. The contrast has traces of modern psychology and does not belong in the story. Karin becomes beautiful when she succeeds in persuading her mother that she must be permitted to wear the fine dress. It is a solemn day for her to ride to church with the St. Mary candles. This atmosphere of beauty, of simple lyricism, jars against the naturalistic details. It is a difficult and not always happy synthesis of epic stylization and detailed observations of cultural history.

The ride to the church is described in a few short Swedish-pastoral scenes, beautiful in their epic tone. Karin has promised her mother:

"Oh, mother, I will be so dignified riding to church—you shall see. And Blackie will lift his hoofs as quietly as if he were walking in a pilgrimage, and I won't look either to the right or to the left, only straight ahead and think of the candles and the Holy Virgin."

The idyllic pictures are few. B uses camera angles typical of his reserved attitude toward the medium. The two riders—Ingeri has been permitted to come along—move along the shore of a lake. We see them among the trees, in dark silhouette against the light water. Karin begins to sing. A bit later she dismounts to pick flowers. Their dialogue suggests Ingeri's lack of illusion, Karin's naïveté. In anger, Karin hits Ingeri. The idyl is over. They come to the forest.

This short description of threatened summer brings to mind the summer sequences in the films from the beginning of the 1950's, *Illicit Interlude* and *Monika*. In those, too, the summer is always threatened. The drama follows the changes of nature. Autumn means death, also, for man. For B, summer is a central visual idea, an image of the free state of happiness for which his characters are longing. The transitory nature of summer symbolizes the fragile quality in the search for lasting happiness. The first act of *The Virgin Spring* is a mixture, characteristic of B, of the beautiful and the repulsive, the ethereal and the concrete. B's picture of summer has nothing to do with the commercial, cliché-like image that occurs in many Swedish films. Arne Mattsson in *She Danced a Summer* touches on this cliché, even though the picture is considerably more personal than the same director's later, poor films would let us suspect.

Karin's ride ends with a painfully beautiful scene in the forest. Karin sits immobile on her horse, in profile and in an unreal illumination, against a background of the dark forest. Ingeri has remained with the old sorcerer. Karin lets herself be lured into a conversation with the herdsmen. One of them plays a strange, alluring tune on a mouth organ. She follows the herdsmen up into the forest. In this strawberry patch, Karin's life ends. She is vain, boasts of herself and her white hands. That is why she shares her food package with the herdsmen, at first more attracted than frightened by their pretended admiration. The rape and the murder, Töre's vengeance and decision to build a church are all the consequences of this mistake. The legend tells of overcoming death and accepting soiled life, of living on, in spite of shame, of paying for the shame. Ingeri, Märeta, and Töre all have to do this.

*The Virgin Spring* could be regarded purely as a directing commission. Provided with given material, one might think, B has striven to translate the text into pictures as adequately as possible. But this is not the whole truth. Within its frame, *The Virgin Spring* reflects exactly the same moral B has earlier proclaimed. It is the thought of the honorableness of him who is defeated, the honor of humiliation, in other words, a direct continuation of *The Magician* despite the fact that that film dealt with artists. B has been able to mold this central theme on subjects as widely apart as *The Virgin Spring*, *The Naked Night*, and *The Devil's Wanton*. As an artist he stands on the side of the lost ones, the innocent sufferers. He knows that the borderline between sin and virtue is thin and very vague. The thought of a release and a cleansing from evil haunts him. The interesting thing is not the kind of churches and the series of promises that are the result of Töre's crime, but his struggle and self-inflicted pain.

From this soil, B's film poem grows to a general universal effect. This is actually strange, since so many of the questions that seem to preoccupy B can be traced to Swedish society, its forms of association, and its lonelinesses. In spite of its openness to impulses, Swedish society can appear like a hothouse, nauseatingly shut off from the world. This may have to do with the fact that no artistic experience, no fiction can take the place of the direct experience of suffering. Swedish artists have themselves not seen the physical background of the moral and general philosophical debate from which they, nevertheless, have drawn much of their inspiration. Behind Eliot's *The Waste Land* and Hemingway's desperate, observant prose, Sartre's and Camus' philosophic discussions, there exists a real, desolate world, war-ravaged, brutal, and naked. In Sweden this was all an impression from the outside, as when Bertil and Rut in *Three Strange Loves* observe the begging children in Germany and give them food. The remarkable thing is that of all B's films *The Virgin Spring* comes closest to the European experience of evil. As a parable of our time's destructive forces, the film is more successful than several of B's tales of the present. What may hurt the spectator in *The Devil's Wanton* is the film's dependence upon poor literature.

It is undoubtedly correct to look upon *The Virgin Spring* as an expression of cinematographic asceticism, a principle that many regard as mocking the mobility of the film art. But Japanese film has most effectively demonstrated that movement in pictures does not consist only of swift rides over the hills, or automobile chases through big cities, but can just as well signify the movement of a man's thoughts. The film art's chief means of expression are motion and contrast, but the spectator's immobility can underscore the brutality of the scene, as in *The Virgin Spring*. Everything is told directly.

Thus Töre's morning meal is like an altar painting. The camera stands still. The individual shots are very long. We can agree with Vernon Young that the film "is as strictly composed as a sonnet, pictorially: each image contains, predicts or recalls every other image—the sustained reverberation of a bell, in which the original note and the final overtone sound as a continuum to the ear. This is the most compactly visual of all Bergman's films, the dialogue more sparse even than that in *Gycklar-nas Afton* (*The Naked Night*), the narration as artfully paced."[7] Young also points out that the placing of the camera in space, more than its movement, determines the style of the film. His assertion about visual power may seem surprising, but is correct. In the scene of the rape the camera is immobile, and records the event almost without changing shots. All through the film we meet the same static compositions without any greater effect of depth. What is important occurs within one single scene. The impression of horror and distance is enhanced, just as the silent-film technique in *The Naked Night* (the flashback) established distance in an epic way. We are reminded of the country fair jugglers and the peep-show operators whom B praises so highly. Perhaps B believes that their technique was similar:

"By all means, borrow my machines and duplicate what I am doing. Take your time. Learn to be agile with your fingers, learn how, just in the right moment, to divert the attention of the audience with your spiel, learn speed, and the mysterious illumination! You will still not do what I am doing, you will still fail. You see, I perform magic! I conjure!"[8]

Not even in moments of the greatest emotional stress does B lose his grip. He uses sound effects of frightening realism. When Karin has been ravished, she staggers around in silence. She emits horrible sounds. Her face is changed. She is an animal. Then a quick shot as she lies on the ground in her death coma and lifts up her face. She blinks a few times. Then her head falls down and she is dead.

This sequence became the subject of an intensive debate in Sweden. There were different opinions as to whether the sequence was meaningful for the film as a whole. But the entire picture really builds on this scene, and on its parallel, Töre's vengeance.[9] It is, however, obvious that the film shots have quite another force, a more immediate emotional effect than the lines in the legend-song in which the crime is described:

> First she was three herdsmen's wife,
> Then she gave up her young life.

They took her by her golden hair,
And led her to a forest lair.

They took her by the golden lock,
And placed her 'gainst a birchtree stock.

They severed then her lovely head—
A spring welled up upon that stead.

It is, to start with, an impossible task directly to recreate the old song. The verse rhythm, the combination of words, the alliteration give the legend quite another, more naïve tone. Nothing like this exists in the film. In some places, however, the film's and the legend's meaning and feeling become identical. Consider, for instance, the transference of the scene by the spring. Ingeri moistens her face with water from the spring, and is redeemed from her external guilt. Only now does her face acquire a certain beauty and harmony. This is a film poem on the basis of the legend, an independent creation. The same is true of Töre's preparation for his revenge. He cuts down a birch. We see the man grasping the tree, swinging on it, felling it to the ground, and falling himself. Afterward he takes a steam bath, beats himself with the birch twigs. The impression of an interplay of natural forces, far from both Christianity and paganism, is never stronger than here.

Most frequently, however, Ulla Isaksson's manuscript is full of literary effects of the type B usually avoids. Her scenario prose never achieves the double, contrasting and complementing impact that heightens the impression of *The Seventh Seal*, although the words have literarily associative functions.

The fixed quality of the film, its transitions between idyl and violence, piety and blood become a weapon in B's hand. It belongs to his equipment, this feeling for violent changes, for quickly altering the line of vision. On the other hand, I have a feeling that there is something unfinished, unresolved in the film, that it, like *The Naked Night*, is an experiment. Despite his ability to create an epic distance, I do not believe that historic material is B's real domain. In everything he does, he remains saturated with contemporary ideas. His pictures are the questions and assertions of a modern man. The historic disguise does not always have the desired effect.

*The Virgin Spring* is a film one does not easily forget. Aside from the fact that it contains a poetic element, it has a strong, almost nauseating feeling of the nearness of death—the stench of a corpse. Perhaps this is necessary for the film's character of a reckoning. The tradition of the film has trained the spectator to expect strong effects, strong sentiments. Until recently, film art has worked with a more violent, a more quickly oscillating field of emotions than literature. Antonioni's pictures are blamed for being slow, literary, since they refrain from certain traditional commonplaces. The purpose of B's shockers, with the strong effects, is not only an artistic purpose for its own sake, but may consist of an attempt to arouse the public from cool indifference and emotional slumber. Perhaps B in *The Virgin Spring* expresses the same opposition morality and uncomfortable attitude as Luis Buñuel once formulated:

"If it were possible for me, I would make films which, apart from entertaining the audience, would convey to them the absolute certainty that they DO NOT LIVE IN THE BEST OF ALL POSSIBLE WORLDS. And in doing this I believe that my intentions would be highly constructive. Movies today, including the so-called neo-realist, are dedicated to a task contrary to this. How is it possible to hope for an improvement in the audience—and consequently in the producers—when every day we are told in these films, even in the most insipid comedies, that our social institutions, our concepts of Country, Religion, Love, etc., etc., are, while perhaps imperfect, UNIQUE AND NECESSARY? The true "opium of the audience" is conformity; and the entire, gigantic film world is dedicated to the propagation of this comfortable feeling, wrapped though it is at times in the insidious disguise of art."[10]

The shocks that B communicates in *The Virgin Spring* may conceivably be founded on more or less the same conviction. B has never hesitated to admit the conditions under which an artist of the film is forced to labor. He must seduce, conquer, or shock great masses of people, for whom subtlety in artistic expression perhaps actually becomes an obstacle rather than a help. The subtle element in *The Virgin Spring* is its asceticism, its keeping aloof from subtleties, the film's "difficult simplicity." The rape and the murder are dramatically justified. They are at the same time visual shocks of the kind that belongs to the essence of the film, to its history.

Töre knows of no other way to live than to avenge. He cannot entrust action to a judicial or executive authority. In a community as primitive as that of medieval Sweden this was the natural course. Modern man has become isolated from such chances of getting an immediate outlet for his desire to create a balance between the forces of good and evil. But the religious part of the film, its miracles, its promise, seem only to comprise a dramatic ornament. The religious element becomes a question of form, a manner in which reality can be understood in a manner rich in contrasts.[11]

Two children form the poles around which Töre's action circles. One is Karin, who is ravished and slain because she for a moment forgot her promise to her mother not to look to the right or to the left. Another is the herdsman lad, on whose fate is lavished little or no sentimentality: "Still, there is something in the eyes of that boy that gives the film a completely timeless dimension, cutting straight through the medieval stylizing. The surrender and the impotence which the boy's eyes express are also the fright and helplessness of a 'child of our time,' in the century of the extermination camps."[12] In such moments, B's cinematographic action reaches a self-evident simplicity, the fruit of his long struggle with the medium, his constant attempt to present a human situation truthfully. In spite of different disguises, this situation is always the same, that of the human being who is confronted with the question: How is it possible to live in this world?[13]

WINTER LIGHT. Gunnar Björnstrand (*Tomas*) and Ingrid Thulin (*Märta*).

THE VIRGIN SPRING. Axel Düberg (*The thin one*) and Birgitta Petterson (*Karin*).

THROUGH A GLASS DARKLY. Lars Passgård (*Minus*) and Harriet Andersson (*Karin*).

The cast of NOT TO SPEAK ABOUT ALL THESE WOMEN with
Ingmar Bergman. (seated) Karin Kavli, Bibi Andersson, Harriet
Andersson, Gertrud Fridh, Barbro Hiort af Ornäs, Eva Dahlbeck,
and Mona Malm. (standing) Allan Edwall, Georg Funkquist,
Ingmar Bergman, and Jarl Kulle.

THE SILENCE. The sisters, Ingrid Thulin (*Ester*) and Gunnel Lindblom (*Anna*).

# 11

## CHAMBER PLAYS

In a conversation, Kafka indicated his opinion about the contrast between literature and poetic writing. Literature was dissolution and narcotics, poetry its opposite, essence. Asked whether poetry was related to religion, Kafka denied this, but said that poetry and prayer were closely allied.[1] One is reminded of these words when contemplating three films by B, by himself collected into a trilogy under the joint title of *Chamber Plays*. The pictures, *Through a Glass Darkly*, *Winter Light*, and *The Silence*, were made during the years 1960 to 1962.

It is possible that *Through a Glass Darkly* and *Winter Light* will be compared by certain critics to religious rites. But, though the latter moves in time between two divine services, it is the attributes of the prayer that we are made to think of. A deepening and a change of B's views on the director's task has taken place, and the questions are perhaps no longer asked with the same relentless bitterness as Marie's in *Illlicit Interlude*, when she expresses herself on the meaninglessness in life. But it is not difficult to detect the continuity in the work, the bridge across the years up till today. As earlier, B discusses the possibilities of faith and doubt. Some of his characters have arrived at an absurd belief in God, at a tragic but proud view of life which, though it may be said to be akin to Kierkegaard's, still must be regarded as B's own.[2]

Chamber plays, in the Strindberg sense of the term, cover short spans of time with few actors, and possess something of the character of intimate music. Chamber plays make use of the subtlest nuances of the soul. *Wild Strawberries* is not a chamber play, but a novel in film form, a retrospective look across a whole life. *Through a Glass Darkly* and *Winter Light* indicate, in the words of the characters, situations that have taken place in the past, but take place with frightening sharpness in the present moment. The former picture covers twenty-four hours in time; the latter, not much more time than the film itself, some hours between twelve and three during a Sunday in November. *The Silence*, too, covers a very short space of time, but formally it deviates from the other two, because B here returns to a freer narrative style.

The similarities between the three chamber plays are evident from some indications about the spiritual climate in which they are set. Over the whole trilogy hovers a feeling of threat and defeat. In *Through a Glass Darkly* the characters are isolated on an island in the archipelago; in *Winter Light* the actors appear deserted and inconsolable; in *The Silence* the leading persons cannot communicate at all with their surroundings. One might say that B on a psychological plane interprets the feeling of terror which has become common with many people in our world today, the alienation which can be tied to very concrete experiences of dehumanization and mechanization in our culture. B has been accused of allowing his own strange milieus and characters to express his inability to delineate modern society. But we can just as easily imagine that these persons become symbols of psychological reaction patterns of wide scope.

The parts of the trilogy are ascetic, the first two visually, the last orally. B seems to be possessed by an endeavor to make these pictures as naked as possible, although *The Silence* in a way means a return to a freer visual style. In *Through a Glass Darkly* and *Winter Light*, however, B has peeled off everything that appeared to him unessential.

## Through a Glass Darkly

The immediate inspiration of *Through a Glass Darkly* is some words in the first epistle of Paul to the Corinthians, thirteenth chapter: "For now we see through a glass, darkly; but then face to face: now I know in part; but then I shall know even as also I am known." The words refer to the meeting with God, when all barriers shall fall. They refer to the moment of death, of perfection, when man is regarded as being united with his God. *The Seventh Seal* also gained its direct inspiration from the Bible, in Revelation. Both films expand from Christian thought. *Through A Glass Darkly* tells of persons who for one reason or another have been driven to isolation. The film concerns Christian conceptions of love. It is not, however, a drama of faith but a description of man's chances to live.

The picture begins with water reflections. We see four persons walk toward the shore after a swim. The spectator may through association think that these people on an island are the last survivors, remnants of a desolate, splintered civilization. The four are David, the author, his daughter Karin, his son Fredrik, known as Minus, and Karin's husband, Martin, who is a physician. David has recently returned from Switzerland where he has been working on his latest novel. Evening falls, the men put out their nets, brother and sister go to fetch the milk. The homecoming is celebrated with a dinner. David presents gifts to the others, but he has just revealed that he will soon set out again, this time as a tour leader for a group going to Yugoslavia. After dinner, Karin and Minus put on a play for their father. It tells how a poet promises to follow the Princess of Castile in love and unto death. He regrets his promise. The following morning David and Martin leave in the motorboat. Karin and Minus are alone. Suddenly reality breaks up for Karin, who earlier has been a patient in an insane asylum and is hypersensitive to sounds and sights. She hides in the wreck of a ship. Her illness breaks out. David and Martin return. They telephone for an ambulance helicopter. After a terror-filled revelation in an empty room, Karin is carried away. David and Minus remain alone. David discloses his faith to Minus. This is the plot of the film.

Earlier, the picture had been given the working title of *The Wallpaper*, and was intended to be done in color. B had long been considering doing a color film, but he had found that those who work in this medium seldom undertsand its properties. After long preparation and intensive testing, B directed his first color film, *Not To Speak About All These Women*, in the summer of 1963. The film will not be shown before 1964; according to B's own statements, he has tried to use color in an antinaturalistic way.[3]

The title *The Wallpaper* covers the central theme in *Through a Glass Darkly*. In a room up in the summer house, Karin is accustomed to listen to voices, wait for visions. She stands turned toward a wallpaper, spotted by dampness, bulging and old. There is a door in the wall. She imagines that God will show Himself in this door. But when in the night she enters the room, her experiences are described as if she were possessed by sexual perversion. She falls on her knees, bends down. Her legs are spread apart. Her schizophrenia has strong hysteric touches.

The final sequence begins with David and Martin finding her alone in the room. She is talking to herself. She knows that her waiting will be fulfilled. She is prepared. She asks her husband to kneel beside her. After a moment's hesitation, he obeys. The conclusion comes in a frighteningly condensed scene. Through the window is seen the helicopter that comes to pick her up. Its sound fills the room. Karin experiences a tremendous reaction of terror. She cowers in a corner of the room. She receives supernatural powers. This, too, seems to be tied to the sexual. In the morning, the conversation between Karin and Martin has revealed that she does not feel sexual desire for her husband.

The downdraft of the helicopter causes the wallpaper door to open. David and Martin overpower Karin. She gets a tranquilizing injection, and relaxes. It is then she can tell of the god that came:

"He came up to me, and I saw his face. It was a loathsome, evil face. And he climbed up on me and tried to penetrate me. But I warded him off. And all the time I saw his eyes. They were cold and calm. When he could not enter into me, he quickly climbed up on my breast and my face and then on to the wall."

A moment later she says: "I have seen God."

Few explanations of this are offered. Perhaps we can say that Karin finds the truth that others of B's figures have arrived at, that God is a void, that the void is the certainty of death. She, who is more sensitive, reacts more violently. She has waited in vain. Therefore she is prepared to leave this world, which is that of normal people, for another, that of the insane asylum. When talking to her father she begs to be spared the electric shocks. She does not want to return. Another interpretation of her experience and her almost voluntary flight into her illness is that B has once more wanted to show the spectator an intellectual jigsaw puzzle which one can interpret as one wishes.

In the play enacted for the father, it is Karin who takes the part of the Princess of Castile. In the play it is indicated that she is closer to her father than to her husband. Martin regards her coolly, with love, but evidently without really understanding her. She cannot sleep that night. She finds her way to the room with the wallpaper, then to her father, who is sitting at his desk, laboriously correcting his manuscript. When he has left, she discovers his diary, in which he has written:

"Her illness is hopeless, but with occasional periods of lucidity. I have long surmised it, but the certainty nevertheless is almost insufferable. To my horror I discover my curiosity. The compulsion to register the progress, concisely to note her gradual dissolution. To utilize her."[4]

An intensive search has been made for the sources of Karin's personality, of her experiences. It is handy to quote an interview from the middle of the 1940's, in which B expressed his desire to "make a film about an insane asylum, which would reflect the mental world and the imaginings of a schizophrenic, and how for him existence gets out of kilter a quarter of a turn." Or one may refer to one sequence left out from *The Devil's Wanton*, where Birgitta-Carolina visits an artist in his room. His experiences are exactly like Karin's in *Through a Glass Darkly*. Of course, with the eagerness to unmask B which is typical of Swedish intellectuals, there have been found literary connections, in an American short story with a similar theme,[5] and in Strindberg's play *Easter*.[6] It is clear that the inspiration from Strindberg, the kinship with Strindberg, makes itself felt everywhere with B. But the questions in this film are a clear continuation of B's own statement of problems since 1944. That he borrows and uses the ideas of others is well known. Interesting, though, is his ability to utilize these ideas in a personal manner. Perhaps he writes the same drama, but the variations are great. It is not the construction of the plot that interests, not the similarity between individuals from literature, but their dramatic life.

Karin's mental illness is not explained. It is, however, dependent upon her relationship to the world around her. It is a matter of love and one's ability to reach one another, but the construction has nowhere the same old Protestant severity as with Dreyer. All live in some form of confinement. This applies especially to David. When during the dinner he tells about his projected trip, his children are dejected. He tries to break the sadness by distributing presents. Then he goes to his own room to look for his tobacco. There he stands alone, while sobs shake his body. Like a crucified one, he reaches for support, and stares out into empty space. His figure is unmercifully delineated. His breakdown corresponds to his daughter's.

In the play the children act out for him, he recognizes himself all too well. The camera often lets the spoken lines be reflected in his face. It expresses weariness, coolness, forced interest, and wounded feelings. When Minus promises to follow the princess into death and the grave, he says: "That is an easy sacrifice, Princess. For what is life to a *real* artist?" The parable ends with Minus "going home and sleeping on the matter." The princess remains alone in her grave, just as David has left all the others. In the night he sits at his desk, correcting his book. The scene indicates his fatigue, coolness, and aridity. It exudes satiety. He has lost his strength, as Minus tells him— spiritually. Once B asked himself: "I still know that what I tell myself is a delusion and that eternal anxiety calls to me: What have you done that will endure? Is there a single meter in your films that will stand the test of the future, a single line, a single situation that is irrevocably true?"[7]

In one form or another he has swung between disgust and fascination in his relation to art. Nowhere is the disgust as differentiated as in this picture, in which David becomes almost a parody of an unsuccessful figure, in spite of the story's strange final words. Material and structure have undergone a symbiosis. A more artless fashioning B has never achieved. There is not an unnecessary gesture, not a superfluous camera movement. Romanticism and the baroque ornaments have disappeared. People are described without illusion. All the stronger appear the tense contrasts between darkness and light, silence and voices. It is perhaps not necessary to emphasize that this stylizing is considerably more difficult to achieve than the baroque in *The*

*Naked Night*. B has never narrated so clearly and cleanly as in this film.

David is an unsuccessful writer. The thought of success, of the burden of work, devours him. Even if the film approaches the hint of an answer, David appears doomed. He seems to have existed entirely for his own perfection. During a decisive conversation with Karin he confesses that he went to Switzerland only because he could not endure her illness. And he has done it once before:

"When mother became ill, I went away, and left you with grandmother. I had my novel to think of. When mother died I had my first big break-through—I had arrived, and that meant more to me than her death. I rejoiced in secret, and still I loved your mother in my confused and selfish way. Oh, Karin, how our eyes smart when we see ourselves!"

The same contradiction between the happiness of private life and professional success haunts the main character in *Wild Strawberries*. The question can never be answered since it appears to be wrongly posed. It is, however, dramatically warranted in *Through a Glass Darkly* for the purpose of underscoring Karin's loneliness and misery. Perhaps B also wants to show that David's behavior is the fundamental reason for Karin's defeat in life.

This criticism expresses a crisis situation. Do artists really have the right to analyze the problems of others if they cannot solve their own? On the boat trip David is accused by Martin of coldness. Martin says ironically that David finds his consolation in religion, in unfathomable grace. Still, his God seems very unconvincing. David then tells him that while in Switzerland he was firmly resolved to commit suicide. The car in which he planned to drive down a ravine developed engine trouble and remained hanging over the rim of the abyss. He saved himself. Like Albert in *The Naked Night* he dares to take the step outward, but he, too, fails in his attempt at self-destruction. From this action, David reveals, grew love: love for others.

Only the broken in spirit can find a new life. This is the film's main theme, an old Christian thought and a modern artistic idea. For that reason, each and every one of the participants must go to his doom. B shapes this thought with superb artistic strategy. Still, the description of the four persons in *Through a Glass Darkly* is only a variation of a motif often recurring with B. The interesting thing is not the suicide or the defeat as such, but the ability almost without any rhetorical gestures to create an artistically convincing reality.

The movement of the film is the soul's. Karin, the most sensitive of them all, is most tormented by isolation, loneliness, of which the island becomes a physical symbol. Martin, comfortably ensconced in his work and his everyday life, cannot understand her, though he loves her. And yet we should not regard Martin as a wholly negative figure. He is perhaps limited, but his strength lies in the field of activity that he masters. Minus experiences puberty as a terror; he fears the leap into the adult world. David has unceasingly thought only of himself. And yet he is closest to her. He can forgive her (it is indicated that she and Minus commit incest in the wrecked ship) because he himself needs forgiveness. The drama is unfolded in two parallel actions, Karin-Minus, David-Martin. As types, all the persons in the picture are divergent. Minus writes a great deal, like his father. He is disgusted with women, overgrown, unsure. All four are unique. That is why Karin chooses between this world and insanity.

"This world" is that of adult, active, normal people, indirectly the world of nuclear weapons and unhappiness, mass destruction and cruelty. The other world can't be worse, even if God were to appear as a frightening spider. Karin longs for peace, freedom, and escape. She belongs among the characters of B's for whom death is a dreadful and tempting possibility. The crisis

she goes through concerns them all, the inability to love un-
selfishly and thereby the inability to surround man with a cor-
don of protection and care. It is therefore a matter of course for
her to choose the reality that is closer to death. This is not possible until she has sunk down in filth and degradation, robbed
of all protective armor. There is in the interpretation a frightful
torture, a physical force that makes Karin the picture's central
figure. Her face is defenseless, ageless, but with great experience.

"When that which is perfect is come," reads the letter to the
Corinthians, "then that which is in part shall be done away."
That which is in part is knowledge, but not love: "And now
abideth faith, hope, love, these three; but the greatest of these
is love." The *now* the Bible refers to is the moment of death,
when man sees his God and is united with him. He returns to
the child's vision. We may imagine that this is what B means,
if we analyze his earlier production. He seeks a stage that lies
at the beginning of life and at its end. Only one who is a child,
who is naïve, can see and love. The moment of certainty is the
moment of death. One of the persons reaches a certitude which
is close to death. That is Karin. Through his suicide attempt,
David has felt the same temptation and tremendous threat.

*Through a Glass Darkly* is almost entirely lacking in music.
The film is strictly restrained in every way. Sounds play, as
previously, a deciding role, as contrasts and omens. As Karin
gets up in the night, she hears the sound of a steamboat whistle.
It is repeated when she is with Minus and suddenly feels the
transformation, her own illness, and the change in nature. As
Martin and David run toward the wreck, their feet scatter
stones. We hear the clucking of the water, the rain, the wind,
weeping, and breathing. The outer stage is limited, too: the
summer house, the stony shore, the pier, the wreck, the garden,
boats, and the helicopter as symbol and reality. More than ever
this drama is isolated from society and time. To be sure, we
know that everything is present and now. Otherwise the film

could occur anywhere, at any time. Still, this is an exaggeration. B describes the spiritual struggle of modern man. He poses questions that have become actual by the threat of death and terror, questions typical both of the culture of Nordic society and of the Western world.

B's camera follows the person who speaks, seldom the one who listens. He again avoids extreme close-ups. Only during the conversation between Karin and Minus in the beginning of the film does he make a long sweep. At times, the transitions between the pictures are drawn-out and hesitant, as when the helicopter disappears in the sky. This technique has already been used in *Illicit Interlude*. The dramatic aspect of the dialogue is built on a strong feeling for the characters' facial contrasts, on spatial relations. This placing in space the theater can never imitate, although two persons on a stage can be screened off to intimacy. Only the film can create the concentration that gives B's lines their meaning.

His way of presenting his actors has little consistency. He almost never uses the depth compositions that Gregg Toland brought to mastery in some films of the 1940's. His naturalism broadens beyond naturalism. In the commonplace details he finds evil and good omens, just as Strindberg did. Simple occurrences achieve a deep added meaning.

Surprisingly enough, we find that *Through a Glass Darkly* is akin to comparative tendencies in other important modern films. B pays less and less regard to external action. Within the framework of the scene, he tries to deepen the image of the participants, to penetrate them, like a microscope. The short sequence becomes autonomous. Let us consider the dinner sequence, which begins with Martin cutting his finger as he opens beer bottles. The reactions of the cast to the food (which David has prepared), to David's announcement of his forthcoming trip, to the presents, the interplay between David and the rest —all aim at a heightened picture of the emotional interplay be-

tween them. What occurs on the screen does not lead the external action forward. The film wants to know something about
man, of the reality in which he moves.

Jean-Luc Godard works in the same manner when he dis-
solves reality into fragments. The only difference is that in *To
the Last Breath* and *A Woman Is a Woman* he uses the camera
in a living manner as a creative medium. He shows other realities.
His exploration takes place in a reality which the eye would not
be able to catch without the aid of the camera. The cutting is
broken up. The pictures tie to each other without any visible external consistency. But the emphasis of the unique value of the
scene is the same. The important thing is the creative attitude
toward the medium, the ability to forget previously acquired
knowledge and to act as if one knew nothing.

I do not believe that B will forsake the personal questions
which he has felt to be urgent. In *Through a Glass Darkly* he has
left behind him the tendencies to artistic self-will which sometimes destroyed the balance of his earlier films, sequences in
which the play with words became meaningless or where the
observation was solely private, where the strength of the feeling
in what was seen did not reach the spectator. Cool restraint is
nothing innate with B, but rather the result of many years' struggle against uninhibited subjective experience. At the same time
he has felt strongly the desire to experiment with the medium,
to test its creative possibilities. The two tendencies threatened
to destroy purity. Hysterical emphasis became an end in itself.

As regards the medium itself, as well as B's development, he
has now gone as far as possible toward a new classicism. B has the
courage and the right in his films to emerge as one who strives
backward. He is opposed to popular tendencies. His path is
not blazed in order to be copied. Its meaning lies in the fact that
it is important for *him*. The road from unrestrained rhetoric
has led to a stylization which may be dangerous as a general
road for the film art to follow. For B, however, it has brought

great results. Even in *The Seventh Seal* and *Wild Strawberries* certain pictures bore the stamp of an antiquated conventionalism. *Through a Glass Darkly* has burned them off.

## Winter Light

It has been said, not without justice, that the somewhat bombastic end of *Through a Glass Darkly* is alien to the film's narrative, its clean and clear entirety. Viewed with *Winter Light*, however, this final sequence becomes explainable, as an introduction to and hint of what B later was to tell. The closing dialogue in *Through a Glass Darkly* forms the nucleus from which B developed the central theme of *Winter Light*.

*Through a Glass Darkly* ends with a conversation between Minus and the father in the latter's study. Karin has been taken away, and Martin has gone with her. The two, father and son, who remain on the island, look out of the window. Minus is plagued by fear and uncertainty. The answer David gives him is that God is love, and that God is encompassed in love. Their love surrounds Karin, who is on her way to the unknown countries.

It is impossible to rid oneself of the feeling that this end is perhaps too obvious, a too conciliatory indication, a compromise intended to disperse the gloominess of the story. As a last line, Minus says: "Daddy talked to me!" This could be regarded as containing something new, a harmony which, in the future, is to mark the father-son relation. The dramaturgic fault with these words is that they almost entirely lack basis in what has gone before. The words as such are not justified by the action.[8] The declaration of faith about God and love makes more sense when it is discussed in *Winter Light*. Since Karin is the dramatic central figure in *Through a Glass Darkly*, the film actually ends with her being sent away.

The main character in *Winter Light* is Pastor Tomas Ericsson, a widower of middle age. The part is played, like the father in *Through a Glass Darkly*, by Gunnar Björnstrand. But it is not his acting or his person, but the meaning of the story that shows the accord between the two films. Exactly the same words which the father uses to his son in *Through a Glass Darkly*, Pastor Ericsson is said to have used in his sermons: "God is love and love is God. Love is the proof of God's existence. Love is found as something real in man's world." These words, applied to the father-pastor, achieve a strangely ironic meaning, since neither of these persons seems to live up to his gospel. The doctrine is helpless and crippled, because the proclaimers of the doctrines are themselves weak.

*Winter Light* is a more difficult film than *Through a Glass Darkly* for reasons that have a certain fundamental importance for the interpretation of B's art. In this book I have tried to show that B's Christianity is so complicated and at the same time so general and capable of being regarded from a non-Christian viewpoint that it can be replaced by any faith. I maintain that B's inspiration is Christian, but that his film dramas can apply to all people. The question of what he believes in, or if he believes in anything, therefore becomes of no concern, so long as the nonbeliever or the believer in something else manages to penetrate into B's world, the world of his characters. The moral discussion in his films, the question of the possibilities of choice, often builds on Christian conceptions and is worked into a Christian symbolism. B's art, however, would lack universal validity if its problems applied only to Christians.

The possibilities of love and living together are discussed in both *Through a Glass Darkly* and *Winter Light*. In the latter picture, however, some central sections seem to be direct descriptions of Christian rites, executed in such a way that one who cannot share the emotional content of the scenes is also unable to experience the meaning of the film. The difficulty of finding a way to the film is thus increased. One feels a great distance between one's self and the action and is forced to regard what happens too much from the outside. At the same time, *Winter Light* has carried B a bit toward a greater immobility in the narrative, a development that has been foreshadowed earlier, and which happily is broken with *The Silence*, B's later work.

A synopsis of the action in *Winter Light* in analytical form gives an idea of the difficulties of transferring B's vision, difficulties that apparently exist even for B himself. *Winter Light* is the shortest feature film B has made. Pastor Tomas Ericsson serves in a small parish somewhere in central Sweden. The picture opens with a communion service in the medieval church of Mittsunda. Tomas is the officiant. Present are all the persons who play a role in the subsequent action: the school teacher Märta Lundberg, the fisherman Jonas Persson and his wife Karin, Fredrik Blom, Algot Frövik, and the sexton Aronsson. The communion service is told with documentary, immediate sharpness, with a concentration on the human face and on minute details that is almost unique in B's production.

Over the film's introduction hovers an atmosphere of early winter, the November winter as one experiences it in Scandinavia. The first words in the manuscript indicate this: "It is twelve o'clock on a Sunday toward the end of November. Dusk is falling over the plains, and the wind carries a raw dampness from the marshes to the east." The shots of the landscape around the church interpolate the story of the communion. One gets a feeling of cold and of abandonment. Although the communion in a Christian sense is a kind of release and deliverance, there remains through the entire film the same mood of doomsday and death. This is found in the words, but even more in the images, in their blackness, their strangely enigmatic life.

*Winter Light* is a film about people whose emotional balance has been jolted. Nothing in the film appears to be in equilibrium. It is a trying, nerve-tingling film. B has himself said of *Winter Light* that it is the first film where he does not posture for the audience. Perhaps he means, and we can agree with him, that *Winter Light* in some way is closed within itself. It appears to be made without any consideration for the spectators' existence, without any consideration for a public. In this manner the film stands by itself, independently, in B's production.

The scenes after the communion delineate the themes of conflict that move around Tomas, the pastor. He is an unhappy man. One feels, all through the story, what the pastor describes as God's silence. No one is able to reach the clergyman. He has lost the ability to commune with his God. Obviously, this means on the earthly plane that he has lost the ability to talk to other people and to understand their motives. Religiously and humanly, he is sterile, as was the father in *Through a Glass Darkly* on an artistic plane.

Tomas's paralysis is shown in his relationship to Märta Lundberg and fisherman Persson and his wife. After the morning service the Perssons come to Tomas. The wife does the talking. She is expecting a child. She reveals her husband's worry. He has read in the papers about the Chinese, that they are educated to hate. They will acquire atomic weapons. Perhaps they will also destroy the earth. Tomas asks Jonas Persson to come back later for a private talk. But when Jonas returns, he has to listen to a monologue by the minister, in which he voices his own fear and uncertainty. One gets the impression that Tomas is trying to console himself rather than the fisherman Persson. He has loved his God from selfishness, his God has been a spider god, a monster (a verbal coincidence with *Through a Glass Darkly*). Tomas has not been able to combine reality with his Christianity, as an anecdote about his past permits the spectator to surmise:

"I knew nothing of cruelty or evil. I was like a little child when I was ordained. Then everything came all at once. I became by chance a seamen's chaplain in Lisbon. This was during the Spanish civil war, and we had a front row seat. I refused to see and understand. I refused to accept reality. I and my God lived in a world, a special world, where everything tallied. All around us the bloody real life was in the throes of agony. But I didn't see it. I turned my eyes to my God."

Considering that Jonas Persson has called on the minister for a personal (and general) problem, considering the feeling of alarm that has gripped him, we can understand that the pastor's comments cannot help him. The minister's words and work, like the father's in the preceding film, thereby take on something of parody as well as great irresponsibility and an extreme self-absorption.

A short time passes after the conversation between the two. An old woman who was present at the communion service enters the church and reveals that Jonas Persson has shot himself. It is then a matter of the technique of the film that Persson's death does not concern the spectator. The suicide seems to have occurred immeasurably far from the present. It is only with the visit the minister later makes to the home of the Perssons, to inform them of the death, that we come to understand the scope of the tragedy, a misfortune that strikes the pastor harder and deeper. For he is partially guilty, a man who wants to help but cannot help.

The complex of emotions connected with Persson's feelings and actions B has earlier interpreted and touched upon. Doomsday has never been far from his characters. As early as *The Seventh Seal* we got a picture of the threat of nuclear weapons. Never before, however, has B more clearly revealed the mechanism of psychological terror than he has done here in these chamber plays.

The dominating conflict in *Winter Light* is, however, enacted between Tomas and Märta Lundberg. She is 33 years old, a public school teacher in the community. She is rather ugly, with an almost twisted face, wears an old worn sheepskin coat and moves stiffly, hesitantly. She wears glasses, is nearsighted. After the morning service, she brings Tomas coffee; but he has his own coffee. Everything she does to come closer to Tomas seems to be wrong. She loves Tomas. She has sent him a long letter, which he reads when alone, just before Jonas Persson is expected to return for their conversation. B lets Märta Lundberg speak the letter, in one long close-up into the camera, instead of using a more conventional technique. In one place, though, the reading is interrupted by an inserted scene which Märta narrates. This scene appears to be a mistake.

It is a confession she is making. Like the actor Johan Spegel in *The Magician*, she asks Tomas to "use" her. This prayer Spegel addressed to the unknown. For Märta Lundberg the supplication means something else. The letter ends with these words: "I love you and I live for you. Take me and use me. Inside all false pride and pretended independence I have only one wish: to live for somebody. It is becoming terribly difficult."

A decisive conversation between them takes place in the bare classroom where Märta teaches. The talk is a continuation of her letter, and forms, emotionally, a high point in the film. Märta's care for Tomas is getting on his nerves. His mind is still fixed on the memory of his dead wife, whom he asserts he has loved. He is a man who does not seem to understand love as a mutual condition of dependence. He has only sought imprisonment and chains. At the same time he wants to flee from the imprisonment. For Märta he becomes at last a zero, a nonentity. She weeps, and this weeping of abandonment is the film's only moment of emotional release.

Still she accompanies him (at his request) to Frostnäs for the second service of the day. The film covers a period of time not much longer than it takes to enact it. In spite of this, almost every scene appears to be loaded with imports and hidden meanings that are threatening, sickening, and depressing. It may be said that *Winter Light* does not deal with what it seems to deal with—the menace of atomic weapons, God's silence—but rather, fundamentally, with the problem of belonging together which B so often has described.

Two scenes, in which B in a fruitful fashion seems to have assimilated influences from the outside (I am thinking particularly of Antonioni's *La Notte*), illustrate at the same time the feelings of distance and lack of contact which are characteristic of *Winter Light*. The first scene is the minister's visit to a desolate place by a waterfall where Jonas Persson has been discovered dead. Of the conversation carried on there, only snatches can be understood. Everything else is drowned in the roar of the water. In this black, forest-shadowed November it suddenly begins to snow. When Tomas and Märta are driving, they have to stop for an approaching train. A minute earlier Tomas has told her that his parents always wanted him to become a minister. The rest of what he says cannot be heard, but we may suppose that it has to do with parental fixation, under the pressure of which he has lived.

The service at Frostnäs, which closes the picture, confirms the themes earlier taken up in the story.

In the forenoon, the rheumatic Algot Frövik has indicated that he wants to speak to the pastor. Now at Frostnäs he comes out with his errand. He has read in the gospels about the sufferings of Christ, and has found that the physical torment was not the worst, for it lasted only four hours. The worst was the moment of doubt, when Jesus found himself forsaken by God and man. The disciples were asleep, all was silence. This was God's silence, the same one that Tomas says he feels.

While Frövik is talking to Tomas, Märta learns the truth about the minister's wife in the meeting room of the church. Tomas loved his wife until her death, without for a moment noticing her falseness.

The end is the tragic part. When the church bells have stopped ringing, calling the worshippers to the service, nobody from the congregation has shown up, except Märta. Tomas still decides to officiate, defying the silence and his doubts. He praises his God, although he is shut off from Him. It is possible to imagine that the relationship of Tomas-Märta will continue in the same defiance, without Tomas's comprehending what he has done wrong, why he acts in such a constricted manner.

Of its kind, *Winter Light* is the most impressive film B has created. One may also, however, view it from a critical perspective, with respect to both the style and the perceived meaning. The movement of the film, the individual compositions, the essence of its cinematography are the result of great and loving care. But in its narrative style there is a touch of calculation, which prevents the spectator from being surprised. One often meets exactly the images and the attitudes one has been expecting. The spontaneous movement is gone, and has been replaced by a masterly asceticism, which also can become academic. *Winter Light* may appear too evenly gray in its character.

The author David and pastor Tomas Ericsson seem to symbolize the breakdown of the metaphysical questions. David is partly a hypocrite. Tomas has chosen to take orders out of consideration for his parents. He has wished for a God who would give him security. But in the moment of examination which constitutes the film he realizes his failure. It does not matter whether God exists or not. The world is easier to explain without Him. Man is freer. To learn to love is to learn the possibilities of communion and consolation, and it is toward these things that the characters are striving.

Strangely enough, a parallel can be drawn between *Winter Light* and *The Devil's Wanton*, in spite of the very different cinematographic movement. "If God does not exist, all is permitted." This peculiar maxim makes the starting point for both

*The Devil's Wanton* and *Winter Light*. The characters in these two pictures are not quite ordinary people. They are both attracted to and threatened by the judging authority known as God, who could be called the Father. They seek a way of revolt, but seek security just as much. They are half-hearted and remain tied to problems that have to do with the existence of the Father and of security. The difference between *Winter Light* and some of the earlier pictures is that in *Winter Light* is seems more difficult to translate the statement of problems to a non-Christian plane.

The central personality in the film is Tomas. But the one who has most to give, dramatically, is Märta, for whom the problem of belonging is the main thing. If her striving is viewed in isolation, a rather strange circumstance may be observed. As with many other women of B's, she can realize herself only through the man. She is unhappy about the drawn-out dissension with Tomas. Although she appears independent and clear-sighted, it is assumed she lacks the strength for independence and a life of her own. The image she desperately tries to hold on to is that of woman as a serving and faithful being. It is a philosophy and a way of life which possibly to a great extent is tied up with patriarchal thinking, evident in those of B's films for which he himself has written the manuscript. (The women in *Crisis* and *Brink of Life* are different.) Comments of this kind make possible the allegation that B's idea of society is antiquated, or builds on the bourgeois moral code of the past. The problem is not that simple, but it is worth noting.

In its analysis of the moment, its winter mood, *Winter Light* is perhaps the most adequate expression of B's striving for stylistic perfection. He describes a breakdown of certain ideas which obviously are or have been relevant to him as an artist. He tells of a psychological threat which is released in self-destruction. He continues on the way where possibilities are still open.

### The Silence

When shooting of *The Silence* started, B explained that this film concluded a trilogy which began with *Through a Glass Darkly*.[9] *The Silence* is connected with the two previous films, but at the same time one can say that it is a preface to something new. In a very distinctive manner the cinematographic form reveals two contrasting paths in B's development. On the one hand, there is the striving for ascetic bareness; on the other hand, there is the tendency to an almost tasteless baroque style, as if there was a synthesis of Dreyer and Fellini.

*The Silence* is the mature B's masterpiece. *Through a Glass Darkly* is superior in human content and expressive power, but as a pure film achievement *The Silence* is more convincing. In the latter the dramatic substance can be said to have been thinned out almost to the point of annihilation. So highly has B developed his talent for subtle nuances that in *The Silence* he can let almost nothing happen and still keep his audience captivated.

*The Silence* is not built around the dialogue, but proceeds from the visual. Its dialogue is very scanty. It follows naturally on the two preceding works of the trilogy in that it, too, does not touch upon current problems of society except in a symbolic, indirect way. But the feeling of threat and destruction, of irritation and the collapse of emotions, is apparent all through the narrative.

A short recapitulation of the film's events gives an idea of this: On a train bound from somewhere to somewhere are two sisters, Ester and Anna, and the latter's son, Johan. The sisters are in their thirties. Of their past we learn that their father, who is dead, was an undisputed, dominating authority. Ester has been deathly ill for a long time. By profession she is a translator, an

intellectual. A strong rivalry, bordering on hatred, exists between the sisters. Ester spies on Anna, watches her, and seems
long to have dominated her. One senses that Ester's childless-
ness is a source of inhibitions. Anna is a creature of instincts;
Ester reflects about everything. The sisters are two poles of the
same soul.

The trip is interrupted in a strange city, since Ester must
rest. The language spoken in this city is one unknown to the
three travelers and is almost completely unrelated to their own.
The city is called Timoka or Timokas. B has explained that this
is the dative form of the Estonian word meaning executioner.
In other ways, too, the language appears to be a loan from the
Finno-Ugric tongues. For instance, Ester learns the expression
for "hand" in the strange language: "*kasi*"—Estonian for hand.
For B, the point seems to be the alienation, the noncommunica-
tion in itself. But behind the barriers of language there are other
obstacles to understanding between Ester, Anna, Johan, and the
others. The social reality in Timoka is completely different.
Only the music—Bach—remains as a common denominator.

The two sisters and Johan establish themselves in an old hotel
with frightening corridors, draperies, doors, old paintings, and
other objects. The description of this milieu, as well as the street
on which they live, takes up much space in *The Silence*. Johan
explores the corridors. Sound and light produce the impression
of frightening, oppressive reality. More strongly than ever before, B has managed to emphasize the role of the surroundings
in the narrative.

Since the sisters cannot read the language of the country and
do not understand what is being said, we do not really know
where we are, in what period of time. Everything in this landscape assumes grotesque, dreadful dimensions. One hears alarm
sirens, sees soldiers. A tank rolls down the street. The setting
may be imagined as Central Europe of the refugees and the
homeless, in a postwar period or a period of waiting for a war.[10]

*The Silence* may therefore be said to reflect or build on experiences familiar to great parts of Europe's population—but not to the Swedes. Anna, Ester, and Johan are some kind of displaced persons, always fleeing from something. This flight becomes for B an excuse to treat their personal problems. As always before, he succeeds in translating general problems into individual human drama. This enormous sensitivity is a key to his success. Although the discussions among the actors may concern abstract events, we can always measure the importance of these problems for the persons themselves, their inner life, their happiness or lack of it.

Ester is ill, stays in bed, drinks and smokes. She seems paralyzed by hatred and envy, perhaps because she knows she will die. She tries to learn a few words in the strange language. An old floor waiter keeps her company. When she remembers the past, it is summer, the Northern summer, she thinks of. Summer, which in some earlier films by B assumed a concrete form and became one of the main actors in the narrative, is transformed in *The Silence* into a swiftly passing recollection.

When Ester tries to cheer up Johan, it is the same summer she depicts for him.

Anna feels the oppressive atmosphere of the hotel, and takes a walk. In a nearby bar she meets a waiter-bartender, to whom she quickly feels herself attracted. He is younger than she. They seem to agree to meet in the hotel. Johan sees them enter a room. He tells this to Ester. She goes to find her sister in the room, where some wild scenes of wordless passion are enacted. Hatred appears when Ester accusingly tries to stop her sister.

A limitless solitude surrounds the film's two women. The end of the story is that Johan and his mother resume their journey, while Ester is left alone to die.

*The Silence* did not change much on the way from manuscript to finished film. The basic character is the same, and there are few abridgments. The visual pattern is already found in the manuscript. This confirms a peculiarity in B's film work, which perhaps has been overlooked. He lacks an original, innovating visual inspiration of the sort which Rossellini, Antonioni, or Fellini (to mention but Italians) possess. During the production of his films, B cannot greatly change the pattern which he has already given. This is also hinted at in some anecdotes told by B himself. He was an autodidact of the film, without any intimate knowledge of the possibilities of that medium. While producing some of his earlier films, he would often go to the cinema and be influenced by the films he saw. Thus he worked (if one may exaggerate somewhat) from day to day, and he followed the pattern of the film he had seen on the previous night. In another connection, B speaks about the effect Visconti's *La terra trema* would have had on him if he had seen that film when it was made, instead of more than a decade later.

In *The Silence* the narrating style is independent but not original. Thanks to the fortunate circumstance that the film in a way has three parallel plots, Ester, Anna, and Johan, B can achieve mobility and surprise in the narrative. In this film he works with the technique of pictorial shocks. He has an ability to captivate the spectator which is not surpassed by many contemporary directors. One needs only to think of certain unexpected scenes, for example, when Johan visits a group of dwarfs performing in town. He goes to their hotel room; they receive him with delight, dress him up as a girl, and dance around him. The scene has no clearly stated significance; it just is there.

The shocks are spread throughout the entire film: Johan's wanderings and discoveries, the bar where Anna meets the waiter, the picture of a starving horse in the street, the tank passing by the hotel, Ester's attacks of illness. But B's skill is expressed primarily through the quick cuts from scene to scene and in his ability to grasp, with short characteristic pictures, an entire life situation. It is all the more surprising that in certain scenes between the two sisters B degenerates into long, monotonous sequences and irritating pan shots, instead of resorting to quick and effective cutting. These are breaches of style that can only be explained by the fact that B here, just as sometimes earlier, allows the literary content of the scene to dominate, rather than the image as independent expression.

In other respects, *The Silence* is a film in which B's creation of a free visual form reaches an unusually high level. Both interiors and exteriors have the right atmosphere of unreality, with realistic details as points of support for the eye. The black-and-white image in *The Silence* has a unique richness of shading, which the photographer Sven Nykvist has attained through an unusual exposure of the negative. The images are created with a extraordinary feeling for shadows and light, but this never becomes an end in itself, estheticism. Both the composition of the images and the play of shadows have a strong dramatic meaning. The old truth that only what is well planned can appear to be improvised is confirmed once more.

The effect of disharmony, which constitutes the basis of the drama in *The Silence*, could not, however, have been achieved through pure imagery alone. B has always had the ability to let silence speak and to make the most of pauses. This time he has gone even further. In *The Silence* we are dealing with a creative innovation in sound montage. Realistic effects are remarkably few. B is not interested in those details which lack dramatic meaning. He stylizes; he emphasizes particulars. Nothing in the soundtrack can be said to be entirely accidental. We are dealing with an extraordinarily sensitive musical composition, in which the phrasing does not consist of tones such as we traditionally conceive them, but of all the sounds of reality. There is no music in the film, but Ester tunes in Bach on the radio. It is a bridge of understanding to that other world, which is the city of Timoka. It is a language which the old waiter also understands.

In Swedish society today the motive of economic security as

a factor in human conduct has been partly pushed into the background. This is not true for all citizens, but it is valid for large
segments of society. That is why it can be said that B's disengage-
ment from social questions and his indifference to what can be
considered as contemporary Swedish problems are both understandable and symbolic. The social question which remains to
be solved, when outward security has been achieved, is the
question of balance on the personal level, in the inner life. This
aspiration can never lead to a definitive result, since perfection
and happiness are remote mirages which man sets up for himself.
The dreamer, who in a moment of exaltation demands everything, has now been replaced in B's art by the realist, who is content with the simple compromises of life. Anna goes to bed with
the bartender in the gloomy hotel room, aware that this moment
will not last.

It is strange that in B's film creations the image of man is at
the same time extremely abstract and obtrusively physical. It is
a contrast which appears in the making of *The Silence*. Dissonant
elements are fused together superbly. As in his earlier films, B
gives few answers. He draws the picture of a human being's
terminus, a zero position almost beyond despair. Neither Ester
nor Anna can be free any more. One can see them as a cinematographic expression of the struggle between psyche and bodily
existence which the creative writer has described in all ages.
Ester and Anna are pure types, and yet they are living persons.

In the printed Swedish edition of the manuscript of *The
Silence*, one reads about "God's silence—the negative print," B's
formulation of what the film is about. The expression is preten-
tious and curiously misdirected. Swedish critics have also followed the same line, when they tried to interpret *The Silence*
as a Christian film—because, forsooth! it deals with the absence
of God. But nowhere does one seem to discover among the
persons in the film motives of action which have anything to do
with Christian questions. B goes back once more to the struggle

for authority which is so central to his films. Now he has finally given up the use of Christian symbolism which has seemed to be too little adapted to the real content of his films. When their father died, Anna says, Ester no longer wished to live. But just as the father had dominated Ester, so did Ester determine Anna's actions. At the end of the film, Anna has perhaps been freed from this, but it has not made her happier.

There is a peculiar disgust apparent in *The Silence*, a contempt for mankind which earlier had been seen in B's films only in glimpses. It is not connected with the fact that what the persons do is so dishonorable, but with B's' continuing tendency toward irrationalism. The conscious, consciously acting person is still for him something of an exception. Even so, the trilogy which B completed with *The Silence* becomes in its way as valuable as Antonioni's great film trilogy. The stubbornness and passion with which B handles his material are unique. It is not the critic's business to suggest that he use different material.

## Not To Speak About All These Women

B's first color film, which is both a farce and a comedy, carries this long title. It was made during the spring and summer of 1963 and is expected to have its Swedish premiere sometime in 1964. In this film B has assembled many of the actors who have been successful in his earlier films. But the central figure is a man, Cornelius, who is writing the biography of the great musician Felix.

The manuscript, which is written by B in collaboration with Erland Josephson, contains B's usual mixture of invention and autobiography. The great master Felix is permanently invisible. In his house live seven women who at some time or other have been his mistresses. His secretary and servant keep the most intriguing secrecy round the master's life. Cornelius is a some-

what ridiculous but serious-minded person who makes up his
mind to expose the secrets about the master.

The dialogue in *Not To Speak About All These Women*
sounds mostly stale and uninspired. It is really hard to become
enthusiastic about this manuscript, full of eclecticism as it is. B
uses the technique of the silent film period (the film is supposed
to be taking place in the twenties), and the film is rich in color.
Also, some of the situations as such have comic value. The film's
technical production is certainly going to obtain good results.
One's attitude toward the whole, the intention, is more skeptical.

*Not To Speak About All These Women* is a relatively harmless divertissement made with the purpose of entertaining, of
creating relaxation after the arduous effort demanded by the
trilogy. The farce is somewhere between *Smiles of a Summer
Night* and *The Devil's Eye*, perfumed like the former, uninspired like the latter. This does not exclude the fact that B in
his way can create a work which appeals to the public. My
analysis of B's films has taken no position toward such questions. Popular success is never a measure of a film's value, but
merely a measure of what seems to attract the public at a given
moment.

It is, of course, another matter that B has often displayed
almost crude, public-attracting features in his films. *Not To
Speak About All These Women* consciously courts the public,
and even *The Silence* does this, although on a much more subtle
level. Here is expressed the dependence of film art upon an in-
dustry, and perhaps also the desire of a film artist to be flattered
and talked about. It is a human trait.

With some obvious exceptions, film art for B has seldom
been a play with images. It was therefore possible for him to
reach the seriousness of prayer, the power of confession. He has
permitted his imagination to associate freely. On the basis of

personal material and subjective questions, he has staged a series of films which in their compact effect are without parallel in modern motion pictures. This does not mean that they cannot be surpassed, or that other paths are closed.

The play with images is executed by artists who do not feel any responsibility extending beyond the borders of art. But even if the work of art is an answer in itself, action in itself, a rebuttal is needed, a spectator, a protest or an agreement. B feels this responsibility. His development has meant a continuous release from the narrow problems to which his society and his own milieu have given rise.

Like Tolstoy, he has inquired about the meaning of art, whether it has any purpose except to gratify man for a moment. In this endeavor, B has come to ask more questions than he can ever answer. He has posed great, metaphysical questions, about the existence of God and of a judging or delivering authority. Perhaps he has at last found that all this is meaningless so long as man cannot solve the simple problems of living with others, so long as he cannot enjoy the moment which is his life.

Film art may seem time-bound, inhibited, because the gestures shown belong to a specific epoch. The words are our words on this very day. But this inhibition is at the same time a strength, since prose fiction can never achieve the same sensitivity of real life. The popularity of film among the broad masses depends not only upon the fact that it is the art form of the age of democracy and mass communication, but just as much upon the directness with which it can speak to all, or to selected groups. Possibly in some future and happier time B's problems may seem petty. Nobody, however, can seriously deny that they symbolize an epoch.

An evaluation of B's artistic aim becomes warped if it hews to his own general and theoretical pronouncements. We might imagine that B would agree with the ethico-esthetic view with which Tolstoy ends "What is Art?" Pained by the inadequacy of art and its insufficient contact with the advancement of a suffering humanity, Tolstoy wrote:

"The task for art to accomplish is to make that feeling of brotherhood and love of one's neighbour, now attained only by the best members of society, the customary feeling and the instinct of all men. By evoking under imaginary conditions the feeling of brotherhood and love, religious art will train men to experience those same feelings under similar circumstances in actual life; it will lay in the souls of men the rails along which the actions of those whom art thus educates will naturally pass. And universal art, by uniting the most different people in one common feeling by destroying separation, will educate people to union and will show them, not by reason but by life itself, the joy of universal union reaching beyond the bounds set by life.

"The destiny of art in our time is to transmit from the realm of reason to the realm of feeling the truth that well-being for men consists in their being united together, and to set up, in place of the existing reign of force, that kingdom of God—that is, of love—which we all recognize to be the highest aim of human life.

"Possibly in the future science may reveal to art yet newer and higher ideals which art may realize; but in our time the destiny of art is clear and definite. The task of Christian art is to establish brotherly union among men."[11]

BIOGRAPHICAL NOTES

NOTES TO THE BOOK

BIBLIOGRAPHY

FILM INDEX

# Biographical Notes on Bergman

(Ernst) Ingmar Bergman was born July 14, 1918, in the university city of Uppsala, fifty miles northwest of Stockholm. He passed his college entrance examination in 1937, after which he fulfilled his national defense conscription service. When this was finished, he began studying at the University of Stockholm, where he received his B.A. degree. Almost simultaneously with his university studies, he commenced his theatrical activities as an amateur director in a religious society.

Bergman is the son of a Protestant minister. This churchly, Christian inheritance has exerted a strong influence upon him, something which Bergman himself has emphasized in a lecture, "Det att göra film." In this he states: "When one is born and reared in the home of a minister, one has a chance at an early age to catch a glimpse behind the scenes of life and death. Father conducts a funeral, father officiates at a wedding, father performs a baptism, acts as a mediator, writes a sermon. The devil became an early acquaintance, and, in the way of a child, it was necessary to render him concrete. It was here the magic lantern came in, a little tin box with a kerosene lamp (I can still remember the smell of hot sheet metal) and the gaily colored glass slides. Little Red Riding Hood and the Wolf, among others. And the wolf was the devil, a devil without horns, but with a tail and wide, red jaws, strangely tangible, but still impalpable, the representative of evil and seduction on the nursery's flowery wallpaper."

The Protestant milieu made Bergman brood over such questions as guilt and reconciliation, punishment and forgiveness. He was surrounded by culture and tolerance, but few surroundings are congenial and tolerant enough to accept fully violent revolt and violent self-assertion of the kind that were to characterize Bergman's work, at least at the beginning of his career.

There is reason not to overemphasize the Protestantism in Bergman's formative years, but to concentrate rather on the bourgeois aspect of his background. Since the nineteenth century why the middle class made its definite emergence in Swedish society, it has retained and carried on certain customs and outlooks on life. It is a matter of forms of life which appear hermetically sealed beside the open and mobile society which has become a reality. It is known in modern history that members of the middle class who revolt become revolutionaries in politics and art. It is equally well known that in many of these who revolt the escape from their origin has taken an apolitical character, that criticism concentrates almost entirely on particulars, forgetting the foundations of the way of life that is being criticized. A lack of community interest can therefore, as is probably the case with Bergman, harmonize admirably with a criticism of certain individual representatives of the bourgeoisie: the pedants, the clergy, the bureaucrats, the military, the spokesmen of power.

The old middle-class way of life has, as a pattern, taken on a fixed, settled rhythm. Adolescence is marked by the influence of paternal authority. The father is often the distant Power, the mother represents what is near and intimate, mysterious and sensual. The father watches over both the home and the world outside. Life is supposed to follow a definite rhythm. The home

offers protection, but also paralysis and isolation. The family
is still the center of life. The young ones are habituated to an
existence in which certain habits seem self-evident. The sum-
mers are spent in the country, in a villa owned by the family. A
certain tolerance exists, but it does not stretch so far as to permit
criticism of the fundamentals on which the middle-class way of
life is built. At the end of the school years, the college entrance
examination is passed, after which the children supposedly begin
their university studies, preferably to follow in their father's
footsteps (as far as the oldest son is concerned). After a period of
revolt, the majority reconciles itself to the ideals the preceding
generation has left it.

The foregoing sketch of a bourgeois life is by no means lifted
from Bergman's biography, but it probably corresponds to the
general course of events he experienced. If one does not wish
to submit the personal development of an artist to a regular
psychoanalysis, one can only suggest the auspices under which
the coming of age took place.

Between the years 1938 and 1944, when Bergman took the step
toward the professional theater, he directed some twenty plays
on amateur stages in Stockholm. One of these, *The Death of
Punch*, also marked his debut as a dramatist. Bergman continued
his very uneven, but interesting, dramatic production until the
middle of the 1950's when his drama *Painting on Wood*—the
latest one up to now—was produced. It forms a preliminary
study for *The Seventh Seal*. Bergman considers today that he can
no longer write plays, since his dialogue is entirely built according to the demands and specific possibilities of the film.

The year 1944 was an important one in Bergman's development. Two years earlier he had come into contact with Sweden's
leading film producer, Svensk Filmindustri, for which he re-
wrote novels and other literary material, which was never
screened. He also turned in manuscripts of his own. One of these
was *Torment*, which was filmed in 1944 under the direction

of Alf Sjöberg and served to carry Ingmar Bergman's name out into the world. In *Torment* Bergman himself worked as an assistant to the director, and the following year he was regarded as ready to make his debut as a full-fledged motion picture director.

But 1944 was important also in another respect: Bergman inaugurated his brilliant professional theatrical career. Aside from the other Northern countries, Germany, and perhaps eastern Europe, there is nothing comparable to the position which the theater enjoys in Sweden. The City Theater in Hälsingborg, of which Bergman was appointed director in 1944, was a small playhouse in a rather small city of southern Sweden. The theater had deteriorated, artistically as well as economically. In two years Bergman managed to get it on its feet. One of the authors he was interested in then—as he is now—was August Strindberg. His B.A. dissertation at the university concerned Strindberg. And Bergman has long had plans to film something by that dramatist, but the plans unfortunately have never been realized. In the spring of 1963 he staged Strindberg's *Ghost Sonata* on Swedish television.

In the spring of 1946 he moved from Hälsingborg to the Gothenburg Theater, where he exerted a similar rejuvenating influence. After interludes in various places he inaugurated, in 1952, at the Malmö City Theater, a career that lasted until the end of 1958 and founded his European fame as a stage director. The playhouse is one of the most modern in Europe. Under Bergman's direction it developed into something unique in Sweden as regards ensemble acting and artistic harmony. The repertory, which Bergman himself staged, varied between drama and operetta, but was constantly distinguished by the same artistic discipline.

At the Malmö City Theater several actors were then active who either earlier had been, or later were to become, Bergman's foremost interpreters, such as Harriet Andersson, Bibi Andersson, Ingrid Thulin, and Max von Sydow. Bergman has became widely famous both in the film and in the theater for his instruction of actors, for his ability to extract from even unknown and untried faces a maximum of genuine power of expression. During the time Bergman has been active in film and in the theater he has discovered and created more new actors than any other Swedish director.

A summary of Bergman's activity in the theater shows that between 1938 and 1962 he staged about seventy productions, in addition to some thirty radio theater performances and five television presentations. If we at the same time bear in mind his dramatic output and his movie work, we get an idea of his enormous working capacity.

Bergman left the Malmö City Theater in 1959 and accepted a post as director at the Royal Dramatic Theater in Stockholm. There, and at the Royal Opera in the capital, he has, however, staged only one production. His presentation of Stravinsky's *Rake's Progress* at the Opera will surely become a classic.

Bergman's present position is about as follows:

As a film director he works currently only for Svensk Filmindustri, although a joint production with an American company has been discussed. Svensk Filmindustri has produced most of Bergman's films, but it must be recalled that some of the most daring ones, such as *The Devil's Wanton* and *The Naked Night*, had other producers—Lorens Marmstedt and Rune Waldekranz/Sandrews, respectively.

The drafts of both these films were submitted to Svensk Filmindustri, but were rejected. It was only *Smiles of a Summer Night* that made Bergman an economically successful director. If any single person should be mentioned who was of importance to Bergman, it is probably the head of Svensk Filmindustri, Dr. C. A. Dymling (dead two years), whose personal encouragement meant much to him.

Today, Bergman is the leading director at Svensk Filmindustri, and acts as a sort of artistic counselor. This means that the course of Swedish production to a decisive degree will be influenced by Bergman's own decisions.

On January 14, 1963, Ingmar Bergman was chosen to head Sweden's national theater, the Royal Dramatic Theater in Stockholm. For the immediate future his new position will require Bergman to be bound more closely to the stage than he has previously been, since the management of such a large and diverse institution as Sweden's national theater demands strength and time. The first two performances that Bergman directed for the theater were *Who's Afraid of Virginia Woolf?* and Hjalmar Bergman's *Sagan* (The Myth). Earlier he had successfully staged the latter play in Malmö.

In spite of his new position Bergman's film work will continue. During 1963 two of his films were premiered; during 1964 his color comedy *Not To Talk About All These Women* will appear, and at the same time Bergman is probably preparing an international production for 1965.

Bergman is married to the pianist Käbi Laretei, by whom he has a son. From earlier marriages he has six children. He lives in a villa near Stockholm, seldom moves outside the borders of Sweden, and, in spite of his international outlook, seems Swedish to an almost nationalistic degree.

# Notes

## 1 · FAME AND SIGNIFICANCE

1. Penelope Houston, "Into the Sixties," *Sight and Sound*, XXIX, No. 1 (Winter, 1959-1960), p. 5.
2. "Det förtrollade marknadsnöjet" (The enchanted pleasure of the market), *Biografbladet*, No. 3 (Autumn, 1947).
3. *Ibid.*
4. Guido Oldrini, "Lo sfondo culturale della critica su Ingmar Bergman," *Cinema Nuovo*, No. 144 (March-April, 1960).
5. Cited from Bengt Holmqvist, *Svensk 40-talslyrik* (Stockholm, 1951), p. 8. The history of ideas of the Swedish forties is yet unwritten.
6. Karl Vennberg in the anthology *Kritiskt 40-tal* (Stockholm: Karl Vennberg and Werner Aspenström, 1948), p. 241.
7. Guido Aristarco, "Da Dreyer a Bergman," in *Film 1961*, edited by Vittorio Spinazzola (Milan: Feltrinelli Editore, 1961).
8. Oldrini, "Lo sfondo culturale della critica su Ingmar Bergman."
9. "Varje film är min sista film" (Every film is my last film), *Filmnyheter*, Nos. 9-10 (May, 1959), pp. 1 ff.
10. "Det att göra film" (The making of films), *Filmnyheter*, Nos. 19-20 (December, 1954).
11. Lionel Trilling, "Bergman Unseen," *The Mid-Century*, No. 20 (December, 1960), p. 6.
12. This is what Arnold Hausen insists in his great work *Sozialgeschichte der Kunst und Literatur*, Band II (Munich, 1953).
13. Jurgen Schildt, "Brev till Ingmar Bergman," *Vecko-Journalen*, 15 (1958).
14. Henri Agel, *Les grands cinéastes* (Paris: Editions Universitaires, 1959).

15. The critic is Bengt Idestam-Almquist.
16. "Om att filmatisera en pjäs" (On making a film of a play), *Filmnyheter*, No. 4 (1946), pp. 6 f.
17. *Kris* (Copenhagen: Det Danske Filmmuseum, 1960).
18. Ulla Isaksson, *Nära Livet* (Stockholm: Rabén & Sjögren, n.d.), p. 15.
19. *Ibid.*
20. Eric Rohmer, "Voir ou ne pas voir," *Cahiers du Cinéma*, No. 94 (April, 1959), pp. 48 f.
21. Louis Marcorelles, "Rétrospective Bergman," *Cahiers du Cinéma*, No. 85 (July, 1958), p. 13.
22. Isaksson, *Nära Livet*, p. 40.
23. Jean Béranger, *La grande aventure du cinéma suédois*, edited by Eric Losfeld (Paris: Le Térrain-Vague, 1960).
24. Antonio Napolitano, "Dal settimo sigillo alle soglie della vita," *Cinema Nuovo*, No. 151 (May-June, 1961).
25. I owe this thought to Fereydoun Hoveyda, "Le plus grand anneau de la spirale," *Cahiers du Cinéma*, No. 95 (May, 1959).
26. Bergman, "Fisken. Fars för film" (The Fish: A farce for film), *Biografbladet*, No. 4 (Winter, 1950-1951), pp. 220 ff.; No. 1 (Spring, 1951), pp. 18 ff.; No. 2 (Summer, 1951), pp. 85 ff.; No. 3 (Autumn, 1951), pp. 110 ff.
27. Jacques Siclier, *Ingmar Bergman* (Paris: Editions Universitaires, 1960), p. 12.
28. Bengt Idestam-Almquist, *Classics of the Swedish Cinema: The Stiller & Sjöström Period* (Stockholm: Swedish Institute, 1952), p. 10.

## 2 · THE ROAD FROM *TORMENT*

1. Lars Ahlin, *Bark och löv* (Stockholm: Albert Bonniers förlag, 1961), pp. 17 f.
2. Lasse Bergström, "Maskspel med ödets avsikter," in *Skott i mörkret, filmessäer* (Stockholm: Wahlström & Widstrand, 1956), p. 7.
3. See Eugene Archer, "The Rack of Life," *Film Quarterly*, XII, No. 4 (Summer, 1959), p. 6.
4. Stig Dagerman: Opinion expressed in the periodical *40-tal*, No. 1 (January, 1947), p. 9.
5. This theme is suggested in Bengt Petersen's introduction to the film, Det Danske Filmmuseum, March, 1953.

6. Uttalande om Hets i filmens programblad, 1944.
7. See the announcement of the film in "Rétrospective Bergman" and Bengt Chambert's article, "Ingmar Bergmans 'Det regnar på vår kärlek,'" Biografbladet, No. 4 (Winter, 1946), pp. 235 ff., in which the author refers to a speech by Bergman at Uppsala the previous spring in which he depicted Carné as one of the few great directors.
8. Chambert, "Ingmar Bergmans 'Det regnar på vår kärlek.'"
9. Gerd Osten, Nordisk Film (Stockholm: Wahlström & Widstrand, 1951), p. 69.
10. Siclier, Ingmar Bergman, p. 22.
11. Where no other source is given, certain statements by B himself are cited from conversations with him during the year 1961. Dialogues cited from the films are generally taken from the manuscripts but corrected according to what the actors actually say.
12. Uttalande om Eva i filmens programblad, Stockholm, 1949.
13. Hugo Wortzelius, "Eva—en ingmarbergmansk vändpunkt?" (Eva—a turning point for Ingmar Bergman?) Biografbladet, No. 2 (Summer, 1949).
14. Erik Ulrichsen, "Skepp till Indialand," Det Danske Filmmuseum Programblad, n.d.
15. Wortzelius, "Ensamhet och gemenskap" (Loneliness and Togetherness), Biografbladet, No. 4 (Winter, 1947).
16. Ulrichsen, "Skepp till Indialand."
17. The statement about Rossellini was found in the Göteborgs-Tidningen, July 5, 1948, in a coverage of the shooting of the last scenes of the film.
18. F. D. Guyon, "Ingmar Bergman," Premier Plan, No. 3 (November, 1959), pp. 20 f.
19. Monthly Film Bulletin (January, 1953), p. 9.

3 · THE DEVIL'S WANTON

1. Filmen om Brigitta-Carolina, Stockholms-Tidningen, March 18, 1949, p. 4.
2. Bengt Idestam-Almquist in Stockholms-Tidningen, March 20, 1949.
3. The short story is kept in the archives of Svensk Filmindustri.
4. Bergman, Kinematograf, Biografbladet, No. 4 (Winter, 1948), pp. 240 f.

5. Jerker A. Eriksson, "Ingmar Bergmans 'Fängelse,' " *Nya Pressen,* May 21, 1953.
6. Jean Douchet in *Cahiers du Cinéma,* No. 95 (May, 1959), pp. 51 ff.
7. Jerker A. Eriksson, "Ingmar Bergmans 'Fängelse.' "
8. The song is mentioned in Georg Svensson's review in BLM (*Bonniers Litterära Magasin*), No. 4 (April, 1949), pp. 315 ff.
9. "Filmen om Birgitta-Carolina" (The Film about Brigitta-Carolina), *Stockholms-Tidningen* (March 18, 1949), p. 4.
10. Erik Ulrichsen, "Ingmar Bergman and the Devil," *Sight and Sound, XXVII* (Summer, 1958), p. 224.

## 4 · SUMMER AND DEATH

1. Harry Schein in BLM, No. 3 (1950), pp. 232 f.
2. *Sydsvenska Dagbladet,* Malmö, September 9, 1945.
3. *Hälsingborgs Dagblad,* January 24, 1946.
4. Ingmar Bergman berätter om en film om det bästa som finns (Ingmar Bergman tells of a film about the best there is), 1951.
5. Stated in Fritiof Billquist's *Ingmar Bergman—teatermannen och filmskaparen* (Stockholm: Natur och Kultur, 1960), p. 151.
6. John Simon, "Ingmar the Image-Maker," *The Mid-Century,* No. 20 (December, 1960), p. 13.
7. Jacques Rivette in *Cahiers du Cinéma,* No. 84 (June 1958), pp. 45 ff.
8. Osten, *Nordisk film,* p. 45.
9. Harry Schein, "En ny Bergman?" (A New Bergman?) BLM, No. 9 (November, 1951), pp. 713 f.
10. Jean-Luc Godard, "Bergmanorama," *Cahiers du Cinéma,* No. 85 (July, 1958).
11. Peter John Dyer in his review, *Monthly Film Bulletin* (March, 1960), p. 33.
12. Siclier, *Ingmar Bergman,* p. 71.
13. Rakel och biografvaktmästaren (Rakel and the Movie Doorman) in *Moraliteter* (Moralities) (Stockholm: Albert Bonniers förlag, 1948).

## 5 · THE NAKED NIGHT

1. Alf Montán's interview with B in *Expressen,* September 15, 1953.
2. "Varje film är min sista film," 1959.

3. The pen name "Filmson" in *Aftonbladet,* September 15, 1953.

4. "Det att göra film," 1954.

5. Jerker A. Eriksson, "Gycklarnas afton," *Nya Pressen,* April 20, 1954.

6. Carl Björkman in *Dagens Nyheter,* September 15, 1953.

7. Opinions on music in films in *Biografbladet,* No. 4 (Winter, 1949-1950), pp. 246 f.

8. Ib Monty, Det Danske Filmmuseum, duplicated program, May, 1957.

9. Jos Burvenich, "Thèmes d'inspiration d'Ingmar Bergman," *Collection Encyclopédique du Cinéma,* Edit. Brussels: Club du livre de cinéma, No. 4 (March, 1960).

10. Archer, "The Rack of Life," p. 9.

11. Siclier, *Ingmar Bergman,* pp. 84 f. When B made *The Naked Night* he had not seen *The Blue Angel.*

12. Louis Marcorelles, "Rétrospective Bergman," p. 12.

13. Ado Kyrou has analyzed this theme in a review in *Positif,* No. 27 (February, 1958), pp. 38 ff.

14. Erich Rohmer, "Oeuvre truculente et blaséé la nuit des forains nous révèle le visage du plus grand cinéaste suédois Ingmar Bergman," *Arts.*

15. This thought is advanced by Siclier in his "Le style baroque de La nuit des forains de Ingmar Bergman," *Etudes cinématographiques,* Nos. 1-2 (1960).

16. Archer, "The Rack of Life," p. 15.

17. *Ibid.*

18. *Ibid.,* p. 16.

19. Siclier, "Le style baroque . . . de Ingmar Bergman."

## 6 · INTERLUDE

1. From articles by Hanserik Hjertén and Olof Lagercrantz respectively in *Expressen,* February 3, 1956, and *Dagens Nyheter,* March 10, 1956.

2. Jouko Tyyri, "Kvinnans skratt," *Hufvudstadsbladet,* February 16, 1957.

3. In his review of *En lektion i kärlek* in *Combat,* December 14, 1959, Pierre Marcabru was the first to compare this film with *Smultronstället.*

4. Jean Wagner in *Cahiers du Cinéma,* No. 103 (January, 1960), pp. 58 ff.

5. Jean Collet, "Rêves de femmes," *Télé-ciné*, No. 85 (October, 1959), Fiche No. 342.
6. Jerker A. Eriksson, "Anemisk teknik," *Nya Pressen*, September 17, 1955.
7. Georges Sadoul, "Ingmar Bergman et le cinéma suédois," *Les Lettres Françaises* (June 27, 1956).
8. This theory of the presentation of past time in the film is brought out in Siegfried Kracauer, *Theory of Film* (New York: Oxford University Press, 1961).
9. Tyyri, "Kvinnans skratt."
10. *Ibid.*
11. Béranger, *La grande aventure du cinéma suédois*, p. 246.
12. The theme is considered by Mauritz Edström in *Dagstidningen/ Arbetaren*, 1956.

## 7 · THE SEVENTH SEAL

1. Carolina Blackwood, "The Mystique of Ingmar Bergman," *Encounter*, XVI, No. 91 (April, 1961), pp. 54-57.
2. "Varje film är min sista film."
3. Marianne Höök in *Svenska Dagbladet*, February 17, 1957.
4. Andrew Sarris, "The Seventh Seal," *Film Culture*, No. 19 (1959).
5. *Moraliteter*, 1948.
6. Uttalande om det sjunde inseglet i filmens utländska program-blad, Stockholm: Svensk Filmindustri, 1957.
7. Johan Chydenius, "Det sjunde inseglet," *Nya Pressen*, October 6, 1958.
8. Blackwood, "The Mystique of Ingmar Bergman," p. 55.
9. Napolitano, "Dal settimo sigillo alle soglie della vita."
10. Ivar Harrie, "Ingmar Bergman vill vara Sveriges Kaj Munk" (Ingmar Bergman wants to be the Kaj Munk of Sweden), *Expressen*, March 2, 1957.
11. Sarris, "The Seventh Seal."
12. Blackwood, "The Mystique of Ingmar Bergman," p. 55.
13. Harry Schein, "Poeten Bergman," BLM, No. 4 (April, 1957).
14. "Varje film är min sista film."
15. The conception that an art which discusses man's conditions for existence is the social art of our time is advanced with great

brilliance by Villy Sörenson in his collection of essays, *Hverken —eller* (Copenhagen: Gyldendal, 1961). I have not, however, been able to work it into my book.

16. Jos Burvenich, "Ingmar Bergman à la trace de Dieu," *Art d'Eglise*, No. 113 (1960).
17. Colin Young's review of the film in *Film Quarterly*, XIII, No. 3 (Spring, 1959), pp. 42 ff.
18. From Sartre's *Le Être et le Néant*, p. 137; quoted in Iris Murdoch, *Sartre: Romantic Rationalist* (New Haven, Conn.: Yale University Press, 1953), pp. 43-44.
19. "Staden. Hörspel" (The City: A radio play). In *Svenska Radiopjäser 1951* (Stockholm: Sveriges Radio, 1951), pp. 49 ff.
20. Napolitano, "Dal settimo sigillo alle soglie della vita."
21. Schein, "Poeten Bergman."
22. Rudolf Arnheim, *Film as Art* (Berkeley: University of California Press, 1958), particularly the last essay, "A New Laocoön: Artistic Composites and the Talking Film," and also Kracauer's above-mentioned *Theory of Film*. Unfortunately, too much in our contemporary film esthetics discussion is based on Arnheim's opinions.
23. Napolitano, "Dal settimo sigillo alle soglie della vita."
24. Sarris, "The Seventh Seal."
25. *Ibid.*
26. Eric Rohmer in *Arts*, April 23, 1958.

## 8 · WILD STRAWBERRIES

1. *Works* of August Strindberg, 11 (Stockholm: Albert Bonnier förlag, 1946), p. 348.
2. Frédéric Durand, "Ingmar Bergman et la littérature suédoise," *Cinéma 60*, No. 47 (June, 1960).
3. Hoveyda, "Le plus grand anneau de la spirale."
4. Lawrence S. Kubie, *Practical and Theoretical Aspects of Psychoanalysis* (New York: International Universities Press, 1950; Praeger Paperbacks, 1960), p. 20.
5. Bengt Idestam-Almquist, *Classics of the Swedish Cinema*, p. 48.
6. See "Delar av ett tal till minne av Victor Sjöström" (Excerpts from a speech in memory of Victor Sjöström), *Sight and Sound*, XXIX, No. 2 (Spring, 1960), p. 98.
7. These circumstances have been pointed out by Bengt Idestam-

252    NOTES FOR PAGES 157-185

Almquist in a comparison between Sjöström and Ingmar Bergman in *Folket i Bild*, No. 7 (1958).

8. Aristarco, "Da Dreyer a Bergman."
9. Eugene Archer in *Film Quarterly*, XIII, No. 1 (Fall, 1959), p. 44.
10. An interview with Sven Thiessen: "Ingmar Bergman does not want to vomit on the audience," *Arbetaren*, August 31, 1958.
11. Eugene Archer in *Film Quarterly* (Fall, 1959), p. 44.
12. Kenneth Cavander in *Sight and Sound*, XXVIII, No. 1 (Winter, 1958-1959), p. 35.
13. "Der Weg nach innen," pen name "ms" in *Neue Zürcher Zeitung*, November 4, 1960.
14. Eugene Archer in *Film Quarterly* (Fall, 1959), p. 44.
15. *Moraliteter.*
16. Jean Collet, "Les fraises sauvages," *Télé-ciné*, No. 85 (October, 1959), Fiche No. 356.

9 · THE ARTIST'S FACE

1. Cited from Edmund Wilson, *The Wound and the Bow: Seven Studies in Literature* (New York: Oxford University Press, 1947; paper edition, 1961).
2. Gilbert Salachas, "Quand Ingmar Bergman prend la parole," *Télé-ciné*, No. 86 (November-December, 1959).
3. Carl-Eric Nordberg, "Det gåtfulla ansiktet" (The mysterious face), *Vi*.
4. Stig Wikander, "Magiker eller frälsare?" *Svenska Dagbladet*, January 4, 1959.
5. Jurgen Schildt asked these questions in his "Brev till Ingmar Bergman."
6. Georges Sadoul, "Ambigu dramatique," *Les Lettres Françaises*, October 8, 1959.
7. Åke Runnquist, "Bakom 'Ansiktet,'" *BLM*, No. 9 (November, 1959).
8. Etienne Dor, "Le visage," *Télé-ciné*, No. 86 (November-December, 1959), Fiche No. 359.
9. Herbert Grevenius, "Vänporträtt av ung man," *Stockholms-Tidningen*, September 16, 1947.
10. Aristarco, "Da Dreyer a Bergman."
11. "Det Förbjudna. Det Tillåtna. Det Nödvändiga" (The Forbidden. The Allowed. The Necessary), *Vi på SF* (April, 1957).

## 10 · THE VIRGIN SPRING

1. Göran O. Eriksson in *Kosmorama*, No. 49 (April, 1960), pp. 154 f.
2. Jean Wagner, "La fontaine d'Aréthuse," *Cahiers du Cinéma*, No. 120 (June 1961), pp. 52 f.
3. Vittorio Spinazzola in *Cinema Nuovo*, No. 150 (March-April, 1961), pp. 150 f.
4. The argument is here developed in support of Louis Marcorelles, "Au pied du mur," *Cahiers du Cinéma*, No. 116 (February, 1961), pp. 51 ff.
5. Victor Svanberg in *Chaplin*, No. 9 (March, 1960), pp. 62 f.
6. In an article in *Stockholms-Tidningen*, October 9, 1960, Sven Ulric Palme has referred to Asta Ekenwall, *Häxan, djävulen och paddan* (The Witch, the Devil, and the Toad) (Stockholm: published by the Fredrika Bremer Association in the jubilee Kvinnovärld i vardande, 1960).
7. Vernon Young in *Film Quarterly*, XIII, No. 4 (Summer, 1960), p. 45.
8. "Kinematograf" (Cinematography), *Biografbladet*, No. 4 (Winter, 1948), pp. 240 f.
9. On February 21, 1960, *Svenska Dagbladet* published a roundup in which most of the participants were of the opinion that exactly these scenes could have been cut from the film without hurting its artistic values. But none of the participants in the roundup was competent in matters of film.
10. Cited from *Film: Book 1, The Audience and the Filmmaker*, edited by Robert Hughes (New York: Grove Press, 1959), pp. 40-41.
11. This motif has been discussed by Göran O. Eriksson in his above-mentioned review in *Kosmorama*.
12. Björn Julén in *Svenska Dagbladet*, February 21, 1960.
13. This chapter is based on Jörn Donner, "Ingmar Bergmans 'Jungfrukällan,'" BLM, No. 3 (March, 1960).

## 11 · CHAMBER PLAYS

1. Gustav Janouch, *Gespräche mit Kafka* (Frankfurt am Main: Fischer Verlag, 1951, 1961.)
2. Guido Aristarco strongly emphasizes the relationship with

Kierkegaard in his essay, "L'aut-aut di David nell'opera di Bergman," *Cinema Nuovo*, No. 159 (September-October, 1962), pp. 383 ff.

3. Even Marlene Dietrich in her *A B C* (New York: Doubleday, 1962, p. 35) knows about Bergman's thoroughness: "When he was planning his first film in color, he sent his entire staff to have their eyes examined for color blindness." This is true.

4. In somewhat similar ways Bergman watched Victor Sjöström during the shooting of *Wild Strawberries*. See *Sight and Sound*, XXIX, No. 2 (Spring, 1960), p. 98.

5. In Swedish, "Den gula tapeten" in *Stora Skräckboken*, edited by Torsten Jungstedt (Stockholm: Rabén & Sjögren, 1959), pp. 321 ff; in English, "The Yellow Wallpaper" in *Ghostly Tales to Be Told*, edited by Basil Davenport (New York: Dodd, Mead, 1950). William Dean Howells, who included "The Yellow Wall Paper" by Charlotte Perkins Stetson Gilman in his anthology, *Great Modern American Stories* (New York, 1920), pp. 320-337, reports that the story was turned down by *The Atlantic* because "it was so terribly good that it ought never to be printed"; he, however, "corrupted the editor of *The New England Magazine* into publishing it" in 1899.

6. The parallel has been analyzed in an insinuating manner and off the point by Stig Ahlgren, "Riset bakom spegeln," *Vecko-Journalen*, No. 47 (November 24, 1961).

7. "Det att göra film," 1954.

8. The treatment of *Through a Glass Darkly* is based on a long review by Jörn Donner in *Dagens Nyheter*, October 17, 1961; the same review has been published in English in *Atlas* (March, 1962), pp. 247 f.

9. Interview in *Dagens Nyheter*, May 29, 1962.

10. It was originally intended to make the film in various Southern and Central European cities, but the plan had to be abandoned and sets were constructed in Sweden. It concerns only the street on which the hotel is situated.

11. Leo Tolstoy, *What is Art? and Essays on Art*, translated by Aylmer Maude (The World's Classics 331; London: Oxford University Press, 1930), p. 288.

# Bibliography

*Ingmar Bergman*

Uttalande om Hets i filmens programblad (A statement on *Torment* in the film program), 1944.

"En kortare berättelse. Om ett av Jack Uppskärens tidigaste barndomsminnen" (A brief narrative about one of Jack Uppskärens earliest childhood recollections), *40-tal*, No. 3 (1944), pp. 5 ff.

"Om att filmatisera en pjäs" (On making a film of a play), *Filmnyheter*, No. 4 (1946), pp. 6 f.

"Filmen slår ihjäl sig" (The film commits suicide), Lecture given at Uppsala students' film studio, May 13, 1946.

*Jack hos skådespelarna* (Jack among the actors). Stockholm: Albert Bonniers förlag, 1946.

"Det förtrollade marknadsnöjet" (The enchanted pleasure of the market), *Biografbladet*, No. 3 (Autumn, 1947).

"Tre tusenfotingfötter" (Three feet of the centipede), *Filmjournalen*, No. 51-52 (1947).

"Kinematograf" (Cinematography), *Biografbladet*, No. 4 (Winter, 1948), pp. 240 f.

*Moraliteter. Tre pjäser: Rakel och biografvaktmästaren, Dagen slutar tidigt, Mig till skräck* . . . (Moralities. Three plays: Rakel and the movie doorman, The day ends early, To my horror . . .). Stockholm: Albert Bonniers förlag, 1948.

Uttalande om Eva i filmens programblad (A statement on *Eva* in the film program), Stockholm, 1949.

"Filmen om Birgitta-Carolina" (The film about Birgitta-Carolina), *Stockholms-Tidningen*, March 18, 1949, p. 4.

"Fisken. Fars för film" (The Fish: A farce for film). Part I: *Biografbladet*, No. 4 (Winter, 1950-1951), pp. 220 ff. Part II: No.

1 (Spring, 1951), pp. 18 ff. Part III: No. 2 (Summer, 1951), pp. 85 ff. Part IV: No. 3 (Autumn, 1951), pp. 110 ff.
"Leka med pärlor" (Playing a game with pearls), *Filmnyheter*, No. 14 (1951),
"Staden. Hörspel" (The City: A radio play). In *Svenska Radiopjäser 1951* (Stockholm: Sveriges Radio, 1951), pp. 49 ff.
"Vi är cirkus!" (We are the circus!) *Film-Journalen*, No. 4 (January 25, 1953).
Uttalande om Sommaren med Monika i filmens programblad (A statement on *Monika* in the film program), Stockholm, 1953.
"Ingmar Bergman om film," *Nya Pressen* (Helsingfors), March 23, 1953.
"Sagan om Eiffeltornet" (Story about the Eiffel Tower), BLM (*Bonniers Litterära Magasin*), No. 9 (September, 1953).
"Trämålning. En moralitet" (Painting on wood: a morality). In *Svenska Radiopjäser 1954* (Stockholm, 1954), Reprinted as a one-act play for amateurs (Stockholm: Albert Bonniers förlag, 1956).
"Det att göra film" (The making of films), *Filmnyheter*, No. 19-20 (December, 1954); a lecture given at Lund, November 25, 1954.
"Filmskapandets dilemma" (The dilemma in making films), *Hörde ni?*, No. 5 (1955), pp. 427 ff.
"Det Förbjudna. Det Tillåtna. Det nödvändiga" (The Forbidden. The Allowed. The Necessary), *Vi på SF* (April, 1957).
Uttalande om Det sjunde inseglet i filmens utländska programblad (A statement on *The Seventh Seal* in the film's foreign program), Stockholm: Svensk Filmindustri, 1957).
"Ingmar Bergmans självporträtt skrivet av honom själv" (Ingmar Bergman's self-portrait written by himself), *Se*, No. 9 (1957), p. 33.
Uttalande om Ansiktet i filmens utländska programblad (A statement on *The Magician* in the film's foreign program), Stockholm: Svensk Filmindustri, 1958.
"Dialog," *Filmnyheter*, No. 11 (September 1, 1948).
"Varje film är min sista film" (Every film is my last film), *Filmnyheter*, No. 9-10 (May, 1959), pp. 1 ff. Also printed separately (Stockholm: Svensk Filmindustri, 1959).
Också separat som särtryck (Also separateness as an impression). Stockholm: Svensk Filmindustri, 1959.
Dagboksutdrag om inspelningen av Jungfrukällan i filmens utländska programblad (Excerpts from a diary about the filming of *The*

*Virgin Spring* in the film's foreign program), Stockholm: Svensk Filmindustri, 1960.

*Four Screenplays.* London: Secker and Warburg, 1960; New York; Simon and Schuster, 1960.

"Delar av tal till minne av Victor Sjöström" (Excerpts from a speech in memory of Victor Sjöström), *Sight and Sound* (Spring, 1960), p. 98.

"Förbön" (Intercession), *Chaplin*, No. 14 (November, 1960), p. 187.

"Artikel under signaturen Ernest Riffe," *Chaplin*, No. 14 (November, 1960), pp. 189 ff.

Uttalande om Djävulens öga i filmens programblad (A statement on *The Devil's Eye* in the film program), Stockholm, 1961.

"Ingmar Bergman ser på film" (Ingmar Bergman looks at films). Bandinspelad intervju om Damen med hunden. *Chaplin*, No. 18 (March, 1961), pp. 60 f.

"Vågskvalp i bakvatten. Bandinspelad intervju." (The sound of waves in a backwater. A taped interview), *Chaplin*, No. 20 (May, 1961), pp. 124 ff.

Uttalande om Såsom i en spegel i filmens programblad (A statement on *Through a Glass Darkly* in the film program), Stockholm: Svensk Filmindustri, 1961.

"Såsom i en spegel. Bandinspelad intervju" (*Through a Glass Darkly:* A taped interview), *Chaplin*, No. 23 (November, 1961), pp. 212 ff.

*Oeuvres.* Paris: Robert Laffont, 1962. (The book includes the scripts of *Sommarlek* and *Gycklarnas afton* in addition to the ones in *Four Screenplays.*)

"För att inte tala om alla dessa skådespelare" (Not to speak about all these actors. A taped interview), *Chaplin*, No. 39 (September, 1963), pp. 178 ff.

*En filmtrilogi.* Stockholm: Norstedts, 1963. (The book contains the scripts of *Såsom i en spegel, Nattvardsgästerna* and *Tystnaden,* with a short introduction by the author.)

Books, Essays, and Articles about Bergman

(Note: A personal selection by the author. Film reviews have been omitted.)

Agel, Henri. *Les grands cinéastes.* Paris: Editions Universitaires 1959.

Ahlgren, Stig. "En skön själs bekännelse," *Vecko-Journalen*, No. 17 (April 28, 1956).

———. "Riset bakom spegeln," *Vecko-Journalen*, No. 47 (November 24, 1961).

Allombert, Guy. "Le septième sceau," *Document Image et Son*, No. 119 (February, 1959).

Alpert, Hollis. "Bergman as Writer," *Saturday Review*, XLIII (August 27, 1960).

———. "Style is the Director," *Saturday Review*, XLIV (December 23, 1961).

Archer, Eugene. "The Rack of Life," *Film Quarterly*, XII, No. 4 (Summer, 1959).

Aristarco, Guido. "I volti e le possibilità astratte," *Cinema Nuovo*, No. 141 (September-October, 1959).

———. "Da Dreyer a Bergman," in *Film 1961*, edited by Vittorio Spinazzola. Milano: Fetrinelli Editore, 1961.

———. "L'aut-aut di David nell'opera di Bergman," *Cinema Nuovo*, No. 159 (September-October, 1962).

Ayfre, Amédée. "Portée religieuse du 'Septième sceau,'" *Télé-ciné*, No. 77 (August-September, 1958).

Azeredo, Ely. "Noites de circo," *Revista de cinema*, No. 22 (April-May, 1956).

Baldwin, James. "The Precarious Vogue of Ingmar Bergman," *Esquire* (April, 1960). (Reprinted in his *Nobody Knows My Name*. New York: The Dial Press, 1961.)

Bassotto, Camillo. "La fontana della vergine," *Cine Forum*, No. 3-4 (May-June, 1961).

Benayoun, Robert. "Docteur Bergman et Monsieur Hyde," *Positif*, No. 30 (July 30, 1959).

Béranger, Jean. "Les trois métamorphoses d'Ingmar Bergman," *Cahiers du Cinéma*, No. 74 (August-September, 1957).

———. "Renaissance du cinéma suédois," *Cinéma 58*, No. 29 (July-August, 1958).

———. "Rencontre avec Ingmar Bergman," *Cahiers du Cinéma*, No. 88 (October, 1958).

———. *Ingmar Bergman et ses films*. Paris: Le Térrain-Vague, 1959.

———. *La grande aventure du cinéma suédois*, Eric Losfeld, ed. Paris: Le Térrain-Vague, 1960.

———. "Ingmar Bergman s'interroge: Dieu est-il méchant?" *Arts*, Paris (April, 18, 1962).

Bettetini, Gianfranco. "Le radici dell'individualista, *Schermi*, No. 29 (January-February, 1961).

———. "Primi piani: Ingmar Bergman," *Rivista del cinematografo*, No. 1 (January, 1961).

Beyer, Nils. "Ingmar Bergman," *Vecko-Journalen*, No. 41 (1947).

Billquist, Fritiof. *Ingmar Bergman—teatermannen och filmskaparen*. Stockholm: Natur och Kultur, 1960.

Björkman, Stig. "Analisi del film," *Cine Forum*, No. 14 (April, 1962).

Blackwood, Caroline. "The Mystique of Ingmar Bergman," *Encounter*, XVI, No. 91 (April, 1961).

Bodelsen, Anders. "Den svenske filmdigter," *Berlingske Aftenavis* (September 25, 1962).

Boris, Jean-Bernard, and Syr, Gérard. "La nuit des forains," *Films et Documents*, No. 127, Fiche.

Brodal, Jan. "Om Ingmar Bergmans filmer," *Arbeiderbladet*, Oslo (August 17, 1963).

Buchwald, Gunnar. "Intervju med Ingmar Bergman," *Berlingske Tidende* (November 20, 1960).

Burvenich, Joseph. "Thèmes d'inspiration d'Ingmar Bergman," *Collection Encyclopédique du Cinéma*, Edit. Bruxelles: Club du livre de cinéma, No. 4 (March, 1960).

———. *Ingmar Bergman zoekt de sleutel*. Den Haag: Lannoo Tielt, 1960.

———. "Ingmar Bergman à la trace de Dieu," *Art d'Eglise*, No. 113 (1960).

———. "Ingmar Bergman scrute la vie," *Christliche Kunstblätter*, Linz an der Donau (February, 1963), Sonderheft Film 63.

Chiaretti, Tommaso. A book on Bergman will be published by Canesi Editore in 1964.

Cole, Alan. "Ingmar Bergman, Movie Magician," *New York Herald Tribune* (October 24, November 1, November 8, 1959).

Collet, Jean. "Rêves de femmes," *Télé-ciné*, No. 80 (January-February, 1959), Fiche No. 342.

———. "Les fraises sauvages," *Télé-ciné*, No. 85 (October, 1959), Fiche No. 356.

Cowie, Peter. *Ingmar Bergman*. Loughton, Essex: Motion Publications, 1961.

Donner, Jörn. "Noter till Ingmar Bergman," *Studio 3, Filmens årsbok 1957*. Borgå, 1957.

——. "Sylvetki wspótczesnych realizatorów szwedzkich," *Kvartalnik Filmovy*, No. 3 (1957).

——. "Ingmar Bergmans billede af Sverige," *Politiken* (February 18, 1962).

——. "Kammerspil," *Kosmorama*, No. 56 (February, 1962).

——. "Traditionen i svensk film I: Victor Sjöströms 'Ingeborg Holm,'" *Dagens Nyheter* (September 4, 1963).

——. "Traditionen i svensk film II: En konstart söker sitt språk," *Dagens Nyheter* (September 10, 1963).

——. "Traditionen i svensk film III: Vägen utför och uppåt," *Dagens Nyheter* (September 14, 1963).

Dor, Etienne. "Le visage," *Télé-ciné*, No. 86 (November-December, 1959), Fiche No. 359.

Durand, Frédéric. "Ingmar Bergman et la littérature suédoise," *Cinéma 60*, No. 47 (June, 1960).

Edström, Mauritz. "Ingmar Bergman och hans värld," *Dagens Nyheter* (April 29, 1962).

——. "Ämnet Ingmar Bergman," *Dagens Nyheter* (December 20, 1962).

Eklann, Thorsten. "40-talistisk filmmoralitet," *Biografbladet*, No. 1 (Spring, 1949).

Elenberg, Fernando. "Una conversación con Ingmar Bergman," *La Prensa*, Buenos Aires (July 2, 1961).

Elmund, Sylvia. "Nattvardsgästerna—en kommentar till Jörn Donners filmkrönika," BLM (*Bonniers Literära Magasin*), No. 3 (March, 1963).

Eriksson, Jerker A. "Ingmar Bergmans 'Fängelse,'" *Nya Pressen* (May 21, 1953).

——. "Gycklarnas afton," *Nya Pressen* (April 20, 1954).

——. "Anemisk teknik," *Nya Pressen* (September 17, 1955).

——. "Ingmar Bergman analyserad," *Hufvudstadsbladet* (May 23, 1962).

Farina, Corrado. *Ingmar Bergman*, Torino: Centrofilm, Quaderni di documentazione cinematografica, 1959.

*Filmklub-Cinéklub*, No. 20 (November, 1959-January, 1960). Special issue of the Zurich periodical on Ingmar Bergman.

Fischer, Gunnar. "Sommarlek med Ingmar Bergman," *Biografbladet*, No. 2 (Summer, 1951).

*Flashback 1: Ingmar Bergman*, edited by Alberto Tabbia, Edgardo Cozarinsky. Buenos Aires: Vaccaro, 1958.

Fleischer, Frederic. "Early Bergman," *Encore*, No. 36 (March-April 1962).

Fogelström, Per-Anders. "Ingmar Bergman," *Folket i Bild*, No. 12 (1956).

Forslund, Bengt. "Prästsonen Ingmar Bergman," *Ord och Bild*, No. 10 (1957).

———. "Bergman och Bergman," *Göteborgs Handels- och Sjöfartstidning* (September 23, 1959).

———. "Nära människan," *Projektio*, Helsingfors, No. 4 (1961).

Fovez, Elic, Ayfre, Amédéc, and D'Yvoire, Jean. "Le septième sceau," *Télé-ciné*, No. 77 (August-September, 1958), Fiche No. 333.

Gauteur, Claude. "Ingmar Bergman," *Cinéma 58*, No. 27 (July-August, 1958).

*Gefängnis*, Kleine Filmkunstreihe, Heft 22. Göttingen, 1961.

Godard, Jean-Luc. "Bergmanorama," *Cahiers du Cinéma*, No. 85 (July, 1958).

Grasten, Bent. "Kris," Det Danske Filmmuseum (November, 1960).

Gravier, Maurice. "Ingmar Bergman et le théatre suédois," *Etudes cinématographiques, textes sur théatre et cinéma*, No. 6-7 (1960).

Grevenius, Herbert. "Vänporträtt av ung man," *Stockholms-Tidningen* (September 16, 1947).

Guyon, F. D. "Ingmar Bergman," *Premier Plan*, Lyon, No. 3 (November, 1959).

Guyonnet, René. "Sur quatres films d'Ingmar Bergman," *Temps Modernes*, No. 142 (December, 1957).

Hardy, Forsyth. *Scandinavian Film*. London: The Falcon Press, 1952.

Hedblom, Oscar. "Ingmar Bergman lyssnar," *Expressen* (July 20, 1963).

Hjertén, Hanserik. "Fallet Bergman eller Sommarnattens Falska Leende," *Filmfront*, No. 1 (1956).

Hopkins, Steven. *Bergman and the critics*. Stockholm: Industria International, 1962.

Hoveyda, Fereydoun. "Le plus grand anneau de la spirale," *Cahiers du Cinéma*, No. 95 (May, 1959).

Höök, Marianne. *Ingmar Bergman*. Stockholm: Wahlström & Widstrand, 1962.

Idestam-Almquist, Bengt. *Dramma e rinascita del cinema svedese*. Roma: Bianco e Nero Editore, 1954.

——. Article in Filmbook, *Orbis*, Uppsala, 1951.

——. "Victor Sjöström och Ingmar—mötet mellan två stora i svensk film," *Folket i Bild*, No. 7 (1958).

Jarvie, Ian. "Notes on the Films of Ingmar Bergman," *Film Journal* (Melbourne), No. 14 (November, 1959).

Kracauer, Siegfried. *Theory of Film*. New York: Oxford University Press, 1961.

Khouri, Walter Hugo. "Notas sôbre Ingmar Bergman," in Program Notes given out at the Film Library of the Museum of Modern Art, São Paulo, 1955.

Kyrou, Ado. "Ingmar Bergman et quelques autres," *Positif*, No. 17 (June-July, 1956).

Lefevre, Raymond. "Sourires d'une nuit d'été," *Image et Son*, No. 109 (February, 1958). Fiche.

——. "La nuit des forains," *Image et Son*, No. 125 (November, 1959), Fiche.

Leirens, Jean. *Le cinéma et la crise de notre temps*. Paris, 1960.

Linder, Erik Hj. "Ingmar Bergman," *Stockholms-Tidningen* (December 31, 1953).

Luritzen, Einar. *Swedish Films*. New York: The Museum of Modern Art Film Library, 1962.

McGann, Eleanor. "The Rhetoric of Wild Strawberries," *Sight and Sound*, XXX (Winter, 1960-1961).

Marcabru, Pierre. "Les interrogations de Bergman," *Arts* (April 19, 1961).

Marcorelles, Louis. "Un auteur moderne: Ingmar Bergman," *France Observateur*, No. 12 (1958).

Marmstedt, Lorens. "Ruda eller Gamba," *Obs!*, No. 18 (September 13, 1950).

Napolitano, Antonio. "Dal settimo sigillo alle soglie della vita," *Cinema Nuovo*, No. 151 (May-June, 1961).

Nordberg, Carl-Eric. Series of articles in *Expressen* (May 18, 20, and 26, 1959).

*Nuovo spettatore cinematografico, II*, Nos. 5, 6 (1959). Special issues on Ingmar Bergman.

Nykvist, Sven. "Photographing the Films of Ingmar Bergman," *American Cinematographer* (October, 1962).

Nystedt, Hans. "Ingmar Bergman om Kristus och Tomas," *Svenska Dagbladet* (April 21, 1963).

Oldin, Gunnar. *Fakta om film*. Stockholm: Norstedts, 1957.

———. "Ingmar Bergman," *American-Scandinavian Review*, XLVII (Autumn, 1959).

Oldrini, Guido. "Lo sfondo culturale della critica su Ingmar Bergman," *Cinema Nuovo*, No. 144 (March-April, 1960).

———. A book on Bergman will be published by Cinema Nuovo Editore in 1964.

Ollier, Claude. "La prison," *Nouvelle Revue Française*, Paris, No. 78 (1959).

Olsson, Jan Olof. "Gossen i mörkrummet," *Dagens Nyheter* (August 22, 1955).

Osten, Gerd. *Nordisk Film*. Stockholm: Wahlström & Widstrand, 1951.

———. *Den nya filmrealismen*. Stockholm: LTs förlag, 1956.

Pedersen, Warner. "Ingmar Bergman," *Information* (May 25, 1949).

Persson, Göran. "Den erotiska kvadraten," *Arbetet* (March 25, 1960).

Petersen, Bent. "Hets," Det Danske Filmmuseum (March, 1953).

———. "Samtal med Ingmar Bergman," *Social-Demokraten* (November 8, 1953).

Renzi, Renzo. "Bergman e l'abolizione dell'Inferno," *Cinema Nuovo*, No. 163 (May-June, 1963).

"Rétrospective Bergman," *Cahiers du Cinéma*, No. 85 (July, 1958).

Rohmer, Eric. "Présentation d'Ingmar Bergman," *Cahiers du Cinéma*, No. 61 (July, 1956).

Runnquist, Åke. "Bakom 'Ansiktet,'" BLM, No. 9 (November, 1959).

Sadoul, Georges. "Ingmar Bergman et le cinéma suédois," *Les Lettres Françaises* (June 27, 1956).

Salachas, Gilbert. "La nuit des forains," *Télé-ciné*, No. 73 (March, 1958), Fiche No. 324.

———. "Jeux d'été," *Télé-ciné*, No. 78 (October, 1958), Fiche No. 339.

———. "Quand Ingmar Bergman prend la parole," *Télé-ciné*, No. 86 (November-December, 1959).

Sarris, Andrew. "The Seventh Seal," *Film Culture*, No. 19 (1959).

Saxtorph, Erik S. "Ingmar Bergman og Alf Sjöberg overför hinanden," *Kosmorama*, No. 20 (October, 1956).

Schein, Harry. "Poeten Bergman," BLM, No. 4 (April, 1957).

Schildt, Jurgen. "Brev till Ingmar Bergman," *Vecko-Journalen*, No. 15 (1958).

Siclier, Jacques. *Ingmar Bergman*. Bruxelles: Club du livre de cinéma, No. 12-13 (1958).

———. *Ingmar Bergman*. Paris: Editions Universitaires, 1960.

———. "Le style baroque de La nuit des forains de Ingmar Bergman," *Etudes cinématographiques*, No. 1-2 (1960).

Simon, John. "Ingmar the Image-Maker," *The Mid-Century*, No. 20 (December, 1960).

Sjöman, Vilgot. "Spänningen Ingmar Bergman," *Vi*, No. 14 (1957).

———. *L-136, Dagbok med Ingmar Bergman*. Stockholm: Norstedts, 1963.

*Spiegel, Der*, No. 44 (October 26, 1960). Cover story on Ingmar Bergman.

Stempel, Hans, and Ripkens, Martin. "Ingmar Bergman," *Filmkritik*, München, No. 9 (September, 1962).

Stolpe, Sven. "Mni vän Ingmar Bergman," *Bildjournalen*, No. 30 (1955).

H.A.T. "Una superación de Bergman," *Film*, Montevideo, No. 21 (June, 1954).

Thiel, Reinold E. "Wie in einem Spiegel" (in Ingmar Bergman, *Wie in einem Spiegel*, Drehbuch). Hamburg: Marion von Schröder Verlag, 1962.

*Time*, LXXV (March 14, 1960). Cover Story on Ingmar Bergman.

Trilling, Lionel. "Bergman Unseen," *The Mid-Century*, No. 20 (December, 1960).

Tyyri, Jouko. "Kvinnans skratt," *Hufvudstadsbladet* (February 16, (1957).

Ulrichsen, Erik. "Skepp till Indialand," Det Danske Filmmuseum, programblad, n.d.

———. "Ingmar Bergman and the Devil," *Sight and Sound*, XXVII (Summer, 1958).

Vermilye, Jerry. "An Ingmar Bergman Index," *Films in Review* (May, 1961).

Waldekranz Rune. *Film från hela världen*. Stockholm: Wahlström & Wildstrand, 1956.

———. "Akademikeren och drömmefabrikken," *Kosmorama*, No. 22 (December, 1956).

———. *Swedish Cinema*. Stockholm: Svenska Institutet, 1959.

Widerberg, Bo. *Visionen i svensk film*. Stockholm: Bonniers, 1962.

Wikander, Stig. "Magiker eller frälsare?" *Svenska Dagbladet* (January 4, 1959).

Wood, Robin. "A Toad in the Bread," *Definition*, No. 3 (1961).
Wortzelius, Hugo. "Ensamhet och gemenskap," *Biografbladet*, No. 4 (Winter, 1947).
——. "Eva—en ingmarbergmansk vändpunkt?" *Biografbladet*, No. 2 (Summer, 1949).
——. "A Decade of Swedish Films," *Biografbladet*, No. 4 (Winter, 1949-1950).
——. "Bergman, il regista piú discusso del recente cinema svedese," *Cinema*, No. 53 (December 30, 1950).
——. "Discorso su Ingmar Bergman, Cinema svedese ieri e oggi," *Quaderni delle FICC*, No. 4 (1952).
——. "Jack och Joakim Naken, Samtal med Ingmar Bergman," *Perspektiv* (1951).
d'Yvoire, Jean. "Sourires d'une nuit d'été," *Télé-ciné*, No. 62 (October, 1956), Fiche No. 289.

Besides reviews in the Stockholm daily press, reviews and articles in the following periodicals have been used: *Bianco e Nero* (Rome), *Biografbladet* (Stockholm), *Biografägaren* (Stockholm), *Cahiers du Cinéma* (Paris), *Chaplin* (Stockholm), *Cinéma 55-* (Paris), *Cinema Nuovo* (Milan), *Definition* (London), *Film Culture* (New York), *Film Journal* (Melbourne), *Film Quarterly* (Berkeley, California), *Films in Review* (New York), *Image et Son* (Paris), *Kosmorama* (Copenhagen), *Monthly Film Bulletin* (London), *Positif* (Paris), *Sight and Sound* (London), *Télé-ciné* (Paris).

# Film Index

1) Year filmed 2) Date of Swedish premiere 3) Produced by (company) 4) Production manager 5) Scriptwriter 6) Director 7) Director of photography 8) Music composed by 9) Set designer 10) Film editor 11) Assistant director 12) Choreographer 13) The cast

TORMENT (British title: Frenzy) (Hets)
1) 1944 2) Oct. 2, 1944 3) Svensk Filmindustri 4) Harald Molander 5) Ingmar Bergman 6) Alf Sjöberg 7) Martin Bodin 8) Hilding Rosenberg 9) Arne Åkermark 10) Oscar Rosander 11) Ingmar Bergman 13) Stig Järrel (*Caligula*), Alf Kjellin (*Jan-Erik Widgren*), Mai Zetterling (*Bertha Olsson*), Olof Winnerstrand (*The school principal*), Gösta Cederlund (*Pippi*), Stig Olin (*Sandman*), Jan Molander (*Pettersson*), Olav Riego (*Director Widgren*), Märta Arbiin (*Mrs. Widgren*), Hugo Björne (*The physician*), Gunnar Björnstrand (*A teacher*), Curt Edgard, Anders Nyström, Birger Malmsten

CRISIS (Kris)
1) 1945 2) Feb. 25, 1946 3)Svensk Filmindustri 4) Lars-Eric Kjellgren 5) Ingmar Bergman from Leck Fischer's play "Moderdyret" 6) Ingmar Bergman 7) Gösta Roosling 8) Erland von Koch 9) Arne Åkermark 10) Oscar Rosander 13) Dagny Lind (*Ingeborg*), Marianne Löfgren (*Jenny*), Inga Landgré (*Nelly*), Stig Olin (*Jack*), Allan Bohlin (*Ulf*), Ernst Eklund (*Uncle Edvard*), Signe Wirff (*Aunt Jessie*), Svea Holst (*Malin*), Arne Lindblad (*The Mayor*), Hjördis Pettersson

IT RAINS ON OUR LOVE (Det regnar på vår kärlek)
1) 1946 2) Nov. 9, 1946 3) Lorens Marmstedt for Sveriges Folk-

biografer 5) Ingmar Bergman, Herbert Grevenius from Oscar Braathen's play "Bra mennesker" 6) Ingmar Bergman 7) Hilding Bladh, Göran Strindberg 8) Erland von Koch 9) P. A. Lundgren 10) Tage Holmberg 13) Barbro Kollberg (*Maggi*), Birger Malmsten (*David*), Gösta Cederlund (*Man with umbrella*), Ludde Gentzel (*Håkansson*), Douglas Håge (*Andersson*), Hjördis Pettersson (*Mrs. Andersson*), Julia Caesar (*Hanna Ledin*), Gunnar Björnstrand (*Herr Purman*), Magnus Kesster (*Bicycle mechanic*), Sif Ruud (*His wife*), Åke Fridell (*The pastor*), Benkt-Åke Benktsson (*The prosecutor*), Erik Rosén (*The judge*), Sture Ericsson (*Kängsnöret*), Ulf Johansson (*Stålvispen*)

WOMAN WITHOUT A FACE (Kvinna utan ansikte) 1) 1947 2) Sept. 16, 1947 3) Svensk Filmindustri 5) Ingmar Bergman 6) Gustaf Molander 7) Åke Dahlqvist 8) Erik Nordgren 9) Arne Åkerman 10) Oscar Rosander 13) Alf Kjellin (*Martin Grandé*), Gunn Wållgren (*Rut Köhler*), Anita Björk (*Frida Grandé*), Stig Olin (*Ragnar Ekberg*), Olof Winnerstrand (*Director Grandé*), Marianne Löfgren (*Charlotte*), Georg Funkquist (*Victor*), Åke Grönberg (*Sam Svensson*), Linnea Hillberg (*Mrs. Grandé*) Calle Reinholdz, Sif Ruud, Ella Lindblom, Artur Rolén, Björn Montin

A SHIP TO INDIA (Skepp till Indialand) 1) 1947 2) Sept. 22, 1947 3) Lorens Marmstedt for Sverige Folkbiografer 5) Ingmar Bergman from Martin Söderhjelm's play "Skepp till Indialand" 6) Ingmar Bergman 7) Göran Strindberg 8) Erland von Koch 9) P. A. Lundgren 10) Tage Holmberg 13) Holger Löwenadler (*Captain Alexander Blom*), Birger Malmsten (*Johannes Blom*), Gertrud Fridh (*Sally*), Anna Lindahl (*Alice Bloom*), Lasse Krantz (*Hans, a crewman*), Jan Molander (*Bertil, a crewman*), Erik Hell (*Pekka, a crewman*), Naemi Briese (*Selma*), Hjördis Pettersson (*Sofie*), Åke Fridell (*Manager of music hall*), Peter Lindgren (*A foreign crewman*)

NIGHT IS MY FUTURE (Musik i mörker) 1) 1947 2) Jan. 17, 1948 3) Lorens Marmstedt/Terrafilm 4) Allan Ekelund 5) Dagmar Edqvist from a novel of the same name 6) Ingmar Bergman 7) Göran Strindberg 8) Erland von Koch 9) P. A. Lundgren 10) Lennart Wallén 13) Mai Zetterling (*Ingrid*), Birger

Malmsten (*Bengt Vyldeke*), Bengt Eklund (*Ebbe*), Olof Winner-strand (*The pastor*), Naima Wifstrand (*Mrs. Schröder*), Bibbi Skoglund (*Agneta*), Hilda Bergström (*Lovisa*), Douglas Håge (*Kruge*), Gunnar Björnstrand (*Klasson*), Åke Claesson, John Elfström, Sven Lindberg, Bengt Logardt, Marianne Gyllenhammar, Barbro Flodquist, Ulla och Runne Andreasson

PORT OF CALL (Hamnstad)
1) 1948 2) Oct. 18, 1948 3) Svensk Filmindustri 5) Ingmar Bergman from a synopsis by Olle Länsberg 6) Ingmar Bergman 7) Gunnar Fischer 8) Erland von Koch 9) Nils Svenwall 10) Oscar Rosander 13) Nine-Christine Jönsson (*Berit*), Bengt Eklund (*Gösta*), Berta Hall (*Berit's mother*), Erik Hell (*Berit's father*), Mimi Nelson (*Gertrud*), Birgitta Valberg (*Assistant to Vilander*), Hans Strååt (*Mr. Vilander*), Nils Dahlgren (*Gertrud's father*), Harry Ahlin (*Skåningen*), Nils Hallberg (*Gustav*), Sven-Eric Gamble

EVA
1) 1948 2) Dec. 26, 1948 3) Svensk Filmindustri 5) Ingmar Bergman, Gustaf Molander from a synopsis by Ingmar Bergman 6) Gustaf Molander 7) Åke Dahlqvist 8) Erik Nordgren 9) Nils Svenwall 10) Oscar Rosander 11) Hans Dahlin 13) Birger Malmsten (*Bo*), Eva Stiberg (*Eva*), Eva Dahlbeck (*Susanne*), Stig Olin (*Göran*), Åke Claesson (*Fredriksson*), Wanda Rothgardt (*Mrs. Fredriksson*), Inga Landgré (*Frida*), Hilda Borgström (*Maria*), Axel Högel (*Johansson, a fisherman*), Lasse Sarri (*Bo as a 12 year old*)

THE DEVIL'S WANTON (Fängelse, Prison)
1) 1948-1949 2) Mar. 19, 1948 3) Lorens Marmstedt/Terrafilm 5-6) Ingmar Bergman 7) Göran Strindberg 8) Erland von Koch 9) P. A. Lundgren 10) Lennart Wallén 13) Doris Svedlund (*Birgitta-Carolina*), Birger Malmsten (*Tomas*), Eva Henning (*Sofi*), Hasse Ekman (*Martin Grandé, film director*), Stig Olin (*Peter*), Irma Christenson (*Linnéa*), Anders Henrikson (*Paul*), Marianne Löfgren (*Mrs. Bohlin*), Carl-Henrik Fant (*Arne*), Inger Juel (*Greta*), Curt Masreliez (*Alf*), Åke Fridell, Bibi Lindqvist, Arne Ragneborn, Rune Lindström (*The pastor, role omitted*)

THREE STRANGE LOVES (Törst, Thirst)
1) 1949 2) Oct. 17, 1949 3) Svensk Filmindustri 4) Helge Hagerman

5) Herbert Grevenius from Birgit Tengroth's short story "Törst" 6) Ingmar Bergman 7) Gunnar Fischer 8) Erik Nordgren 9) Nils Svenwall 10) Oscar Rosander 12) Ellen Bergman 13) Eva Henning (*Rut*), Birger Malmsten (*Bertil*), Birgit Tengroth (*Viola*), Mimi Nelson (*Valborg*), Hasse Ekman (*Doctor Rosengren*), Bengt Eklund (*Raoul*), Gaby Stenberg (*Astrid, his wife*), Naima Wifstrand (*Miss Henriksson, the dancing teacher*), Sven-Eric Gamble (*The worker*), Gunnar Nielsen (*The assistant*), Estrid Hesse (*A patient*), Helge Hagerman (*A pastor*), Calle Flygare (*Another pastor*), Else-Merete Heiberg, Monica Weinzierl, Herman Greid

TO JOY (Till Glädje)
1) 1949 2) Feb. 20, 1950 3) Svensk Filmindustri 4) Allan Ekelund 5-6) Ingmar Bergman 7) Gunnar Fischer 8) Felix Mendelssohn, W. A. Mozart, B. Smetana, Ludwig van Beethoven 9) Nils Svenwall 10) Oscar Rosander 13) Maj-Britt Nilsson (*Martha*), Stid Olin *Eriksson*), Victor Sjöström (*Sönderby*), Birger Malmsten (*Marcel*), John Ekman (*Mikael Bro*), Margit Carlquist (*Nelly, his wife*), Sif Ruud (*Stina*), Rune Stylander (*Persson*), Erland Josephson (*Bertil*), Georg Skarstedt (*Anker*), Berit Holmström (*Lisa*), Björn Montin (*Lasse*), Carin Swenson, Svea Holm, Svea Holst, Agda Helin, Maud Hyttenberg

WHILE THE CITY SLEEPS (Medan staden sover)
1) 1950 2) Sept. 8, 1950 3) Svensk Filmindustri 4) Helge Hagerman 5) Lars-Eric Kjellgren from a manuscript by P. A. Fogelström from a synopsis by Ingmar Bergman 6) Lars-Eric Kjellgren 7) Martin Bodin 9) Nils Svenwall 10) Oscar Rosander 11) Hugo Bolander 13) Sven-Erik Gamble (*Jompa*), Inga Landgré (*Iris*), Adolf Jahr (*Iris's father*), Elof Ahrle (*Basen*), Ulf Palme (*Kalle Lund*), Hilding Gavle (*Hälaren*), John Elfström (*Jompa's father*), Barbro Hiort af Ornäs (*Rut*), Carl Ström (*Portis*), Märta Dorff (*Iris's mother*), Ilse-Nore Tromm, Arne Ragneborn, Hans Sundberg, Lennart Lundh, Hans Dahlberg, Ulla Smidje, Mona Geijer-Falkner, Harriet Andersson

THIS CAN'T HAPPEN HERE (Sånt händer inte här)
1) 1950 2) Oct. 23, 1950 3) Svensk Filmindustri 4) Helge Hagerman 5) Herbert Grevenius 6) Ingmar Bergman 7) Gunnar Fischer 8) Erik Nordgren 9) Nils Svenwall 10) Lennart Wallén 13) Signe

Hasso (*Vera*), Alf Kjellin (*Almkvist*), Ulf Palme (*Atkä Natas*), Gösta Cederlund (*A teacher*), Yngve Nordwall (*Lindell*), Stig Olin (*The young man*), Ragnar Klange (*Filip Rundblom*), Hanno Kompus (*The pastor*), Sylvia Tael (*Vanja*), Els Vaarman (*Woman in the cinema*), Edmar Kuus (*Leino*), Rudolf Lipp (*"Skuggan"*)

ILLICIT INTERUDE (British title: Summer Interlude) (Sommarlek)
1) 1950 2) Oct. 1, 1951 3) Svensk Filmindustri 4) Allan Ekelund 5) Ingmar Bergman, Herbert Grevenius from a manuscript by Ingmar Bergman 6) Ingmar Bergman 7) Gunnar Fischer 8) Erik Nordgren 9) Nils Svenwall 10) Oscar Rosander 13) Maj-Britt Nilsson (*Marie*), Birger Malmsten (*Henrik*), Alf Kjellin (*David*), Annalisa Ericson (*Kaj*), Georg Funkquist (*Uncle Erland*), Stig Olin (*The ballet master*), Renée Björling (*Aunt Elisabeth*), Mimi Pollak (*Little lady*), John Botvid (*Karl*), Gunnar Olsson (*The pastor*), Douglas Håge, Julia Caesar, Carl Ström, Torsten Lilliecrona, Marianne Schüler, Ernst Brunman, Olav Riego, Fylgia Zadig, Sten Mattson, Carl Axel Elfving, Gösta Ström

DIVORCED (Frånskild)
1) 1950-1951 2) Dec. 26, 1951 3) Svensk Filmindustri 4) Allan Ekelund 5) Ingmar Bergman, Herbert Grevenius from a synopsis by Ingmar Bergman 6) Gustaf Molander 7) Åke Dahlqvist 8) Erik Nordgren 9) Nils Svenwall 10) Oscar Rosander 13) Inga Tidblad (*Gertrud Holmgren*), Alf Kjellin (*Doctor Bertil Nordelius*), Doris Svedlund (*Marianne Berg*), Hjördis Pettersson (*Mrs. Nordelius*), Håkan Westergren (*Manager P. A. Beckman*), Irma Christenson (*Doctor Cecilia Lindeman*), Holger Löwenadler (*Engineer Tore Holmgren*), Marianne Löfgren (*"Chefen fru Ingeborg"*), Stig Olin (*Hans*), Elsa Prawitz, Birgitta Valberg, Sif Ruud, Paul Ström, Ingrid Borthen, Yvonne Lombard, Einar Axelsson, Ragnar Arvedson, Rune Halvarson, Rudolf Wendbladh, Guje Lagerwall

SECRETS OF WOMEN (British title: Waiting Women) (Kvinnors väntan)
1) 1952 2) Nov. 3, 1952 3) Svensk Filmindustri 5-6) Ingmar Bergman 7) Gunnar Fischer 8) Erik Nordgren 9) Nils Svenwall 10) Oscar Rosander 13) Anita Björk (*Rakel*), Maj-Britt Nilsson (*Märta*), Eva Dahlbeck (*Karin*), Gunnar Björnstrand (*Fredrik*

*Lobelius*), Birger Malmsten (*Martin Lobelius*), Jarl Kulle (*Kaj*), Karl-Arne Holmsten (*Eugen Lobelius*), Gerd Andersson (*Maj*), Björn Bjelvenstam (*Henrik*), Aino Taube (*Anita*), Håkan Westergren (*Paul*), Kjell Nordensköld, Carl Ström, Märta Arbiin

MONIKA (British title: Summer with Monika)
(Sommaren med Monika)
1) 1952 2) Feb. 9, 1933 3) Svensk Filmindustri 4) Allan Ekelund 5) Ingmar Bergman, P. A. Fogelström, from an idea, synopsis, and novel by the latter 6) Ingmar Bergman 7) Gunnar Fischer 8) Erik Nordgren 9) P. A. Lundgren, Nils Svenwall 10) Tage Holmberg, Gösta Lewin 13) Harriet Andersson (*Monika*), Lars Ekborg (*Harry*), John Harryson (*Lelle*), Georg Skarstedt (*Harry's father*), Dagmar Ebbesson (*Harry's aunt*), Åke Fridell (*Monika's father*), Naemi Briese (*Monika's mother*), Åke Grönberg, Sigge Fürst, Gösta Prüzelius, Arthur Fischer, Torsten Lilliecrona, Bengt Eklund, Gustaf Färingborg, Ivar Wahlgren, Renée Björling, Catrin Westerlund, Harry Ahlin

THE NAKED NIGHT (British title: Sawdust and Tinsel)
(Gycklarnas Afton, Sunset of a Clown)
1) 1953 2) Sept. 14, 1953 3) Sandrews 4) Rune Waldekranz 5-6) Ingmar Bergman 7) Hilding Bladh, Sven Nykvist 8) Karl-Birger Blomdahl 9) Bibbi Lindström 10) Carl-Olov Skeppstedt 13) Harriet Andersson (*Anne*), Åke Grönberg (*Albert Johansson*), Hasse Ekman (*Frans*), Anders Ek (*Frost*), Gudrun Brost (*Alma*), Annika Tretow (*Agda, Albert's wife*), Gunnar Björnstrand (*Mr. Sjuberg*), Erik Strandmark (*Jens*), Kiki (*The dwarf*), Åke Fridell (*The officer*)

A LESSON IN LOVE (En lektion i kärlek)
1) 1954 2) Oct. 4, 1954 3) Svensk Filmindustri 4) Allan Ekelund 5-6) Ingmar Bergman 7) Martin Bodin 8) Dag Wirén 9) P. A. Lundgren 10) Oscar Rosander 13) Eva Dahlbeck (*Marianne Erneman*), Gunnar Björnstrand (*Dr. David Erneman*), Yvonne Lombard (*Susanne*), Harriet Andersson (*Nix*), Åke Grönberg (*Carl-Adam*), Olof Winnerstrand (*Professor Henrik Erneman*), Renée Björling (*Svea Erneman, his wife*), Birgitte Reimer (*Lise*), John Elfström (*Sam*), Dagmar Ebbesen (*The nurse*), Helge Hagerman (*The traveling salesman*), Sigge Fürst (*The pastor*), Gösta Prüzelius (*The*

*train conductor*), Carl Ström, Arne Lindblad, Torsten Lilliecrona, Yvonne Brosset

DREAMS (British title: Journey into Autumn) (Kvinnodröm) 1) 1955 2) Aug. 22, 1955 3) Sandrews 4) Rune Waldekranz 5-6) Ingmar Bergman 7) Hilding Bladh 9) Gittan Gustafsson 10) Carl-Olov Skeppstedt 13) Eva Dahlbeck (*Susanne*), Harriet Andersson (*Doris*), Gunnar Björnstrand (*Consul Sönderby*), Ulf Palme (*Manager Lobelius*), Inga Landgré (*Mrs. Lobelius*), Sven Lindberg (*Palle*), Naima Wifstrand (*Mrs. Arén*), Benkt-Åke Benktsson (*Director Magnus*), Git Gay (*Lady in the studio*), Ludde Gentzel (*Photographer Sundström*), Kerstin Hedeby (*Marianne*), Jessie Flaws, Marianne Neilsen, Siv Ericks, Bengt Schött, Axel Düberg

SMILES OF A SUMMER NIGHT (Sommarnattens leende) 1) 1955 2) Dec. 26, 1955 3) Svensk Filmindustri 4) Allan Ekelund 5-6) Ingmar Bergman 7) Gunnar Fischer 8) Erik Nordgren 9) P. A. Lundgren 10) Oscar Rosander 11) Lennart Olsson 13) Ulla Jacobsson (*Anne Egerman*), Eva Dahlbeck (*Desirée Armfeldt*), Margit Carlquist (*Charlotte Malcolm*), Harriet Andersson (*Petra, the maid*), Gunnar Björnstrand (*Fredrik Egerman*), Jarl Kulle (*Count Carl Magnus Malcolm*), Åke Fridell (*Frid, the groom*), Björn Bjelvenstam (*Henrik Egerman*), Naima Wifstrand (*Mrs. Armfeldt*), Jullan Kindahl (*The cook*), Gull Natorp (*Malla, Desirée's maid*), Birgitta Valberg (*First actress*), Bibi Andersson (*Second actress*)

THE LAST COUPLE OUT (Sista paret ut) 1) 1956 2) Nov. 12, 1956 3) Svensk Filmindustri 4) Allan Ekelund 5) Ingmar Bergman, Alf Sjöberg from a manuscript by Ingmar Bergman 6) Alf Sjöberg 7) Martin Bodin 8) Erik Nordgren, Charles Redland, Bengt Hallberg 9) Harald Garmland 10) Oscar Rosander 13) Olof Widgren (*Lawyer Hans Dahlin*), Eva Dahlbeck (*Mrs. Susanne Dahlin*), Björn Bjelvenstam (*Bo Dahlin*), Johnny Johansson (*Sven Dahlin, 8 years old*), Märta Arbiin (*Grandmother*), Jullan Kindahl (*Alma, the Dahlins' maid*), Jarl Kulle( *Doctor Farell*), Nancy Dalunde (*Mrs. Farell*), Bibi Andersson (*Kerstin*), Harriet Andersson (*Anita*), Aino Taube (*Ker-

*stin's mother*), Jan-Olof Strandberg (*Claes Berg*), Hugo Björne (*Lecturer Björne*), Göran Lundquist (*The little kid*)

THE SEVENTH SEAL (Det sjunde inseglet)
1) 1956 2) Feb. 16, 1957 3) Svensk Filmindustri 4) Allan Ekelund 5-6) Ingmar Bergman 7) Gunnar Fischer 8) Erik Nordgren 9) P. A. Lundgren 10) Lennart Wallén 11) Lennart Olsson 12) Else Fischer 13) Max von Sydow (*Antonius Block, the Knight*), Gunnar Björnstrand (*Jöns, the Squire*), Nils Poppe (*Jof*), Bibi Andersson (*Mia*), Bengt Ekerot (*Death*), Åke Fridell (*Plog, the smith*), Inga Gill (*Lisa, Plog's wife*), Erik Strandmark (*Skat*), Bertil Anderberg (*Raval*), Gunnel Lindblom (*The girl*), Inga Landgré (*The Knight's wife*), Anders Ek (*The monk*), Maud Hansson (*The witch*), Gunnar Olsson (*The church painter*), Lars Lind (*The young monk*), Benkt-Åke Benktsson (*The merchant*), Gudrun Brost (*Woman at the tavern*), Ulf Johansson (*The leader of the soldiers*)

WILD STRAWBERRIES (Smultronstället)
1) 1957 2) Dec. 26, 1957 3) Svensk Filmindustri 4) Allan Ekelund 5-6) Ingmar Bergman 7) Gunnar Fischer 8) Erik Nordgren 9) Gittan Gustafsson 10) Oscar Rosander 11) Gösta Ekman 13) Victor Sjöström (*Professor Isak Borg*), Bibi Andersson (*Sara*), Ingrid Thulin (*Marianne*), Gunnar Björnstrand (*Evald*), Folke Sundquist (*Anders*), Björn Bjelvenstam (*Viktor*), Naimi Wifstrand (*Isak's mother*), Jullan Kindahl (*Agda*), Gunnar Sjöberg (*Alman, an engineer*), Gunnel Broström (*Mrs. Alman*), Gertrud Fridh (*Isak's wife*), Åke Fridell (*Her lover*), Max von Sydow (*Åkerman*), Sif Ruud (*Aunt*), Yngve Nordwall (*Uncle Aron*), Per Sjöstrand, Gio Petré, Gunnel Lindblom, Maud Hansson, Lena Bergman, Monica Ehrling, Göran Lundquist, Eva Norée, Gunnar Olsson, Josef Norman, Anne-Marie Wiman

BRINK OF LIFE (Nära livet)
1) 1957 2) Mar. 31, 1958 3) Nordisk Tonefilm 5) Ulla Isaksson from her short story "Det vänliga, värdiga" in the book, "Dödens faster" 6) Ingmar Bergman 7) Max Wilén 9) Bibi Lindström 10) Carl-Olov Skeppstedt 13) Ingrid Thulin (*Cecilia Ellius*), Eva Dahlbeck (*Stina Andersson*), Bibi Andersson (*Hjördis Pettersson*), Barbro Hiort af Ornäs (*Sister Brita*), Max von Sydow (*Harry*

*Andersson*), Erland Josephson (*Anders Ellius*), Inga Landgré (*Greta Ellius*), Anne-Marie Gyllenspetz (*Social welfare director*), Gunnar Sjöberg (*Dr. Nordlander*), Margareta Krook (*Dr. Larsson*), Lars Lind (*Dr. Thylenius*), Sissi Kaiser (*Sister Marit*), Monica Ekberg, Gun Jönsson, Maud Elfsiö, Inga Gill, Gunnar Nielsen, Kristina Adolphson.—Medical advisor, Lars Engström

THE MAGICIAN (British title: The Face) (Ansiktet)
1) 1958 2) Dec. 26, 1958 3) Svensk Filmindustri )4 Allan Ekelund 5-6) Ingmar Bergman 7) Gunnar Fischer 8) Erik Nordgren 9) P. A. Lundgren 10) Oscar Rosander 11) Gösta Ekman 13) Max von Sydow (*Albert Emanuel Vogler, the mesmerist*), Ingrid Thulin (*Manda Vogler, his wife, disguised, called Aman*), Åke Fridell (*Tubal, Vogler's assistant*), Naima Wifstrand (*Vogler's grandmother, a sorceress*), Lars Ekborg (*Simson, Vogler's coachman*), Gunnar Björnstrand (*Anders Vergérus, counselor of medicine*), Erland Josephson (*Abraham Egerman, the consul*), Gertrud Fridh (*Ottilia, his wife*), Toivo Pawlo (*Frans Starbeck, police chief*), Ulla Sjöblom (*Henrietta, his wife*), Bengt Ekerot (*Johan Spegel, an actor*), Sif Ruud (*Sofia Garp, the Egerman's cook*), Bibi Andersson (*Sara Lindkvist, the maid*), Birgitta Pettersson (*Sanna Fernström, a maid*) Oscar Ljung (*Antonsson, the Egerman's coachman*), Axel Düberg (*Rustan, a servant*)

THE VIRGIN SPRING (Jungfrukällan)
1) 1959 2) Feb. 8, 1960 3) Svensk Filmindustri 4) Allan Ekelund 5) Ulla Isaksson from a fourteenth-century legend 6) Ingmar Bergman 7) Sven Nykvist 8) Erik Nordgren 9) P. A. Lundgren 10) Oscar Rosander 11) Lenn Hjortzberg 13) Max von Sydow (*Herr Töre*), Birgitta Valberg (*Fru Märeta*), Gunnel Lindblom (*Ingeri*), Birgitta Pettersson (*Karin*), Axel Düberg (*The thin one*), Tor Isedal (*The tongueless one*), Allan Edwall (*The beggar*), Ove Porath (*The boy*), Axel Slangus (*Bridge guard*), Gudrun Brost (*Frida*), Oscar Ljung (*Simon*), Tor Borong (*First farm laborer*), Leif Forstenberg (*Second farm laborer*)

THE DEVIL'S EYE (Djävulens öga)
1) 1960 2) Oct. 17, 1960 3) Svensk Filmindustri 4) Allan Ekelund 5) Ingmar Bergman, freely adapted from a Danish radio play 6) Ingmar Bergman 7) Gunnar Fischer 7) Motif from Domenico

Scarlatti 9) P. A. Lundgren 10) Oscar Rosander 11) Lenn Hjortzberg 13) Jarl Kulle (*Don Juan*), Bibi Andersson (*Britt-Marie*), Stig Järrel (*Satan*), Nils Poppe (*The vicar*), Gertrud Fridh (*Mrs. Renata*), Sture Lagerwall (*Pablo*), Gunnar Björnstrand (*The actor*), Georg Funkquist (*Count Armand de Rochefoucauld*), Gunnar Sjöberg (*Marquis Guiseppe Maria de Macopazza*), Axel Düberg (*Jonas*), Torsten Winge (*The old man*), Kristina Adolphson, Allan Edwall, Ragnar Arvedson, Börje Lund, Lenn Hjortzberg

THROUGH A GLASS DARKLY (Såsom i en spegel)
1) 1960-1961 2) Oct. 16, 1961 3) Svensk Filmindustri 4) Allan Ekelund 5-6) Ingmar Bergman 7) Sven Nykvist 8) Johann Sebastian Bach, from suite No. 2, D major for violincello 9) P. A. Lundgren 10) Ulla Ryghe 11) Lenn Hjortzberg 13) Harriet Andersson (*Karin*), Max von Sydow (*Martin*), Gunnar Björnstrand (*David*), Lars Passgård (*Fredrik, called Minus*)

WINTER LIGHT (Nattvardsgästerna)
1) 1961-1962 2) Feb. 11, 1963 3) Svensk Filmindustri 4) Allan Ekelund 5-6) Ingmar Bergman 7) Sven Nykvist 9) P. A. Lundgren 10) Ulla Ryghe 11) Lenn Hjortzberg 13) Gunnar Björnstrand (*Thomas Ericsson*), Ingrid Thulin (*Märta Lundberg*), Max von Sydow (*Jonas Persson*), Gunnel Lindblom (*Karin Persson*), Allan Edwall (*Algot Frövik*), Olof Thunberg (*Fredrik Blom*), Elsa Ebbesen (*The old woman*), Kolbjörn Knudsen (*Sexton Aronsson*)

THE SILENCE (Tystnaden)
1) 1962 2) Sept. 23, 1963 3) Svensk Filmindustri 4) Allan Ekelund 5-6) Ingmar Bergman 7) Sven Nykvist 8) Bo Nilsson, Johann Sebastian Bach 9) P. A. Lundgren 10) Ulla Ryghe 11) Lenn Hjortzberg, Lars-Erik Liedholm 13) Ingrid Thulin (*Ester*), Gunnel Lindblom (*Anna*), Jörgen Lindström (*Johan, Anna's son*), Birger Malmsten (*Bartender*), Håkan Jahnberg (*Hotel waiter*)

NOT TO SPEAK ABOUT ALL THESE WOMEN (För att inte tala om alla dessa kvinnor)
1) 1963 2) Autumn, 1964 3) Svensk Filmindustri 4) Allan Ekelund 5) Ingmar Bergman, Erland Josephsson 6) Ingmar Bergman 7) Sven Nykvist 8-9) P. A. Lundgren 10) Ulla Ryghe 11) Lenn Hjortzberg, Lars-Erik Liedholm 13) Jarl Kulle (*Cornelius*), Eva Dahlbeck

(*Adelaide*), Barbro Hiort af Ornäs (*Beatrice*), Mona Malm (*Cecilia*), Bibi Andersson (*Humlan*), Gertrud Fridh (*Traviata*), Karin Kavli (*Madame Tussaud*), Harriet Andersson (*Isolde*), Georg Funkquist (*Tristan*), Allan Edwall (*Jillker*).—Filmed in Eastmancolor